Be Your Own Stockbroker

The amount of information on stocks and shares available by traditional and electronic methods is increasing. This is encouraging more and more people to organise their own investment strategy without relying on advice from conventional stockbrokers.

The cost savings on commissions to be enjoyed by a DIY approach to investment are substantial. However, anyone considering this should understand the way the market works and how to assess potential investments. Most importantly, they must be fully aware of the financial risks involved.

Be Your Own Stockbroker addresses the issues in an uncomplicated and relatively informal manner. The opinions and recommendations expressed will be of enormous interest to private investors, particularly those who are considering an investment for the first time or believe they could have achieved more than their own 'advisory' stockbroker.

This is one single publication which tackles the 'stockbroking mystique' – head on.

Stephen J Pinner MSI(Dip)
Managing Director, City Deal Services Ltd.

Vintcent's latest book will transform the occasional share-owner into a serious DIY investor. It is unique in its breadth of coverage -- even taking the trouble to explain settlement, the source of many problems for private investors – and avoids becoming bogged down in patent investment methods. Read the book, find a good sharedealing and information service and start making money.

David L Jones
Chief Executive of ShareLink

Charles Vintcent's *Be Your Own Stockbroker* provides readers with a comprehensive and informative guide to investing their money. As he states, common sense, the right amount of information and a reasonable amount of work are required to be a successful investor. Moreover, he demonstrates that by managing your own portfolio, savings are to be gained that enhance the return one may earn.

Fidelity Brokerage's clients tell us that they spend on average four hours per week managing their portfolios. Many investors use the techniques described in Mr. Vintcent's book. A large number of them take advantage of the information sources that he recommends. His cautionary statements provide a sound platform from which investors may avoid the pitfalls that cause them to miss the goals they set for themselves. Most importantly, his book takes the mystique out of managing a portfolio.

I recommend *Be Your Own Stockbroker* to any investor serious about taking investment decisions into their own hands.

David Plucinsky
President, Fidelity Brokerage Services

INVESTOR'S GUIDE

Be Your Own Stockbroker

The secrets of managing your own investments

CHARLES VINTCENT

London · Hong Kong · Johannesburg · Melbourne · Singapore · Washingstone DC

PITMAN PUBLISHING
128 Long Acre, London WC2E 9AN
Tel: +44 (0)171 447 2000
Fax: +44 (0)171 240 5771

A Division of Pearson Professional Limited

First published in Great Britain in 1995

This edition published in 1997

© Pearson Professional Limited 1997

The right of Charles Vintcent to be identified as author of this work
has been asserted by him in accordance with the Copyright, Designs
and Patents Act 1988.

ISBN 0 273 62686 8

British Library Cataloguing in Publication Data
A CIP catalogue record for this book can be obtained from the British Library

10 9 8 7 6 5 4 3 2 1

Typeset by Northern Phototypesetting Co. Ltd, Bolton
Printed and bound in Great Britain by Bell and Bain Ltd, Glasgow

The Publishers' policy is to use paper manufactured from sustainable forests.

Contents

Acknowledgements   *ix*

Introduction: Take charge of the health of your wealth   *xi*

1 THE BROKER, THE MARKET AND YOU   **1**

Being your own stockbroker   2

The London Stock Exchange   3

Dealing   7

Payment   9

Share registry   10

Broker services   12

Summary   15

2 SETTLEMENT   **17**

Part 1: the changes   20

Part 2: services linked to the settlement system   23

Part 3: advantages and disadvantages of the three options   30

Summary   31

3 GETTING TO GRIPS WITH STOCKS AND SHARES   **35**

Part 1: shares   37

Summary   51

Part 2: derivatives   52

Summary   66

4 GATHERING YOUR SHARE INFORMATION   **69**

Share information   71

Share price information   72

Information from other sources   82

Speculative buying   86

Summary   86

5 INTERPRETING SHARE INFORMATION   **89**

Market data and how to use it   90

Charts   93

The IC/Coppock Indicator   97

	Forecasting future PER	101
	Summary	104
6	**COMPANY REPORTS AND ACCOUNTS**	**107**
	New issues	109
	Reading a set of accounts	109
	Factors affecting the company	112
	Indices	114
	Summary	126
7	**MAKING THE MOST OF MANAGED FUNDS**	**129**
	Investment trusts	131
	Unit trusts	138
	Other managed funds	142
	Personal Equity Plans (PEPs)	144
	Summary	150
8	**CAPITAL GAINS TAX – A VOLUNTARY TAX?**	**153**
	CGT – the basics	154
	Rights issues	159
	More ways of reducing your liability to CGT	161
	CGT computation for monthly savings in investment and unit trusts	164
	Summary	169
9	**BUILD YOUR OWN STRATEGY**	**173**
	Part 1: overall factors to consider	174
	Summary	187
	Part 2: personal strategic planning	187
	Summary	195
10	**SHARPENING YOUR INVESTMENT TACTICS**	**197**
	Some basics	198
	A portfolio for income and growth	199
	A portfolio for growth alone	215
	Creating a portfolio for growth	220
	A portfolio for income	223
	A portfolio for trading	225
	A portfolio for inheritance tax planning	226
	Summary	229

11	THE ROLE OF INFORMATION TECHNOLOGY (IT)	233
	Data required	234
	Charts	237
	What are the signals?	242
	How do we interpret the signals?	244
	Further interpretation of charts	252
	Summary	257
12	GETTING THE MOST FROM FINANCIAL ADVISERS	259
	General advice on do's and don'ts	260
	Questions you should ask your financial adviser	261
	Execution-only service versus full advisory service	262
	Summary	263

Conclusion 265

Appendix 1: Registrars 269
Appendix 2: Firms of stockbrokers offering execution-only services 279
Appendix 3: Client agreement forms 299
Appendix 4: Regulatory authorities 307
Appendix 5: Glossary of Stock Market Terms 309

Index 317

Acknowledgements

I have received a great deal of help in writing this book from many sources. I wish to thank Mrs Pat Broughhall for her enthusiastic help and advice, and particularly my friend Phil Barnes, whose patience and tolerance with my inept wrestling with computers deserve a medal.

I am also indebted to the *Investors Chronicle*, Reuters, Extel, Datastream, the Stock Exchange, LIFFE, the Association of Investment Trusts and the Association of Unit Trusts for allowing me to reproduce material which they kindly supplied.

▶ You don't have to be a mathematical genius to be a good stockbroker, nor is there any great mystique involved.

Introduction

Take charge of the health of your wealth

There is a conviction, widely held, that being a stockbroker somehow gives you access to secret ways of making money fast, and that members of 'the club' are privy to all sorts of information not available to outsiders!

If that were true, not only would this book remain unwritten, but all stockbrokers would be millionaires and would be dealing for themselves alone.

It is said that stockbroking is an art, not a science, and there is a grain of truth in that. But only a grain, not much more. The secret to being a successful stockbroker requires two main things.

First, knowing which stocks and shares to buy in order to achieve high income or above average growth. This demands that you are fully conversant with the capabilities of each 'tool of the trade', so that you do not expect results from a particular type of stock or share which it is incapable of producing.

Second, it requires the ability to analyse the important financial information about companies in order to find those which are cheap to buy, but whose share price is more likely to be going up rather than down.

This book will show you exactly how to do all of that, and it will save you a great deal of time by showing you what areas of data you should concentrate your research on and the yardsticks you should use to measure the company's performance against, so that you avoid the more risky shares. It will show you how the professional fund managers go about choosing shares to buy for their funds, as well as explaining how to save money on your dealing costs.

> It is said that stockbroking is an art, not a science, and there is a grain of truth in that. But only a grain, not much more.

You can do all this yourself and improve the performance of your own portfolio however large or small it may be.

Do you like paying Capital Gains Tax?

Most people don't, and as it is often regarded as a voluntary tax, you owe it to yourself to keep such contributions to the Inland Revenue to the absolute minimum. This book will show you how to manage your investments so that you reduce such liability as far as possible, which is exactly the sort of guidance you should get from a good stockbroker. Now you can do it all for yourself, and you do not have to be an accountant to work out the computations. It is all here in the book in step-by-step worked examples, and this knowledge will enable you to reduce your expenses because you will not have to pay an accountant to do it for you any more.

Are you aware that the new settlement system called CREST makes share certificates redundant?

This book will explain all the options open to you using broker nominee companies. It tells you the questions you should ask so that you understand all the 'extra' charges which you might incur, as well as describing the benefits and risks attached to pooled nominee accounts.

Did you know that you can save yourself at least 3 per cent when you buy unit trusts?

You don't have to be a mathematical genius to be a good stockbroker, nor is there any great mystique involved. What you do have to have is the time to do your homework thoroughly and keep a constant watch on your investments to monitor their progress. This book will show you how to set reasonable and achievable targets for your capital to hit, and with the availability of up-to-date information now so widespread, you can manage your own funds with the same expertise as the professionals do for themselves.

This book will guide you through all the steps needed to create your own tailor-made portfolio, whether you are an investor or a trader, and it will equip you with all the fundamental knowledge required for you to be your own stockbroker in all but dealing with market makers and settlement.

This book will describe how information technology (IT) can make your record keeping and essential analysis easier and quicker and make you more successful, particularly if you learn how to interpret the signals which charts are exhibiting. It will make your investment performance really satisfying. You could become complacent!

Now read on.

▶ If you want to manage your own investments, make your own decisions, choose your own stocks, monitor the performance of your portfolio and compute your liability to capital gains or income tax, then you have to know how the market works and the roles of market makers and stockbrokers.

1

The broker, the market and you

Being your own stockbroker

The London Stock Exchange

Dealing

Payment

Share registry

Broker services

Summary

This chapter explains briefly how the stockmarket works and the role of a stockbroker. It describes what is involved in dealing in stocks and shares and the contractual liabilities which arise.

Chapter 1 is devoted to explaining those aspects of dealing which you cannot do yourself. It describes the functions of a stockbroker and the range of services which are available.

It covers:

- buying and selling;
- settlement, including rolling settlement;
- commitment to pay;
- commitment to deliver;
- share registry;
- nominee accounts.

A glossary of terms used is given in Appendix 5.

BEING YOUR OWN STOCKBROKER

You may ask why this book has been called *Be Your Own Stockbroker* when in fact you can not be one without passing exams and being authorised by a regulatory authority.

The point is that if you want to manage your own investments, make your own decisions, choose your own stocks, monitor the performance of your portfolio and compute your liability to capital gains or income tax, then you have to know how the market works and the roles of market makers and stockbrokers.

You will still have to use the services of a stockbroker, but you will be confident that you are as well-informed as possible about the whole process, and that you can give specific instructions to deal with a full understanding of what your commitments are, as well as having researched carefully the reasons for making a sale or purchase.

It is important that you know 'who' is responsible for 'what' and whether you wish to incur certain costs for services which you feel you can do for yourself. Unfortunately, nowadays nothing is for free, and if you can save costs it will be to your advantage.

Let us begin by explaining what the market is and who controls it.

THE LONDON STOCK EXCHANGE

The London Stock Exchange is a market in which stocks and shares can be bought or sold every working day during market hours. Part of its function is to maintain an orderly market in those stocks and shares which are listed on the exchange. It has the essential advantage that most shares can be liquidated at any time if needs be.

Regulatory authority

Since the Financial Services Act in 1986, the market has been regulated by the Securities and Futures Authority (the SFA). The SFA is responsible for two main functions.

First, it lays down rules which govern the conduct of member firms and those individuals who are authorised to deal with market makers, as well as those giving investment advice to members of the public.

> Unfortunately, nowadays nothing is for free, and if you can save costs it will be to your advantage.

Second, it is responsible for receiving and investigating complaints from the investing public. Owing to the complexities of the different types of shares and the various ways in which capital is often reconstructed, particularly as a result of takeovers, mergers and recapitalisation, a large proportion of the complaints which are received arise because of a lack of understanding on the part of the public.

Nevertheless, each one is investigated and receives a reply and an explanation. If it is found that there has been malpractice, then remedial action is taken. The powers of the SFA are wide and deep. In effect it polices the regulations. It makes detailed examinations of the dealing records of individual clients and their financial standing to ensure that the advice given was neither reckless nor commission-oriented. Their officers are particularly concerned to find whether a portfolio of any client has been 'churned': that is to say, whether shares have been bought and sold too frequently so that suspicion is created that the transactions were made for the benefit of the broker rather than to the client's financial advantage.

The rules which govern the conduct of members are covered by codes of practice, and anyone found to be infringing them is likely to be fined or have their authorisation rescinded, which effectively prohibits them from carrying on business.

It is very important to understand the rudiments of how it all works. Here is a brief summary of the principal roles of the main players.

The market

The market consists of market makers and brokers. The public cannot deal with a market maker direct.

There are many technical reasons why this is so, but the most important ones are concerned with payment and delivery of stock and share certificates, and we explain these aspects later in more detail.

A broker has to be authorised individually by the SFA to deal with the market makers, and he can only do so if associated with, or employed by, a firm which is a member of the Stock Exchange.

Role of a market maker

A market maker runs a 'shop' and you buy shares from him or sell them back to him. The rules insist that all share transactions must go through a market maker.

The market makers act as retailers of shares and display their prices during working hours. The prices may vary (sometimes considerably) during the day, depending on a number of influences. For example, if holders of very large amounts of a share decide to sell (or a lot of holders of small amounts), then the market makers will reduce the price which they are prepared to pay for the share. The converse is true also; if there is a consistent and large enough demand for a share, then the market makers will increase the price.

> ...The public cannot deal with a market maker direct. ....

Share price movement

More often than not it is quite simply supply and demand which dictates the prices. Often the answer to the question, 'Why has the price of XYZ Company fallen?', is that there are more sellers than buyers. Facile maybe, but very often there is no tangible reason to account for the fall in price.

Never forget that the market maker has to pay cash on settlement day for shares which have been sold to him, so that unless he can sell them on to someone else very quickly, he will reduce the price of the share to discourage others from selling more of the same to him.

Thus his stock or 'book', as it is called, will vary from that of another market maker dealing in the same share. If he has too many he is said to be 'long', and if he has too few he is said to be 'short'. Frequently, this can be seen from the prices which he displays on the dealing screen when compared with those of another market maker.

Role of a broker or agent

The prime role and essential reason for being a broker is to act as an agent on behalf of his client. He must put his clients' interests first, above his own or anything else, and he must get the best price for his client, whether buying or selling. His job is to argue, haggle, beg, cajole or use whatever guile is necessary to buy shares at the lowest prices and to sell shares at the highest prices for his clients.

You can use the services of a stockbroker simply to execute your instructions, or you can ask that he acts as an adviser in addition. The distinction is important, and you must be aware of the ramifications between the two distinct and different roles.

Remember that whether you choose to be advised by a stockbroker, or do all your own research and construct a portfolio particularly suited to your own needs, you will have to have your dealing done by someone who is authorised.

There are various types of firm who can carry out your instructions and we shall consider later the advantages, disadvantages and costs, for the services which they offer. If, however, you choose to use a stockbroker, then you should be aware of what you can expect from him. If you are going to act as your own adviser, then you will have to be able to do everything a stockbroker does other than deal with a market maker and effect settlement.

Let us look at the two main reasons why you have to use brokers and market makers. Essentially it boils down to payment and settlement.

Settlement is explained in more detail later (see Chapter 2) as the methods have undergone fundamental changes.

Commitment to pay

When the broker has found a market maker offering the share at the best price to buy, he gives an oral order, e.g., 'I buy 2,000 Shell at 708p'. In so saying he has committed his firm to paying the market maker £14,160 ten working days later. **This period will soon be reduced to five days (see Chapter 2).**

If the client, on whose behalf he is acting, does not pay on the due date, then the broker's firm will lose that sum because they must pay the market maker without fail.

Thus by giving an instruction to an intermediary to make a purchase on your behalf, you are creating a contractual liability between yourself and the broking firm to pay on time.

Purchases

The broker is acting as an agent, not as a principal, and therefore, the debt which results is recoverable from the client through the courts. The argument that because the buyer did not pay for the shares means that they do not belong to him is not valid. The instruction to buy is considered to be a contract and as such it is enforceable.

Commitment to deliver

In the same way, when you instruct the broker to sell a number of shares on your behalf, you are contracting to deliver the share certificates to him on or before settlement day, so that he can in turn deliver them to the market maker and get paid. If you do not deliver them on time, there are penalties which will be dealt with later.

The market motto 'Dictum Meum Pactum' or 'My Word is My Bond' should apply equally inside and outside the market.

Once instructions have been given and a commitment made the transaction has to be settled.

Late delivery costs

It is easy to understand why firms of brokers want to be in possession of cleared funds on or before settlement day. When interest rates are high, every day that a broker is kept waiting for funds after settlement day is costing him money. With commission rates as low as they are, and with overheads increasing every year, the cost of borrowing money to finance late payers can easily become intolerable.

Whether the broker charges interest for late payment or not is a matter for negotiation with each firm, but it is fair to say that more and more are imposing such sanctions.

Some firms will not act on a client's instructions until they have cleared funds in their accounts. Whilst this is mandatory in a lot of firms when you deal in traded options, as a general rule it is not practised for equity or gilt transactions by professional firms of stockbrokers or those who have been in existence for some time.

It is acceptable for the first transaction with a firm to whom you are not known, but you should ask a firm that you are considering using what their terms are before you commit yourself. Find out if it is their regular practice to demand cleared funds at all times in advance of executing dealing instructions. The banks are notorious for conducting their business in this way.

Let us look at what you can expect by way of information when you buy or sell a share.

DEALING

It is essential that you are able to deal at a price with which you are happy and which fits in with your plans. This applies whether you are buying or selling. If you are asked to put cleared funds in the hands of your broker before he will deal, you are at a major disadvantage. The price of the share may well have moved up considerably by the time your cheque has cleared so that either you end up getting fewer shares than you had planned, or you may well not want the investment at that price anyway.

There are some exceptions to this advice.

When you buy stock such as gilts or shares which are still in allotment form prior to becoming registered and some foreign shares, cash settlement may be required within 24 hours of the date of purchase. In such cases, you cannot expect your broker to finance your business for nothing.

Reporting

A good stockbroker will always report back to you as soon as he can after he has dealt, telling you the price at which he has executed the bargain.

Unless you have given him a 'limit' order which he is unable to execute because the price is unobtainable, he has to deal on your instructions as soon as is practicable. This is one of the rules imposed by the SFA and you will see the time of dealing shown on the contract note.

Time of bargain

Quite apart from seeking confirmation of the price of a share before you commit yourself to dealing, you should make a note of the time when you gave your instructions over the telephone, for your own protection. Say there is a difference of half an hour between your instructions to deal and the time of execution. Something happens which moves the price considerably against you. You can demand that the broker effects the transaction at the original price quoted and that he bears any loss which might result.

> ... The price of the share may well have moved up considerably by the time your cheque has cleared. ....

Sales

When you sell a share you are contracting to deliver the share certificate and signed transfer form to the intermediary who made the sale.

The contract note will show you the date on which settlement is due to you. Unless you have delivered the share certificate and transfer form before that date, you cannot expect to get paid.

In the same way that the contract to buy creates an obligation between you and the agent, so a similar situation arises when you make a sale. The difference, in this instance, is that whereas you can be sued to reimburse the agent if you default on your purchase debt, you have not created such a debt by failing to deliver a share certificate on time.

You could be penalised for failure to deliver on time, and this is done by the market maker taking steps to protect himself by 'buying in' against you.

Buying in

If you fail to deliver the stock on time, the market maker, who may well have sold your shares onwards to someone else and is obliged to deliver them, simply buys the same amount in the market and charges you with the cost. This cost now becomes a debt which is recoverable in the same way as a purchase debt.

What happens if the price has fallen since the day when you gave instructions to sell?

You will not receive any cash difference because until you deliver the share certificate you are not entitled to any proceeds. Thus you could end up with shares which are unsold and incur a debt as well.

How can you ensure that you do not run such a risk?

This risk can be eliminated by using stockbrokers' nominee companies and this facility is described in more detail later.

PAYMENT

Rolling settlement

We have explained the contractual liabilities both to pay for shares bought, and to deliver certificates for shares sold, in time for settlement day. The Stock Exchange account period used to run for two weeks (and occasionally three weeks) during which you could buy and sell shares without having to pay for them until settlement day which arrived ten days after the end of the account period.This system has been abolished and replaced with rolling settlement.

Under rolling settlement, each transaction must be settled five working days after the dealing date. Previously a statement was sent after the end of a trading account listing all purchases and sales made and showing a net balance either payable or receivable. **Now every day becomes a settlement day.** There is no statement issued for settlement purposes. Each contract note shows clearly the date by which payment must be made for purchases and the date on which you will receive payment for sales, and that is the only settlement information which you will receive.

If you make more than one transaction on the same day then you will receive an advice note showing the net amount due either way and this will accompany that day's contract notes. A monthly summary of transactions which have been made will be sent to you, but this is advisory only. Payment must not be delayed pending receipt of this statement. Brokers expect to be in receipt of cleared funds on settlement day (and, since cheques take at least three working days to clear, you will be expected to make sure that the cheque arrives with them not later than seven days after the date of the relevant transaction). If, as expected, the settlement period is reduced to five days, you will have to send your cheque the day after you have dealt.

.....There is no satement issued for settlement purposes. ....

Let us suppose that for one reason or another you want to postpone payment to a later date.

Extended settlement

You may be able to negotiate a settlement period of up to 28 days from the bargain date, but you will probably be asked to pay 25 per cent of the consideration immediately. Also, since this concession will have to be arranged with the market maker at the time of dealing, you may well find that if you want to alter the settlement period, you have to pay a higher price for the share or accept a lower one if you are selling. Thus, if you bought a share on one day in the expectation that the price will rise within the next nine days, and you want to close the transaction before you have to pay for the purchase under normal settlement terms, your agent would have to negotiate a price for settlement of the sale bargain to coincide with the settlement date of the bought bargain. You can of course arrange for an extended settlement for the purchase, thus leaving a longer period for the possibility of a rise in the share price, before closing the bargain.

 SHARE REGISTRY

When anyone buys shares, a record must be kept showing who owns them and the quantity they possess. All companies must keep a register of shareholders. Small companies keep their own and this is usually the job of the company secretary. Larger companies use a registrar who will act for many listed companies. A list of registrars is given in Appendix 1. It is the job of the registrar to remove from the company register the names of those who have sold their shares, and to add to the register the full names of those who have bought. There is always a time lag between the date of purchase or sale, and the alteration on the register, and this can extend to three months or more, particularly if the share is not traded very often.

The date on which the share appears on, or is removed from, the register must never be taken as the date on which the transaction occurred. This is shown on the contract note. The registrar is responsible for such things as paying dividends, issuing vouchers showing tax deducted and capitalisation values. These are dealt with later.

The entry on the Register is the only real evidence of ownership. A contract note *per se* is not.

Contract note as evidence

Although the contract note is not of itself evidence of registration of ownership of a share in the case of a purchase, it is essential that all 'bought' or 'sold' contract notes are kept safely. The information shown on them is vital for calculating possible liability to Capital Gains Tax (CGT) which is explained in detail in Chapter 8.

Under the present system of share registry, you should expect to receive a certificate in about three to four weeks after you have settled a bought bargain. If it does not arrive you may need your contract note to provide evidence of the transaction.

After I have bought a share, do I have to wait for a share certificate to be in my possession before I can sell?

No. You do not have to have the certificate in your hands before selling the shares. The internal settlement systems within the stock exchange will match up your 'bought' and 'sold' bargains from information recorded on the records of transactions which have to be submitted daily by each member firm.

If I change my address, do I need a new certificate from the registrar?

The registrar will not issue a new certificate if you change your address – you will be identified by your name, which is why he will not accept a name for registration with initials only attached.

However you must tell the registrar if you move – or your broker – otherwise all correspondence, including dividend cheques, will go to your previous address, which could create all sorts of problems.

Indemnity for lost certificates

If you lose a share certificate, you can obtain another one by writing to the registrar. He will send you a form of indemnity for you to complete and return. This form has to be countersigned by a bank.

Needless to say they make a charge and this can vary between £25 and £40. It is something to be avoided.

How does the indemnity protect me?

The immediate effect of lodging an indemnity is rather like putting a 'stop' on a cheque. It alerts the registrar to the fact that a share certificate has been lost or stolen or destroyed. If a request to transfer that certificate out of your name subsequently arrived on his desk and he were to allow the transfer, you would have a case against him for recompense.

Systems of recording shareholdings are changing with the introduction of computerised records and soon share certificates will become redundant.

BROKER SERVICES

Rules and regulations have been drawn up governing the conduct of brokers in order to try to safeguard the investing public. They cover all types of services offered by brokers. In some cases the rules put the client at great disadvantage and this can lead to considerable dissatisfaction and complaint. Sometimes it can lead to substantial financial loss. The regulators do not seem to find this situation anomalous. However brokers have to abide by the rules on pain of losing their licence to carry on business.

A number of broking firms offer a two-tier service and charges vary considerably. A list of firms offering execution-only service, together with their addresses and telephone numbers, is given in Appendix 2.

Full advisory service

A full advisory service enables you to discuss your investment requirements and get advice on individual shares. Each person with whom you deal must be registered with the SFA and have passed examinations to demonstrate their knowledge of stockbroking procedures and market practice and be considered to be a fit and proper person to give advice.

> In some cases the rules put the client at great disadvantage and this can lead to considerable dissatisfaction and complaint.

The only way to get the best results out of this liason is to make sure that you have a really good relationship with your broker. Relationships take a long time to develop but they can be destroyed in a moment. You must find an individual with whom you can get on and who completely understands you, your circumstances and your hopes and aspirations as well as your problems. In other words – a friend.

Execution-only service

The second level is an execution-only service.The staff employed in an execution-only department are not allowed to give any advice under the regulations. You must be careful not to cross the line between asking for information which is allowed under execution-only rules, and asking a question which could be construed as asking for advice, which is not.

You are deemed to be fully aware of all the circumstances surrounding a share and your obligations for settlement if you use an execution-only service. That is one of the reasons why this book has been written.

At this point, I want to sound a word of warning. You might think that as a stockbroker I have an axe to grind, but the warning is not be to construed as being an attempt to influence you to avoid using execution-only services.

A large number of complaints arise for two main reasons.

- The first reason stems from the lack of understanding of the mechanics of capital reconstructions which sometimes occur in companies.

- The second reason stems from the regulations imposed on firms by the codes of practice arising out of the Financial Services Act.

Here is a typical example of how such confusion and complaint can and do arise.

EXAMPLE ✳

The most frequent cases occur when a company decides to reconstruct its share structure. This happens most commonly with smaller property companies.

Sometimes the company's assets values diminish to a point where they do not balance with the share capital. The reasons are usually because of trading losses or massive reductions, values of assets, such as property, in times of deep recession. The alternatives facing the company are either to go into liquidation or consolidate the capital of the company, so that where there were millions of shares in issue with a nominal value of 1p, the company converts them into fewer shares at a ratio of, say, 100:1, and then has a rights issue to raise further capital to save the company.

Let us assume that the market price of the share immediately prior to the reconstruction is ³⁄₄p to sell and 1p to buy.

The company then has another capital consolidation after the rights issue of, say, one new 25p share for every 25 1p shares held after the first consolidation.

Thus a shareholder who had 75,000 shares of 1p nominal value before the two consolidations of capital will now hold 300 shares of 25p, assuming that he did not take up any of the rights.

Existing shareholders will have received notice from the company of the intended reconstructions and rights issue, and indeed they will have been notified of their rights to vote at the meetings called to pass the necessary resolutions. In addition, there will almost certainly have been reports and comment in the press about the intended changes in the company's capital structure.

However, it is inevitable that there will be some investors who have missed the news.

If they decide to sell all or part of their holding, believing that they own more shares than in fact they do, and if they use an execution-only service, the broker is not obliged to point out that there has been a capital consolidation, but a good one will do.

The result can be that more shares are sold in the new form than the shareholder actually possesses and the balance will have to be repurchased in order to deliver the correct number of shares to settle the sale bargain.

If you deal through an execution-only service you are expected to be fully *au fait* with the current situation regarding the shares which you buy and sell, and you have no redress against the stockbroker under such circumstances for failing to point out the change in the share structure.

Client agreements

When you deal with a broker for the first time you will be asked to sign a client agreement form (see Appendix 3).

A client agreement form spells out the terms and conditions of business under which a broker is prepared to act, and by signing it you are acknowledging your understanding and acceptance of all the terms and conditions. You must read the whole document and if you have any questions you must ask for clarification before you sign.

The firm is obliged to supply you with a list of charges for all the services on offer.

If you want to make use of their advisory service you will be asked to provide further information, such as the levels of risk that you will accept, whether you want to invest for short-, medium- or long-term and other investment objectives.

The client agreement does not restrict you from dealing through other firms, but you will have to sign an agreement with each one. It is just as much a protection for the firm as it is for you.

The charges will vary with each firm and you must shop around.

> ## SUMMARY

In this chapter we have looked at certain aspects of how the stockmarket works. We have dealt with those operations involved in dealing and settlement which you cannot do yourself unless you are authorised to trade with the market and have the facilities to effect settlement which a stockbroking firm possesses.

In dealing with the various operations involved, we have restricted the information and comments to those elements which are pertinent to you as the manager of your own investments.

From that particular angle we have described:

- The role of a stockbroker in executing buying and selling orders, and the vital need to establish a good rapport with a broker if you are to get the best results.

- The contractual liabilities for payment which arise between broker and client and broker and market maker when you give instructions to execute transactions. The need to make cleared funds available when you buy, and to deliver share certificates and transfer forms in advance of settlement dates.

- The role of a registrar and his duty to keep records of shareholdings.

- What you can do if you lose a share certificate. the reasons for indemnity forms and their costs.

- The implications concerning payment and prices under rolling settlement. How the reduction in the settlement period demands the ability to finance your purchases at the outset now that the 'account' system has disappeared.

Because the changes which are
taking place will affect every private
investor, it is in your own interests
to understand the fundamental
changes that have taken place.

2

Settlement

Part 1: The changes

Part 2: Services linked to the settlement system

Part 3: Advantages and disadvantages of the three options

Summary

Settlement consists of paying cash for shares which have been bought, or receiving cash for shares which have been sold.

A fundamental change, beginning in July 1996, has taken place in the way in which bargains are settled on the London Stock Exchange. A new computerised system called CREST replaces the old Talisman system and it alters for ever some of the practices to which most of us have become used.

One of the most obvious and striking examples of the changes will be the option to abolish the use of stock and share certificates and to record your share holdings on a computer. The system is designed to reduce the use of paper and to handle as much of the process of settlement as possible by electronic methods.

CREST is needed to remove the enormous and expensive movement of paper around the country which happens at present when shares are traded, and to reduce the risks in exchanging shares for money. Whether the effects of these changes make the overall costs of dealing and holding shares any cheaper for the private investor remains to be seen. The purpose of this chapter is to answer two main questions :

- How does CREST work?
- Will the private investor have to pay more to buy, sell, or hold stocks and shares?

In addition, this chapter answers the following questions :

- Does the ordinary investor have any choice whether or not to use CREST?
- Do the different options increase or reduce the risk of loss, either of securities or money?
- What protection does the ordinary investor have under CREST?
- Does CREST make dealing easier or more difficult?
- How does the share holder know what shares he or she holds if there are no certificates?

In order to answer these questions you must understand:

- how settlement works, and

- the difference between a settlement system, and any services which a broker or financial intermediary offers.

Although the two are interlinked, they are quite separate activities.

This chapter will describe these different elements in simple language and give easy-to-follow examples of the various stages involved in the settlement of a bargain. Also, it will show you what options you have when you are deciding which method to choose for holding (registering) your shares. It will explain the benefits and dangers which are involved in the various choices available, and give you the reasons why you may be better off using one method rather than another.

In order to make the whole complicated subject as simple to understand as possible, the chapter has been divided into three parts

- The first part explains how settlement works now, and how CREST works, in simple language.

- The second part describes the various services offered by brokers and financial intermediaries which are linked to the settlement system.

- The third part shows the benefits and disadvantages of each of the three stated options. These are set out in a table for easy reference (see Table 2.1 on page 31). Also this part lists the questions you should ask your broker, financial intermediary or bank before you commit yourself so that you know exactly what your rights are, what the costs will be, and to help you understand and appreciate the risks involved.

Because the changes which are taking place will affect *every* private investor, it is in your own interests to understand the fundamental changes that have taken place. This will enable you to be better informed so that you can make decisions as to how you want your shares to be held in future. You must be satisfied that you fully understand what seems, at first sight, to be a new and complicated system so that you will be able to choose the arrangements which suit your own particular needs. Your aim should be to understand the different options available to you, and what questions to ask, so that you are confident that you have selected an arrangement which gives you the best value for the administrative costs involved.

PART 1

The changes

This part is concerned with the changes in the settlement system of stock and share transactions carried out on the London and Irish Stock Exchanges. Because a fundamental change is taking place, it is necessary to understand how settlement used to work and how it will work in the future. You will also want to know how it will affect you and your share dealings from now on.

> **Using CREST for settlement gives the market the ability to eliminate the need to hold share certificates.**

Under the old system, private investors did not need to know what was involved in handling all the paperwork when they traded or invested in stocks and shares. You bought shares one day and received a contract note, usually the day after. You were expected to pay for settlement about two or three weeks in the future. In due course, after you had paid for your purchase, you received a share certificate which you kept until the day came when you wanted to sell some or all of the shares. Then, when you made a sale, you signed a transfer form and sent it off to your broker or bank, with the share certificate, and subsequently you received some money. You were not concerned with what happened to your old share certificate or to the transfer form, nor were you interested in the processes which took place, 'behind the scenes', whether you bought or sold.

To most people, the share certificate was tangible evidence of their ownership of that particular share holding. It had their name on it and it could be looked at, if required.

Changes have been introduced into the settlement system over the last year. The old 'account' system has disappeared, and the time allowed to pay for your purchases has been reduced. At present, most bargains are dealt on a standard basis for settlement – five business days from the date of the bargain. It may be possible to arrange an extended period of up to 25 days with a market maker, but this concession will probably become more difficult and be restricted to certain shares only. In August 1997 this standard period is almost certain to be reduced even further to three days. However, the most obvious of the changes is the question of stock and share certificates. Using CREST for settlement gives the market the ability to eliminate the need to hold share certificates. Nevertheless, even though a company has decided to enable its shares to be settled through CREST, a share certificate will be produced for a purchase if the investor wants one.

Note that share certificates will not be issued in future when you buy a share in those companies who have joined CREST unless you demand to have one at the time when you give the order to buy. Under the new system, handling any extra pieces of paper such as share certificates will take longer to process with the real possibility of incurring extra administration costs.

In order to understand why these changes have come about and how they affect you – the private investor – you need to understand some more about the process of settlement. This requires a description of the settlement system CREST itself, as well as the ways in which the brokers or intermediaries are linked in to it.

This part explains only how CREST works. The next part describes the reasons why you have to use the services of a broker or intermediary to use CREST.

The best place to start is to give a brief description of how the settlement of bargains in stocks and shares used to take place.

Dealing

When you instructed your broker to buy or sell a share, he entered into a contract on your behalf with a market maker. If your instruction was to buy some shares, the contract demanded that the market maker would be paid on a certain date in the future. If your contract was to sell some shares, the contract demanded that the market maker would pay your broker in exchange for the relevant share certificates and a signed Talisman transfer form renouncing your claim to ownership. Such purchase or sale contracts were usually made verbally. Written confirmation of these contracts followed on the next day.

Settlement

It was the job of Talisman to 'match up' the records of both the broker and the market maker to ensure that both parties to the contract agreed to all aspects of the bargain. For example, Talisman would have to check that both sides agreed about the correct name and type of share, the same number of shares, the price at which the bargain was struck, and the date for payment.

It was only after all this matching up and checking had taken place that the renounced share certificate and transfer form was sent to the relevant company registrar so that he could remove the name and address of the seller from the register of shareholders of the company and send a new certificate to the buyer.

You will see that it all takes time and quite a lot of paper.

Why was CREST invented?

Talisman was owned and operated by the Stock Exchange. The physical handling of these forms, together with the work involved in checking that all the details on the share certificates and the transfer forms match up, is too expensive in a world where information technology does more and more. The Stock Exchange recognised the need to modernise the settlement process and set up a project called Taurus to devise a suitable electronic system. This project was abandoned in 1993 and subsequently the Stock Exchange has decided that it no longer wants to be involved in the settlement process.

A new system has been devised by the Bank of England, known as CREST, to handle the increasing volume of transactions. This will be cheaper, faster and safer than the old Talisman system, and guards against errors whilst protecting the rights of individual share holders.

How does the new system work?

In order to reduce settlement time and costs, the first thing to be taken out of the settlement process must be the share certificate. All the matching up and checking the bargain details will be done by computer. The register will be kept up-to-date by electronic computer transfers in exactly the same way that a Switch card transfers money from one bank account to another, without the need for writing cheques. In the same way, payment between broker and market maker will be made electronically, thereby saving time, paper and costs.

CREST will automatically record all share transactions between broker and market maker as well as transferring ownership of shares between seller and buyer. It will also debit and credit the accounts of both the buyer and the seller immediately, eliminating the need for almost all the paperwork. There will be no need for share certificates within the CREST system.

Will all shares be dealt with within CREST?

It is envisaged that by April 1997 virtually all companies (possibly more than 3,000) will enable their shares to be settled through CREST. It has been estimated that 85–90% of the volume of trade going through the London Stock Exchange daily consists of shares within the top 250 companies in the FT-SE Index. Shares of companies with relatively small market capitalisation and shares listed on the USM and AIMS market will not immediately be included.

As an individual, it is possible to become a 'sponsored member'.

Will any types of share be excluded from dealing through CREST?

Yes. Government stocks (Gilts) and any fixed interest stocks which bear interest accruing on a daily basis, although these will be settled through a CREST style system early in 1997.

Who can use CREST?

In principle, anyone can have access to, and use CREST. Someone who has access to the CREST system via an accredited network supplier is called a 'user'. The computer costs for preparing for, and connecting to, CREST can range from around £10,000 for a very small user to millions of pounds for highly sophisticated investment houses. Generally, users have to be approved by their regulatory bodies and there are substantial financial requirements. However, as an individual, it is possible to become a 'sponsored member'. This choice is discussed in the next part.

PART 2
Services linked to the settlement system

From mid July 1996, the number of companies whose shares are settled through CREST in the first few months are very small. Gradually more and more companies will join and you will be faced with having to make some decisions in the future when buying or selling shares. This part describes what options will be open to you as the scope of CREST grows until it has become fully operational.

There are two important points to make about the effects that the introduction of CREST will have on the private investor.

- *Although the changes which will come about may seem at first sight to be complicated and confusing to the private investor, they must be kept in perspective. In time, they will become normal practice as is the case in other countries.*

- *The effects arising from tightening up the settlement systems may make it less attractive to insist upon retaining share certificates if the consequence is a rise in administrative costs. The danger to the small investor of financial penalty for late delivery of share certificates and transfer forms can be avoided provided you understand how the new system works and arrange for sufficient time to be available for settlement to take place.*

In this part we examine:

- the reasons for the increasing importance of keeping contract notes;
- a comparison of the settlement procedures for a purchase under CREST and the old system;
- a comparison of the settlement procedures for a sale under CREST and the old system;
- the different options open to you for holding your shares either physically or electronically;
- the different ways in which your shares can be registered under CREST;
- the benefits, disadvantages and potential risks involved under each of these options;
- the questions you should ask your broker when you are faced with having to choose one of these options.

You will have to make some choices in the future when you buy or sell shares, and you will be asked some questions by your broker when you give him instructions. We shall demonstrate what the questions are likely to be, the reasons for the questions, and what options you will have when you are faced with having to make a decision. The best way to do this is to follow the process which takes place from the time you give your broker instructions to buy a share through to the share registration.

*If you want to receive a share certificate, whether the company has joined CREST or not, **you must tell your broker at the time when you give him instructions to buy.***

Before you decide whether you want to retain your right to receive share certificates, we shall examine the increased importance which the contract note has, particularly if you choose to accept electronic share registration.

Contract notes

Whatever option you choose, you will still receive a contract note. As we have said in the last chapter, it is important to stress the fact that a contract note by itself is **not** evidence of ownership. It is only a record of an event, i.e. a purchase or a sale, and it is contingent upon either payment of money or delivery of renounced ownership of stock or shares. However, if you choose electronic share registration, this document is the only one you are likely to receive which relates to a particular and specific transaction. It is not a title deed.

The contract note will also have items of information concerning the transaction which you may need for reference in the future, particularly if you want to confirm details of your holding with the registrar. It is easy to forget the details of a scrip issue, for example, or how many rights you may have taken up. If there are no share certificates for you to count, you may have to confirm your holding with the registrar and he will need an identification reference. This aspect will become clear when we look at the different options for share registration.

Settlement of a purchase

Let us assume that you instruct your broker on Monday to buy 1,000 shares in XYZ Plc at 500p each. You would expect to receive the contract note on Tuesday. If the bargain has been done under current standard practice – for example, five day settlement – payment would be required on the following Monday, i.e. five business days later. Your broker has to pay cash to the market on settlement day, whether or not he has received cleared funds from you. If he does not receive your cheque until Monday morning he will be funding your purchase out of his own money for three days until your cheque has cleared.

How will settlement differ under CREST?

Settlement of bargains for companies within CREST will be done electronically and with all the different operations taking place within a very short period. Checking and matching up all the details on both the broker's and market maker's sides of the bargain will take place on the same day of the trade. Settlement (payment) and changes on the share register will take place on settlement day without there being any paper involved. Thus, for those shares which are held and registered electronically, there will be no reason for any delay in the proceedings nor will there be any danger of incurring financial penalties for late payment or delivery of transfer forms or share certificates *because these will not exist, unless, that is, you have chosen to keep your share certificates.*

Settlement for bargains for companies outside CREST, or for any hold-

For those shares which are held and registered electronically, there will be no reason for any delay in the proceedings.

ing which includes share certificates (even if the company is within CREST) will take longer than for those within CREST and will involve more handling. As more companies opt to have their shares and registration handled within CREST, it is likely that there will be a charge made for the extra work involved. It is because more time is needed for settlement that you will have to declare that certificates are involved *before* the transaction is concluded with the market maker. The reason is that after April 1997 he will be expecting settlement to be completed within three days. As we have shown, settlement on time will be impossible if certificates are involved. It may be that the prices which he is making for any given share are based on the expectation of three day settlement. Thus you should be prepared for the possibility of having to accept a different, and probably worse, price for a transaction if share certificates are involved.

Settlement of a sale

Under the current settlement system, if you deal for five-day settlement, you are expected to have placed your share certificate and signed Talisman transfer form in the hands of your broker within five business days of the bargain date. It is generally recognised by brokers that this period of time is tight and any further reduction would probably make it impossible to operate for physical reasons such as postal unreliability and administration requirements for matching up, etc. The share certificate has to be converted from paper form to an electronic record before the system will accept it. This is called 'dematerialisation' by the Bank of England! Thus it is preferable to negotiate a longer period for settlement when the bargain is struck provided you do not get offered a worse price for the extension.

If you fail to deliver the documents within ten business days of the bargain date, financial penalties are levied on the broker by the Stock Exchange which he will pass on to you.

How will settlement alter under CREST?

The system will deal with sales in exactly the same way as purchases. Because there will be no need for share certificates or transfer forms, the whole process can be completed quickly. The settlement period will be reduced similarly and there will be no possibility of incurring penalties from the Stock Exchange for late delivery. Payment and alteration to the share register will take place on the same day. The important point is that if the 'standard' for settlement of three days becomes established under CREST, any form of settlement which cannot be handled electronically from start to finish will take longer, involve more physical handling of paper, and generate a greater number of separate

> .... **If you fail to deliver the documents within ten business days of the bargain date, financial penalities are levied.** ....

operations to complete the process. Inevitably there are likely to be extra administrative costs incurred which will almost certainly be passed on to the client.

Choices for registration of share ownership

There are two choices facing you, the private investor, and these choices will continue to be faced for the foreseeable future. They are :

- to have your shares registered in your own name and to receive a share certificate (certificated share registration);
- to have your shares registered electronically for purchases in those companies which have decided to use CREST (electronic share registration).

Certificated share registration

If you decide to hold share certificates, whether the company whose shares you are buying has joined CREST or not, you need do nothing other than tell your broker, bank or financial intermediary that this is your wish *at the time you give instructions to buy*. You must also tell him that you hold your shares in certificate form *at the time that you give him instructions to sell*. The shares will be registered in your name and at your address in exactly the same way as before.

Dividends will be sent to you and you will receive the company's report and accounts, and be entitled to attend shareholders meetings and vote if you wish.

Electronic share registration

If you decide to have your shares registered electronically when you buy them, you will need to have them kept in a nominee account managed by your broker, bank or financial advisor. A nominee account will be held in a nominee company which is a kind of electronic share warehouse or depository. Most shares – in terms of value – are now held in nominee companies. You will have to make a decision between the *type of nominee account* in which you want to have the shares registered. There are two different types of nominee account which may be open to you.

Broker nominee designated account

The shares will be bought and registered electronically in the name of the broker's nominee company and 'designated' with your identification code number. This means that they are explicitly identifiable as being your property and can be located upon enquiry provided you can supply the correct designation code. If you arrange to hold your shares in this way, you will probably find that your designation code is included among the various items of data shown on your contract note. This is just another reason for emphasising the importance of keeping your contract notes safely. When the 'standard' settlement period is reduced to three days, you will have to come to some arrangement with your broker as to how payment is to be made on time.

If you have to wait for the contract note before you know what amount is due, and if there is any delay in your receiving it, you will not be able to remit the funds to your broker in time. It will be important to ensure that you do not incur any extra costs should such delays happen. Dividends can be mandated to you or to your bank and they can be identified individually upon enquiry by yourself. The same applies to tax credit vouchers.

Broker nominee pool account

Under this arrangement, the shares will be acquired and registered in exactly the same way as outlined above, except that they will *not* be explicitly identifiable as belonging to any particular individual upon enquiry to the registrar. The only name which will appear on the company share register will be that of the broker's nominee company. (The broker will, of course, have internal systems to recognise your holding within his pool.) There may well be several clients of the broker holding different quantities of the same share and all the individual holdings will be 'pooled' for registration purposes and shown on the register as one holding in the name of the broker's nominee company.

Dividends and tax credit vouchers will be sent to the broker for him to apportion to the different holdings and then pass on to you. There could be delays in your receiving them. Clients using nominee pool accounts will not normally receive company reports and accounts, nor will they receive notices of company meetings or vote forms because these are only sent out from the registrars on the basis of one set per holding on the share register. All the shares in the broker's pool will appear on the register as one holding in the name of the broker's nominee company. It should be noted that the Securities and Investments Board (SIB), the regulator of stockbrokers and investment managers, has said that the question of designated or pooled accounts is equally valid in terms of the safety of investors' interests.

Sponsored member

To be a sponsored member you must be sponsored by a firm which is itself a 'user' of CREST. You will have to make arrangements to provide funds for settlement as they are required. You could do this by giving your broker or financial intermediary access to your bank account using your Switch card, for example, or by instructing your bank to accept payment instructions from him. Alternatively, you could keep sufficient funds on deposit with your broker's bank which he can use to settle any purchases on your behalf. The main advantage to you of this arrangement is that the CREST system recognises you as a shareholder. Your name appears on the company register of shareholders and reports and accounts, dividends and tax vouchers, etc. are sent to you direct. When the 'standard' settlement period is reduced to three days, as a sponsored member you will be able to comply with the new timescale of the market and will avoid incurring any financial penalties for being late with your payments in settlement of your purchases. You will still have to deal through a broker. Being a sponsored member does not give you direct access to the market makers. The shares will be registered electronically.

The advantages of electronic registration

The advantages of having your shares registered electronically via CREST are as follows :

- you reduce paperwork to a minimum when you deal, particularly when administering 'sale' bargains;

- there is no danger of losing share certificates so you avoid the risk of incurring indemnity charges made by registrars for replacing lost certificates, because there will not be any;

- there is no danger of incurring financial penalties for late delivery of share certificates or transfer forms, because these will not be used;

- there should be no delay in completing settlement including registration.

The disadvantages of electronic registration

The disadvantages of having your shares registered electronically via CREST are as follows:

- Most investors will probably feel that the main disadvantage will be the absence of share certificates. However, most of the major stock markets in the rest of the world operate without issuing share certificates. Such practice does not cause a loss of investor confidence, either in the system or in feelings of security.
- The reduction in the settlement period to three days will mean that payment has to be arranged much more quickly.

PART 3
Advantages and disadvantages of the three options

One of the side effects of the CREST settlement system will be an increased dependence on the broker by the investor for records of investments held. Consequently, it is in your own interests to make sure that you are fully aware of what charges are going to be made for the various services which your broker offers. It is also very likely that the administrative charges will vary and so it may be to your advantage to shop around. You should pay particular attention to costs of holding shares in nominee companies and charges for transferring from one nominee company to another.

As a result of the changes, there are bound to be many people who will feel that they want to satisfy themselves about such aspects as safety and how to get access to information when required. You may feel it pertinent to ask your broker some of the questions which are listed here.

- *Is there any charge for having my shares held in your nominee company?*
- *If I decide to sell shares through another broker, are there any extra charges for transferring from one nominee company to another?*
- *How often can I have a list of my current holdings? Is there a charge?*
- *How often can I have a valuation of my portfolio? Is there a charge?*
- *How quickly will I receive dividends?*

- *How can I find out what any of my individual holdings are? Who do I contact? What identification do I need to get this information?*
- *Will I be eligible for share holders' perks if my shares are held in a nominee company?*
- *Will I be able to vote at an AGM?*
- *What amount of insurance cover for each investment in my portfolio in your nominee company do I have under the Investors Compensation Scheme?*

Table 2.1

Advantages and disadvantages of the three options, summarised

	Sponsored member	Designated nominee account	Pool nominee
Is my share holding identifiable on the Register?	Yes	Yes	No
Will I get annual and interim company reports and accounts?	Yes *	Yes *	No *
Might there be any delay in my receiving dividends and tax credit vouchers?	No	No	Maybe
Will there be any fees payable for holding my shares in a nominee account?	Ask your broker	Ask your broker	Ask your broker

* You may have to make special arrangements with your broker.

 SUMMARY

The introduction of the CREST settlement system is a logical development if the London Stock Exchange is to be able to compete successfully. Market trading in investments is not only world wide, but everyone who uses the London market expects the same speed of settlement that is considered normal in other stock markets. Certainly it introduces changes, but they will benefit investors overall.

In this chapter, we have :

- Explained the reasons for the introduction of fundamental changes in the settlement systems used by the London Stock Exchange to make them compatible with major stock markets in the rest of the world.

- Described the different choices which are available to you when deciding whether to hold your shares in paper or electronic form, as well as the benefits and disadvantages inherent in both cases.

- Demonstrated the reasons for the inadvisability in choosing to cling to paper share certficates.

- Drawn your attention to the questions which you should ask your stockbroker so that you are fully aware of any additional costs which may be involved in the future, both in actual transactions as well as in any 'storage charges'.

- Defined the degree of protection as well as the 'rights' attached to the different types of registration accounts available to you.

Unless you are fully aware of the characteristics of the different classes of shares and instruments which are available, you cannot construct your own portfolio to achieve your objective whether it is for income or growth.

3

Getting to grips with stocks and shares

Part 1: Shares

Summary

Part 2: Derivatives

Summary

So far we have explained:

- how the market works;
- the role of a stockbroker.

In this chapter we describe the characteristics of the different types of share or instrument in which you can invest. It is most important to understand:

- the rights attaching to each class of share;
- the factors which influence their prices;
- the problems and dangers in buying shares in overseas markets.

Unless you are fully aware of the characteristics of the different classes of shares and instruments which are available, you cannot construct your own portfolio to achieve your objective whether it is for income or growth.

These are the basic materials from which to construct your self-administered private fund, and unless you know how each one functions you will not be able to get the best use out of them.

A word of warning at the outset
Whenever you give instructions to buy or sell a share or bond or any other instrument, it is vital that you give its full description in your instruction. This is particularly important when you are dealing in gilts, preference shares, loan stock or warrants. Otherwise you will run the risk of buying or selling the wrong stock and the result will be expensive – to you.

This chapter has been divided into two parts in order to separate those instruments which relate directly to the assets of a company, such as shares and secured loan stock, and those which do not, such as options and warrants. Those described in the second part can be much more volatile in price and therefore more dangerous. Although they can often be used to advantage, it is strongly recommended that you do not use them to any great extent in portfolio planning and that you thoroughly understand the pitfalls and hazards surrounding them.

PART 1
Shares

Ordinary shares

When you buy an ordinary share in a company, you are investing in a part of the assets of that company.

Ordinary shares carry the most risk among equities but they reap the greater reward and the market prices will be more volatile as a result. **Price movement of a particular share is linked mainly to supply and demand. Market sentiment will largely depend on the expectations of a company's earnings. Sudden and unexpected change in the company's circumstances which are thought likely to enhance or threaten future prospects can alter the price substantially.**

Because the stock market is usually anticipating a company's earnings six months ahead, the share price will reflect an expected upturn or downturn in its profits.

When you are selecting shares to provide the growth element in your portfolio, the ordinary shares will form the backbone of your construction.

All companies have ordinary shares, and all the ordinary shares in issue in the same class will have the same denomination e.g. £1, 25p, 10p, etc., and the same voting rights. Some companies may have more than one class of share, e.g. 'A' or 'B' and these will probably have different voting rights. They may have different rights to dividends as well. You must specify which class of share you want to buy or sell if there is more than one class in existence.

There is no statutory nominal value for an ordinary share, and theoretically it is possible to issue ordinary shares in any denomination. The usual amounts are 25p, 50p or £1. However, all the ordinary shares in issue for a company must be of the same denomination.

> The share price will reflect an expected upturn or downturn in a company's profits.

The fact that one company might decide to issue shares with a nominal value of 10p, whilst another elects to issue shares with a nominal value of £1 has no bearing whatsoever on the size or quality of the company. A lower denomination merely means that there will be a lot more shares in issue for every £1,000 of capital.

Sometimes a company decides to alter the existing share denomination from, say £1 to 25p. The effect of this is that your holding becomes four times larger than it was, and you would expect the price to be reduced to a quarter of what it was prior to the change.

If a company reduces the nominal value, it is usually because the market price of the share has become out of all proportion to the denomination, and it is felt that a reduction in the price per share will make the share more easily tradeable. Many private investors are put off investing in shares when the price is several pounds, but if the company is progressing well and increasing its profits satisfactorily, the price of the share per se is irrelevant.

Any increase in the number of shares in issue as a result of an alteration in the nominal value of the share price does not mean that the company has distributed capital to the ordinary shareholders. The same amount of capital is in issue to the ordinary shareholder as before. It is simply divided into more shares.

There are occasions when a company moves in the other direction and increases the nominal value of the ordinary shares, and this results in there being fewer shares in issue. Using the same example as above, if the nominal value was to be changed from 25p to £1, your holding would be reduced to a quarter of the number held previously.

Such a move tends to raise a question mark as to the future profitability of the company. If the reason for increasing the number of shares is to make the share price more attractive to potential investors, the reason for reducing the number of shares in issue could be that the share price was so low that investors were avoiding the share for fear that the company was going under. Any such alteration in the nominal value of the shares will be shown in the Extel card for the company. An Extel card is a summary of a company's balance sheet and profit and loss information, together with dividend and earnings history over the last five years. It also gives changes in issued capital, identifies the directors and company secretary, and records the names and addresses of the registrar, bankers, solicitors and the company's registered address.

Scrip or bonus issues

If a company has been making good profits for a number of years or if it has sold an asset at a substantial profit, and it cannot envisage any significant calls on its reserves in the foreseeable future, it may decide to distribute some of the accrued funds by way of a scrip or bonus issue. These distributions are only ever applicable to the fully paid up ordinary shares, not to the preference or any other class of share.

Such a bonus issue will increase the number of shares which you hold, and in due course they will qualify for dividends and all the rights attaching to the ordinary shares.

Shares in lieu of dividend

More and more companies nowadays offer a choice between taking the dividend either in cash or accepting shares in lieu. In both cases the creation of these extra shares represents an increase in the number of shares in issue by the company and an increase in the issued capital.

In the case of a scrip or bonus issue, the share price is likely to drop proportionately by the amount of the number of new shares, so that a bonus issue of 1 for 1 would double the number of shares in issue and you would expect the share price to halve.

However, shares issued in lieu of dividend normally have no effect on the share price because the amounts are relatively small.

Do not overlook the fact that shares taken in lieu of dividend will carry a liability to income tax. As far as the Inland Revenue is concerned, you have received a distribution of cash from the company. The fact that you choose to receive it in shares does not remove the potential liability to income tax which you would have had to face if you had taken the dividend in cash instead of shares.

Bearer shares

Some companies have bearer shares which are not registered in individual names of holders. No companies whose registered address is within the United Kingdom issue bearer shares. They are dangerous to own because if you lose them you can not prove ownership. The best way to regard them is as being similar to a currency note. If it falls out of your pocket and someone else picks it up, how do you prove that it belongs to you?

For this reason, it is very important to specify that you wish to deal in registered shares.

Overseas companies

Many overseas shares, Australian and Hong Kong in particular, have shares which are registered in their native country as well as some being registered in London. Stock which is registered in Australia, for instance, cannot be delivered in London for payment when it has been sold. It has to be sent to Australia which takes time and there is a greater risk of it being lost *en route*. Late delivery in Australia, particularly, will cost you a packet because they have their own rules about 'buying in' against you and they can make whatever price they like in such cases. They do not have to abide by market prices for this purpose.

If you ever decide to buy a foreign stock, make sure that it is either London registered and London delivery, or ask your broker at the time if it can be delivered in London when you want to sell it.

Some foreign shares can be bought either in sterling or the currency of the country of origin. Whatever price you are quoted in sterling, the London agent will have converted the current local currency price into sterling and allowed for the cost of buying or selling the currency in the quotation. Unless you hold that currency already, in an account in your own name, there is no point in buying the share in anything other than sterling.

Foreign currency exchange rates can and do move up and down against the pound, sometimes quite sharply but more often slowly and steadily, and usually in the wrong direction from your point of view. It is often the case that a good profit on an investment in a foreign stock is wiped out by adverse exchange rate movement, so you end up making little or no profit. Sometimes the price of the stock drops quite a lot and the exchange rate moves against you as well, so that two bad elements are compounded into a disaster.

Depots

If you buy shares in European countries, it is advisable, sometimes mandatory, to have the share certificate held in a depot to your order. Needless to say, there is a depository charge but it is much safer from your point of view because the depot is liable for safekeeping and delivery when you sell. In fact, you have no choice when you buy German company shares, because the German government does not allow share certificates to leave the country.

Fixed-interest investments

If ordinary shares are the backbone of a company's capital structure, what is the purpose of fixed-interest investments?

They serve two main purposes.

First they are a relatively cheap way of raising long term money to 'gear up' the capital employed in the company and thus enhance the earnings of the ordinary share. If you can raise extra capital at a cost which is less than you would have to pay to a bank, and provided that money is able to earn more than it costs, then the net surplus earnings are available for the ordinary shares and thus enable larger amounts to be paid out by way of dividends.

Also, in many cases, the fixed-interest stock is not repayable in the normal course of events at the behest of the loan provider in the same way as a bank loan.

Second, because the interest or 'coupon' attached to them has first call in the pay out queue, such instruments are generally considered to be a safer investment than ordinary shares. Thus they are a cost efficient and simpler way of increasing the long-term capital in a company without issuing more ordinary shares and diluting the earnings potential for the ordinary shareholder.

A fixed-interest investment is one which produces a rate of return that is set at its birth, so to say, and which remains unaltered for the rest of its life. Some are pure loans to be repaid at a predetermined date in the future, while some, which are included in the category, have certain options attached to them such as the ability to convert into a different class of share in the future according to a formula which will be different in every case.

The safety of the investment depends entirely on the stability of the enterprise to which it relates.

Gilt-edged securities

Gilts, as they are known, consist of loans issued by the government to fund its spending. The government is borrowing capital from the public and in return it guarantees to repay such monies at a date in the future. It also guarantees to pay a certain rate of interest every year until redemption. The period to redemption is divided into three parts:

- **'Shorts'** are those with a redemption date of less than five years.
- **'Mediums'** are those with a redemption date of between five and 15 years.
- **'Longs'** are those with more than 15 years to go before redemption. There are some which will never be redeemed, such as War Loans.

The interest rate attached to each gilt is called the coupon. Some are fixed for the life of the stock and never vary, and some have their coupon linked to the cost of living index and thus the interest rate payable will vary during their lifetime. When the retail price index (RPI) is low, and their yields are relatively low, they are cheap to buy. However, if you take a long-term view of, say, seven to ten years they can be regarded as a useful hedge against inflation.

How is the rate of interest attached to a gilt selected?

When the government issues a new gilt it does so through the Bank of England. A judgement has to be made as to what rate of interest will be appropriate to attach to the new issue. Sometimes, in times of high interest rates, people wonder why the coupon attached is relatively low at the time of the issue. The reason is because a view is taken of the likely average rate of interest which will pertain during the life of the gilt, and the judgement is not an easy one. On one hand the government does not want to pay out more than it has to during the life of the stock, whilst on the other hand it wants to make sure that it receives as much money as possible by way of subscription for the stock when it is issued which could be at a time when base rates are high and better rates can be obtained from other fixed- interest instruments already in the market.

> The safety of the investment depends entirely on the stability of the enterprise to which it relates.

Since gilts are issued by way of auction, the government is never sure exactly how much money it is going to raise until the auction is over.

The nominal value of each gilt is 100, and on redemption that is the amount which a holder at that date would receive irrespective of what the price had been recently. In fact as the date of redemption draws near the price will move upwards or downwards towards 100.

If the price of a gilt is standing above 100, it is said to be at a premium. If it is less than 100, it is said to be at a discount.

A gilt which is standing at a premium should not be discarded automatically when you are selecting investments for that part of your portfolio which is designed to produce income. The decision to include or reject it depends upon other factors dealt with later in Chapter 10.

New gilt issues

The Bank of England acts as agent on behalf of the government and it, together with the Treasury, agrees the size of the coupon at the time of issue of a new gilt.

If the market is able to get a return from an investment with a similar risk of, say, 8 per cent per annum then they are going to ignore an offer of a gilt with a coupon carrying only 6 per cent.

However, if the government is convinced that during the life of the gilt, say 20 years, interest rates will generally be lower and that 6 per cent per annum is a fair rate to pay for that period, then it will fix the rate at 6 per cent.

So when the gilt is issued to the market the Bank has to sell it by way of auction. It invites tenders from the market and the bid levels will reflect the market opinion of what 100p is worth, together with the value of the coupon, compared with what is currently available in the market.

Gilt data including prices are shown in the newspapers as follows:

- *Name* (e.g. Treasury 8pc 2003). The name means very little from an investor's point of view, it merely serves to identify the stock. You will see other names in the list, such as Exch. which stands for Exchequer, Conversion, Consols which stands for the Consolidated Fund, and War Loan.

- *Percentage* (e.g. 8pc) is the annual rate of interest which will be paid by the government on the stock at a price of 100, irrespective of what price the stock is standing at in the market.

- *The year* (or years) (e.g. 2003) is the year in which the Bank of England will redeem the stock *at 100*. You will see some of the gilts have more than one year shown (e.g. 2001–4). This means that the stock will be redeemed at any time during that period. Some, such as War Loan, are undated which means that they will never be redeemed. There is a separate section for undated stocks.

- *Yields*. There are two yield figures shown for each gilt. There are two columns under the yield heading – Interest and Redemption. The first shows the annual rate of interest which an investment will yield at the current price if you bought it today, and the second shows the yield on the same investment if you held it to the redemption date allowing for the gain or loss on the capital depending upon whether you bought the gilt at a discount or a premium.

- *Price*. This is shown in pence with subdivisions of one penny in 32nds, 16ths, eighths, quarters and halves. The price of each gilt is followed by an indication showing the amount by which the closing price has increased or decreased, or remained unchanged, since the close of business on the previous day.

- *High and Low* columns show the top and bottom of the range which the price has achieved over the last 12 months.
  Some gilt examples are shown in Figure 3.1.

| | ...Yield... | | | ...1994... | |
Notes	Int	Red	Price £	High	Low
Shorts" (Lives up to Five Years)					
Treas $8^3/_4$pc 1997............	8.58	6.28	102	$107^{21}/_{32}$	102
Treas $7^1/_4$pc 1998............	7.18	6.51	101	$109^{19}/_{32}$	$100^5/_8$
Conv 9pc 2000...............	8.50	6.99	$105^7/_8$	$108^{27}/_{32}$	$103^{29}/_{32}$
Undated					
Consols 4pc.....................	8.12	–	$49^9/_{32}$	$59^3/_4$	$46^3/_8$
War Loan $3^1/_2$pc‡..........	7.93	–	$44^1/_4$	$45^9/_{16}$	$41^3/_{16}$
Conv $3^1/_2$pc '61 Aft.........	5.77	–	$60^{11}/_{16}$	$62^1/_4$	$58^9/_{16}$
Treas 3pc '66 Aft.............	8.18	–	$36^{11}/_{16}$	$38^1/_{16}$	$34^9/_{16}$
Consols $2^1/_2$pc.................	7.98	–	$31^5/_{16}$	$38^1/_8$	$29^5/_8$
Treas $2^1/_2$pc....................	8.00	–	$31^1/_4$	$32^3/_{16}$	$29^1/_8$

Figure 3.1 Gilt examples

The gilt prices reflect the view of the market on where interest rates are likely to be over a short period. Usually this affects the 'shorts' more than the 'longs' but they will move to keep yields in line with the overall market in fixed interest securities.

Any profit made on the sale of a gilt is exempt from Capital Gains Tax.

However, the converse is that any losses incurred cannot be used to off-set capital gains made elsewhere. Income arising from investments in gilts is taxed at source at the basic rate prevailing. This currently is 20 per cent.

Gilts are generally considered to be one of the safest investments because of their underlying guarantee by the government, but they do not appreciate or decline in price very much. Unless you are able to deal in very large quantities and trade them frequently at specially negotiated rates, they do not form part of a strategic plan for capital growth for the average investor. They should definitely feature in a plan for income.

Generally the price of a gilt moves in the opposite direction to the movement of interest rates. If interest rates are moving down and you appear to be able to get a better return for your money by buying a gilt, then the demand will push the price up. The converse is true also.

Thus gilt prices are sensitive to interest rates and are not connected to the movement of equity prices in any way.

All gilts are bought and sold on a cash basis and this means that you have to pay for them on the day after you have dealt. It is possible to negotiate deferred settlement but this must be done at the time the dealing instructions are given and the price may be affected.

The price which you will have to pay is made up of two elements: the price of the gilt and the number of days' interest accrued.

Interest attaches to a gilt every day from one payment date to the next. All payments are made half yearly and each gilt has a different payment date. Thus if you want to defer your settlement, the overall cost of the transaction will depend on the number of days of accrued interest to which you are entitled.

Other fixed-interest investments

There are many different investment instruments, in addition to gilts, which carry fixed-interest coupons and the safety of each one varies considerably.

This safety factor cannot be stressed too much or too often. It is with monotonous regularity that clients telephone to say that they have seen a stock which is yielding returns well above average and 'should they have some?'

My reply is to ask, 'how much of your hard-earned capital are you prepared to gamble and risk losing?'

It does not matter whether you are buying an equity or a fixed-interest security, the safer the underlying financial base the less the company concerned has to offer to attract investors. If you do your homework, as we have described in this book, the figures will speak for themselves, and you will avoid being burned by the candle as are so many moths!

The safety factor is dependent entirely on the strength or otherwise of the company or institution to which they are linked. They can be issued by other governments or companies including insurance and industrial companies, and they may have a redemption date or be irredeemable.

Each one will have a predetermined payment date, and the frequency can vary up to four times a year.

Because some of the insurance-linked packages can be very complicated, and with very heavy penalties for early withdrawal, it is vital that you read the small print and fully understand all the implications of such an investment before you commit yourself.

The prices of pure loan stock will not be expected to move in concert

> The safety factor is dependent entirely on the strength or otherwise of the company or institution to which they are linked.

with the all-share index because they are related directly to interest rate levels, actual or anticipated.

However, other forms of fixed-interest investments, such as convertible loans or preference shares or bonds, will follow more closely the fortunes of the ordinary share price of the company to which they are attached. As a result their own price is likely to be more volatile.

Preference shares

Preference shares are so called because they take preference over the ordinary shares in the event of the company being wound up, and preference in the payment of dividend. If the company goes bust and the debts are massive, there is not much solace for the preference share holder because he is unlikely to get any money back anyway.

The number of preference shares in issue is usually considerably smaller than the number of ordinary shares.

Preference shares carry a coupon, or rate of interest, which is linked to the nominal value of the share. This nominal value is usually £1. Thus a 5% £1 preference share will only ever pay 5p per share per annum to the shareholder, irrespective of the market price of the preference share.

A preference shareholder is never given the opportunity to take shares in lieu of dividend.

Preference shares may have no voting rights, except under certain circumstances, or they may have different ones from those of ordinary shareholders and these rights will be described in the articles of association or the company prospectus.

There are variations on the basic rights of preference shares as follows.

Cumulative preference shares

These shares have the right to receive any interest which was due to them, and which was not made in any preceding accounting periods, paid up to date before the ordinary shareholders receive a penny. Obviously, if there have been several years when the payment to the preference shareholders has been missed, the company is likely to be in pretty dire straits. However, there are occasions when there has been a change in management, or an outstanding lawsuit looks like being settled in the company's favour, or some such valid reason exists when it is possible to buy this type of share and make a good profit. This sort of investment, under these circumstances, would definitely be regarded as speculative and should only be undertaken when you have really satisfied yourself that you have got enough real information which can be confirmed by independent sources, as opposed to rumour or opinion to expect the company to prosper.

Participating preference shares

These shares, which are often cumulative as well, have the right to participate in the profits of the company at a level which is predetermined by a formula. The formula will be described in the company's articles and prospectus.

Apart from enjoying the same rights as cumulative preference shares, they have the added attraction of the possibility of receiving extra income. This benefit will depend on the dividend rate declared on the ordinary shares being above a certain level which is usually fairly high.

So in a nutshell, the first call on the profits is made by the preference shares, debentures and loan stock if any. Then follow the ordinary shares, and if there are enough profits remaining to be distributed and the formula allows for it, a further distribution will be made to the participating preference shareholders.

The prices of the preference shares described so far will be influenced generally by the prevailing rate of interest. They will not be directly affected by movements in the price of the company's ordinary shares unless market opinion of the company reflects danger signals.

This dependence on interest rates is common to all forms of fixed interest securities unless they are linked to the ordinary shares in some way, such as convertibles.

Convertible preference shares

These shares, which possess all the same rights as ordinary preference shares (and which can have cumulative rights as well), have an additional right to convert into ordinary shares of the company using a predetermined formula. This right is conveyed to holders of convertible preference shares every year as the anniversary of the option approaches. It is sent to each registered shareholder by the registrar and shows the number of ordinary shares to which his holding is entitled to convert at the current price of the ordinary share.

The option to convert is usually available once a year and in some cases the number of years in which you are allowed to exercise the option is limited, in some cases it is not.

- The right time to exercise an option to convert into ordinary shares is when the dividend payable on the ordinary shares exceeds the rate of interest receivable from the convertible preference share. However, beware of creating a liability to CGT.

- The price will move more in line with that of the ordinary share particularly if the company's earnings are rising steadily.

If you opt for the conversion, you are forsaking the certainty of the income represented by the coupon and joining the ranks of the ordinary share-holders in the expectation that the capital growth together with increasing earnings in the future will be greater than the reduced income receivable by way of dividends.

It is usually the case that the price of a convertible is less than that of an ordinary share, and it frequently said that buying a convertible is a cheap way into the ordinaries.

This is true provided the price of the ordinary share is likely to rise by a sufficient amount to make the conversion worthwhile without any extra payment being made by the holder of the convertible stock. You have to apply the predetermined formula to both prices to see what price the ordinary share must reach for it to be to your advantage to convert, and each company's convertible will have a different one.

Some loan stocks are convertible, some are not, see below, 'Secured and Unsecured Loan Stock'.

Permanent interest bearing shares (PIBS)

Within the last few years, as a way of raising extra funds, some of the building societies issued permanent interest bearing shares ('PIBS') which carried a coupon substantially higher than contemporary gilt yields. There were potential dangers to holders of PIBS in the event of the building society being wound up, but the attraction of the yield coupled with the general assessment of the risk ensured a widespread demand for the stock and the prices went to a premium of 20 to 30 per cent.

In 1993, when the effects of the recession were taking their toll on levels of employment, a lot of people who had been made redundant and who were unable to keep up their mortgage payments had their houses repossessed. The resulting glut of houses for sale depressed the property market with the result that there was a fear in the stock market that some of the smaller building societies might find themselves in financial straits. For a time the premium on the shares of those societies which were considered to be most at risk disappeared, but when the management demonstrated that fears of such potential disasters were groundless, the prices recovered.

Another attraction attached to PIBS is that, like a gilt, any profit captured by an investor is exempt from liability to Capital Gains Tax (see below). However, if the building society were to go bust, the holders of PIBS would receive nothing from the receiver and they would lose all their investment.

> ...... **Another attraction attached to PIBS is that, like a gilt, any profit captured by an investor is exempt from liability to Capital Gains Tax.** ......

Secured and unsecured loan stock

A loan stock can be secured or unsecured.

Unsecured loan stock represents a sum of money which the company has borrowed and which is traded on the market in its own right, and which is not secured on any particular assets of the company. It is less secure than secured loan stock from the investor's point of view. Depending on the cost of money prevailing at the time at which it was raised, and the market opinion of the financial strength of the company concerned, the interest rate which it has to pay to make the stock attractive to investors will be more or less high.

The difference between secured and unsecured loan stock is one of safety of your investment in the event that the company is wound up before the loan is redeemed. Secured loan stock is secured on the assets of the company, and ranks ahead of unsecured loan stock in the distribution of any assets if the company goes into liquidation. As far as a company with a large market capitalisation is concerned, there should be no significant difference in price between the two.

There are some loan stocks which offer a variable rate which is linked to bank base rates.

Debentures are similar to loan stock.

Nominal values

In contrast to preference shares, which are usually issues with a nominal value of £1 per share, the nominal value of loanstock can vary, but is normally £100. Foreign stocks can vary upwards of this figure considerably, and often there are minimum amounts for dealing purposes, sometimes quite large.

Price volatility

By their very nature the prices of gilts and large issues of pure loan stocks do not move up and down like express lifts. If they ever start so doing, then there is something very wrong with the economy and any such significant oscillation will be the signal. Small issues of loan stock (say, £10 million to 20 million) issued by a company may move in this fashion, but this is more of a reflection of market sentiment towards the underlying financial strength of that company as well as anticipated movement in interest rates.

Loan stock prices are related directly to interest rates and their price movement is not connected in any way to that of ordinary shares.

Income tax and Capital Gains Tax (CGT)

Both fixed-interest securities and equities which pay a dividend deduct tax before making a payment to the registered holder of the stock. The current rate of tax deducted is 20 per cent and the recipient has to make a further payment to the Inland Revenue to equite the total payment to his tax level.

If you are a single person, as far as the Inland Revenue is concerned, there is not much that you can do to alleviate this situation. There is some room for reducing the burden of both income and capital gains tax if you are married.

If one spouse is in employment and the other is not, or if both are salaried or receiving wages, but the income levels are different to the extent that the rate of tax varies for each person, then it is sensible to divert some or all of the investment income into the name of the partner in the lower bracket.

All that is required is for the share or stock certificate to be registered in the appropriate name, so that the income arising can be demonstrated as belonging to the one with the lower tax rate.

The share can be bought originally in the name of the spouse, where the income is required, or the share can be transferred from one to the other by way of a gift.

Since there is no inheritance tax applicable between husband and wife, there is no financial penalty for making such a gift, and this concession can be used also to mitigate liability to CGT.

This concession is not available for gifts between generations, so gifts made between parents and children, for example, will be regarded in the same way as if the stock had been sold, and a liability to CGT could arise.

You will have to remember that whilst the transfer is effective legally from the date of the gift, it will take some weeks for the new holder's name to be substituted on the register, and if you leave it too late, you could find that the dividend is paid to the wrong recipient. This can be rectified, but it will involve extra correspondence with the tax inspector which could have been avoided.

A transfer is allowable, in just the same way, for the purposes of mitigating CGT.

Each individual, whether married or single, is allowed to generate up to £6,300 per annum of capital gain without incurring any liability to CGT.

> Sensible management of the family investments should utilise all legal concenssions which are available to keep the tax bill as low as possible.

Now it follows that sensible management of the family investments should utilise all legal concessions which are available to keep the tax bill as low as possible. So when in you are contemplating the sales of any of those investments which have been selected for their growth potential, you should use up the tax-free allowance for both parties. It may mean that you have to transfer one or more shareholdings between spouses.

If the transfer takes place within a few days prior to the sale of a share, the tax inspector may disallow the concession on the grounds that such a transfer was a device to avoid incurring a tax liability. It is generally accepted that a period of three months should elapse between the transfer and subsequent sale of a share, but there are no set rules and it is at the discretion of individual inspectors. The longer the period which can be left between the two actions the better.

The computation of gain or loss adjusted for indexation which arises from a sale of a security is described in detail in Chapter 8.

► SUMMARY

In this part we have described the different types of instrument in which you can deal which are linked directly to assets in the company, or, in the case of gilts, which are backed by a guarantee from the government.

In particular, we have defined those prices are directly affected by company results and those which are linked to interest rates and which are relatively unaffected by industrial activity. These include:

- **Ordinary shares.** Relative to all other instruments they carry the greatest risk, but also they offer potentially the greatest reward. Generally regarded as the backbone of most investment portfolios, they are the providers of capital growth. Their prices will move on company results rather than changes in interest rate, and the price movement is usually a direct reflection of market sentiment towards each individual company.

- **Gilts.** The safest fixed-interest investment, because their repayment is guaranteed by the government. Very little growth potential, but likewise not much downside risk either. Prices are sensitive to interest rate movement, either actual or anticipated.

- **Preference shares.** Fixed interest and more volatile in price than gilts, and without the underlying government guarantee. Their safety is linked directly to that of the company which issues the shares. Price movement linked mainly to interest rate change as with gilts, but a radical change in the fortune of the underlying company can have a considerable influence also.

- **Convertibles.** Fixed interest but with the possibility to switch into ordinary shares if the price is rising sufficiently and consistently. An 'each way' bet. Price movement depends on interest rate changes and the results of the underlying company, roughly equally.

- **Loan stock.** Fixed interest, sometimes with a buy back date. Good quality loan stock is a useful ingredient in an income portfolio. Price movements are for reasons similar to those affecting preference shares.

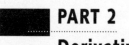

PART 2
Derivatives

Derivatives are so called because they derive their existence from an underlying share to which they are attached.

- They have a price but not a value;
- They do not entitle a holder to share in any asset of the company;
- They do not entitle a holder to any vote in the company's affairs;
- They have a limited life which is defined at the outset;
- At the end of their life they are worthless and they cease to exist;
- Their price during their lifetime is linked to the value of the underlying share to which they are attached.

Options

Options and warrants are derivatives. They are so called because they derive their existence from an underlying share to which they are attached. They do not have any voting rights, nor do they form any part of the issued capital of the company. They simply enable the holder of the instrument to have the right to convert into the ordinary shares of the company at a date in the future if the holder so desires. If the option is not exercised on or before the exercise date it ceases to exist and is worthless.

What is the purpose of dealing in an option?

There are two reasons for dealing in options, namely:

- To protect a holding in a particular share against loss, and
- To make a profit from the movement of a share or the market as a whole, whether it is going upwards or downwards.

As an over-simplification, you can regard an option either as an insurance policy or as a straight bet on the future price of an individual share or the market index.

The option market exists because people want to reserve a position whereby they can buy or sell a share in the future at a price which is quoted and acceptable today.

Naturally enough, if there is a market for something, there are sellers and buyers. If an investor wants to reserve the right to buy a parcel of shares in a company at an agreed price at some date in the future, and chooses to exercise his option subsequently, then the seller of the option must deliver those shares to him at the exercise date.

Likewise, if an investor wants to reserve the right to sell a parcel of shares to the market at today's price, and chooses to exercise his option so to do, then he must be able to deliver the shares to the market subsequent to the exercise date.

- **The option to buy is called a 'call' option.**
- **The option to sell is a 'put' option.**

The price which is agreed at the outset for either is called the 'strike' or 'striking' price. The date for exercising the option is called the 'exercise' date. There are two types of options:

- Traditional options, and
- Traded options.

Traditional option

The market for traditional options is long-established and used to be much more active than it is now.

Traditional options have a life of three months only from the date of purchase and they must be exercised at that time or allowed to expire. They cannot be exercised before declaration day (the day when the option buyer has to decide whether he wants to complete the bargain or let it lapse), irrespective of what the share price has done in the meantime. The purchase of a traditional option is arranged between the person who wants to buy (known as the 'giver'), and the person who is prepared to accept the risk (known as the 'taker').

The 'giver' gives money for either the put or the call depending upon whether he thinks that the price of a particular share is going to rise or fall.

The 'taker' enters into the contract because, in essence, he thinks that he can make a profit.

If the 'giver' chooses to exercise his option, whether it is a put or a call, the 'taker' has to complete the bargain. Thus if the 'giver' has agreed a call option on a share whereby he has the right to buy a parcel of shares in a company at a price of xp, and the price of the share has risen to $xp + 50$ per cent within the three-month life of the option, the 'giver' exercises his right to pay the 'taker' xp per share and the 'taker' must deliver the shares to the 'giver' at that price.

Likewise, in the case of a call option, if the 'giver' exercises his rights to sell shares to the 'taker' at a price agreed at the outset and the price of the share has fallen, then the 'taker' must buy the shares from the 'giver' and the 'giver' must deliver them.

GEC

✴ EXAMPLE Let us assume that the price of the ordinary shares in GEC are 285p bid, 289p offered. The high has been 349p and the low 270p.

You think that the share price is likely to move upwards in the next three months but you do not want to buy at the moment.

It may be that you would like to invest in GEC rather than speculate for a quick profit, but you do not want to buy at the moment, although you expect to have sufficient funds in the future. So you want to reserve your right to buy them in the future at today's price.

You ask for the price of a call option; assume that the option premium is 43p per share in this case.

You will see that the bid price has got to move up to a minimum of 332p (289p + 43p) before you break even.

If you 'give for the call' for 1,000 shares, it will cost £430 plus dealing costs. **This amount is not recoverable whether you exercise the option or**

not. The same applies if you 'give for the put' option.

Thus, if you have taken a gamble on the price of GEC shares moving (upwards in this case) and they do not do so within the life of the option, you will lose £430.

On the other hand, you believe that GEC should form part of your portfolio, and although they have not moved up in price sufficiently, you still believe that they are worth taking up. Since you will not have had to pay commission at the time of taking out the option on the full consideration at the exercise price, there will be no more costs to pay other than Government Stamp Duty, whatever the price has reached when you exercise your option.

You can deal in traditional options in any quantities you choose. For example, you could 'give for the put or call' in 429 shares if you so wished. Most of the money is made by the 'takers' of options.

If you are tempted to become a 'taker' for the call, you should protect yourself by holding the requisite number of shares at the outset. If you 'take for the put' you must be prepared to buy shares at a price above their current market price in order to deliver them if the 'giver for the put' decides to exercise against you.

Traditional options can be arranged between 'giver' and 'taker' in any amounts of a particular ordinary share. You cannot arrange options in any other class of share.

If you have taken out an option on a share, and the share goes ex-dividend during the life of the option and the option is exercised, the dividend must be protected. This means that the 'giver' for the call option must receive the cash equivalent of the dividend from the 'taker' if he exercises his rights subsequently. The same protection of the dividend applies to a put option if it is exercised.

Traded options

Before getting into the details of what are traded options, I should like to make two points at the outset.

First. My advice to anyone who wants to speculate in this extremely volatile market is that you should write off the cost of such a gamble entirely at the outset, and that any profit you might make is a bonus. You should only join in this game if you can afford to lose the money in the first place.

Second. The concept of dealing in something which is not backed by

> .... **You should write off the cost of such a gamble entirely at the outset, and that any profit you might make is a bonus.** ....

any tangible assets, and which has a very short life and which disappears into thin air at the end of its brief period of existence worth absolutely nothing is difficult to comprehend for the average investor. It is also very difficult to explain in simple and clear terms without leaving great big holes in the description which could leave you only partly equipped to understand how and why the the traded option market works and the risks involved.

I have been actively involved in the stock market for years, and I try to make sure that any client of mine really does understand what the risks are, and I would not allow anyone to deal in this market whom I did not feel was able to afford the potential losses.

I have adopted the official description of the component parts involved in traded options, together with illustrations of the mechanics of dealing. Although the descriptions are somewhat stilted, they do cover all the essential facts which you need to understand if you are going to get involved in this market.

There are some similarities between traditional options and traded options.

A traded option confers the right to acquire or sell the ordinary shares referred to in its title in much the same way as a traditional option.

However, there are some fundamental differences between traded options and traditional options. A traded option, as its name suggests, can be traded at any time during its life. You buy and sell traded option puts and calls as opposed to 'giving money'. Instead of 'taking money', you are said to 'write' or 'sell' an option.

You can enter into a bargain by buying at any time and you can terminate your involvement and liabilities at any time by selling. You do not have to wait for a period of time to elapse before you can release yourself.

Traded options are dealt in units called contracts, and each contract consists of 1,000 shares in the underlying company.

Traded options can be dealt in periods of three, six and nine months ahead.

When you buy a traded option you can adopt one of two approaches.

- **Either you can simply bet that the price of the option will rise or fall within a set period in the future.**
- **Or you start by wanting to invest in the share because you have faith in the likelihood of the share price continuing to grow over the months to come.**

If, for some reason, you do not want to pay for a share at a particular moment you can protect your position in the same way as described above for traditional options but at a fraction of the price. Then you can either convert the traded option into the share at the expiry date of the option, or, if you decide not to take up the share, you can sell your option. If you want to take a profit or cut a loss at any time during its lifetime you are free to do so.

Traded options are dealt in every day on the London International Financial Futures Exchange (LIFFE), and bargains are executed using what is called the 'open outcry' system. This means that a dealer shouts the price at which he is prepared to buy or sell, and if the price suits another dealer, the bargain is completed. Prices showing the last transaction are displayed on the dealing screens. Unlike those shown for equities, they are not prices at which you can be sure of dealing. They are only indications of how trading has gone so far that day. They move with a great deal more volatility.

It is important to understand the terminology used in the traded option market. You will see some similarities between these and traditional options, but since the use of the latter is diminishing largely due to their inherent inflexibility, it is worth giving the definitions in full.

Call option

An option that conveys – to the option buyer – the right, but not the obligation, to **purchase** one or more contracts (1,000 ordinary shares per contract) in a specific instrument (known as the 'underlying' instrument) at a fixed price at any time during the life of the option.

Put option

An option that conveys – to the option buyer – the right, not the obligation, to **sell** one or more contracts in a specific instrument at a fixed price at any time during the life of the option.

Exercise

The right to purchase the underlying instrument by the holder of a call, or sell the underlying instrument by the holder of a put.

Upon exercise of an option on equity shares an option seller (writer) will be required to deliver shares at the exercise price (in the case of a call option) or purchase shares at the exercise price (in the case of a put option).

Exercise (or strike) price

The price at which the buyer of a call acquires the right to purchase the underlying instrument and at which the buyer of a put acquires the right to sell the underlying instrument. At any given time, options are available with a range of different exercise prices.

Expiry

The date on which the right conveyed by the option expires. Once an option has expired, it can no longer be exercised and, therefore, ceases to exist.

Premium

The price that an option buyer pays and an option seller (writer) receives for the right conveyed by the option.

How are premiums determined ?

To understand options and the various strategies for employing them, it is vital to have a general knowledge of how option premiums are determined – including the factors that influence whether a given option will increase or decrease in value over its lifetime. Premiums are continuously determined by supply and demand in the trading pits of the exchange. Thus, the premium for a particular option at any given time is a reflection at that moment of supply and demand for that particular option which may well be different for the next trade attempted in the same option.

Option premium = Intrinsic value + Time value

An option's **current premium** is the sum of its **intrinsic** value, if any, and its **time** value.

Intrinsic value

An option has intrinsic value if it would currently be worthwhile to exercise. Such an option is referred to as being 'in-the-money'.

Specifically, a **call** is in-the-money and has intrinsic value if the bid price of the underlying share is above the option's exercise price.

Conversely, a **put** is in-the-money and has intrinsic value if the underlying **offer** price of the share is currently below the option's exercise price.

Time value

This is the amount, if any, by which an option's premium exceeds its current intrinsic value. Time value reflects the willingness of buyers to pay for the **right** conveyed by the option and the willingness for sellers (writers) to incur the **obligations** of the option. In other words, time value represents the value of the possibility that the option will become in-the-money and worthwhile to exercise prior to or at its expiry date.

Variables influencing option premiums

There are five principle variables that influence the level of the option's premium and its response to market events and the passage of time.

1. The underlying share price

All else being equal, call option premiums increase as the price of the underlying shares rises and put option premiums increase as the price of the underlying shares declines (see Table 3.1).

| Table 3.1 | How changes in the underlying share price affect option premiums |

Change in price of the underlying equity	Change in call option premium	Change in put option premium
↑	↑	↓
↓	↓	↑

2. Time remaining to expire

An option's time value is influenced by the length of time remaining until expiry. The less time remaining for the option to move into the money, the less likely it is to do so within the allotted time. Accordingly, the time value component of an option's premium tends to decline with the passage of time. At expiry, time value is zero (see Figure 3.2).

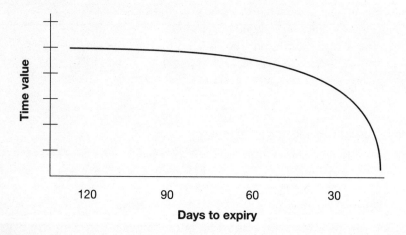

| Figure 3.2 | Time erosion of option premium |

3. Volatility

Option premiums are influenced by current and expected volatility. In volatile stocks, buyers are willing to pay more for the rights associated with an option and sellers (writers) will demand more to compensate them for the additional risks incurred. The more volatile the stock, all else remaining the same, the higher the premium. The importance of volatility in option pricing is considerable and it is made up from two separate elements, historical and implied volatility.

Historical volatility is a figure derived from a share's past price movements. This figure varies according to the time period used in the calculation. It is by no means precise.

Implied volatility is the level of volatility implied by the current premium of an option when the underlying share price, the exercise price, the interest rate and the time remaining to expire are known quantities. Implied volatility reflects the market consensus of expected volatility.

4. Interest rates

Interest rates also influence option premiums. Since buying call options rather than shares leaves capital that can be invested to earn interest, higher interest rates tend to make call options relatively more attractive, thus increasing call option premiums. In the case of put options, higher interest rates tend to increase the opportunity costs involved in holding stock and buying puts, thereby resulting in lower put option premiums. It should be noted, however, that changes in interest rates tend not to have a significant effect on equity option premiums (see Table 3.2).

Table 3.2 **How changes in interest rates affect equity option premiums**

Interest rates	Call premium	Put premium
↑	↑	↓
↓	↓	↑

5. Dividends

Holders of put and call options are not entitled to receive dividends paid on the underlying shares unless they own them. When shares are marked 'ex-dividend', the dividend payment has the effect of lowering the share price. It might be expected, therefore, that an ex-dividend announcement should result in a fall in call option premiums and a rise in put option premiums, but this will have been taken into account in the prices well in advance of the ex-dividend date.

It is essential to understand fully these five principal variables, because they are the elements which exert the greater part of the influences on the premiums of traded options. But there is another aspect to add to your grasp of the subject, and it is this. The instrument called a traded option is rather like an amoeba. It is constantly changing shape because one variable might be exerting a positive influence whilst two or more variables could be exerting a negative influence **at the same time**. For example, you could have bought a traded option where the premium should be increasing as a result of the price movement of the underlying share (a positive influence), but the time to expire might be running out and the implied volatility might be acting against you also (two negative influences). Thus you could find that a profit which should be increasing is actually evaporating, and possibly quite fast.

The strategic use of options

Option strategies fall into two main categories:

- the management of investment risks and returns;
- trading.

In either case the maximum that you can lose is the cost of the premium which you paid for each contract. On the other hand, the profit potential is enormous, particularly when compared to the return on capital employed if you were to buy the underlying shares in the expectation of a rise in price.

> The instrument called a traded option is rather like an amoeba

You will see that you can buy long put options (around nine months ahead) to protect an existing holding in a share if you think that there is a danger of the share price dropping during the lifespan of the option. You can buy long call options in a share whose price you expect to increase, either to protect the purchase price because you would like to buy the stock but do not have the funds at the time, or simply to make extra profits whether you own the stock or not.

Two examples of the gearing effect of options are given in Figures 3.3 and 3.4.

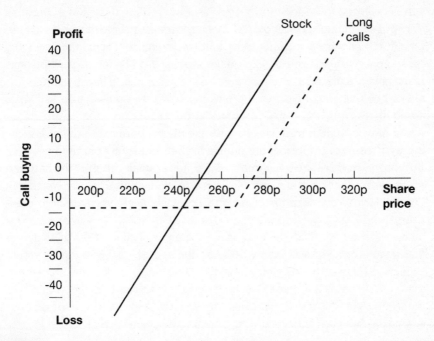

Figure 3.3 The gearing effect of options: call buying

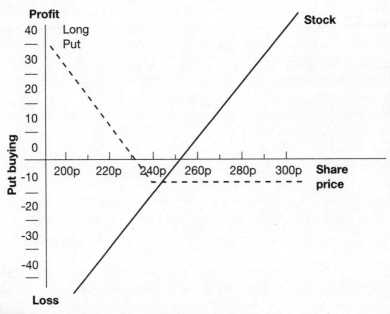

Figure 3.4 The gearing effect of options: put buying

EXAMPLE 1 In the first example (call buying) we shall assume that on 1 November the share price of XYZ plc is standing at 254p and the premium for an April call option with an exercise price of 260p is 14p. You expect the price to rise significantly.

You buy one XYZ plc call at a premium of 14p. Net outlay is £140 (14p x 1,000 shares).

At expiry in April the call will be worth the market price of the shares less the 260p exercise price, or zero if the share price is below 260p at expiry.

If, however, the share price rose to 300p, for example, at any time between buying the call option and expiry of the option, the option would be worth 40p (300p – 260p). Your net profit by making a closing sale of the option or by exercising it is £260 (40p – 14p premium cost x 1,000) less dealing expenses. This represents a profit of 185 per cent. If the share price had not risen at all during that period, or had fallen below 260p by the end of April, the option would expire worthless and you would lose the premium of £140. The break-even share price at expiry, in this example, is 274p (exercise price of 260p plus 14p premium). At any share price above 274p, you would realise a profit of whatever amount the share price exceeds the break-even share price.

EXAMPLE 2 In the second example (put buying) we shall assume that the share price of XYZ plc on November 1 is 254p. You expect the share price to fall sharply. You buy one XYZ plc April 240p put option at a premium of 6p. The cost of the option is £60 (6p x 1,000). If, between the purchase date and the expiry of the option, the price does not drop below 240p, it will not be in your interests to exercise the option, and your loss will be £60. If, at expiry, the price of the underlying share is 234p, you break even. The gain of 6p on the XYZ plc put option when exercised is the same as the 6p cost of the option. The option is worth the £60 you paid for it, with neither a gain nor a loss. At any price below 234p the gain realised through the exercise is greater than the 6p cost of the option. For instance, were the share price to decline to 220p at expiry, the put option would be worth 20p then. Your net gain would be 14p (20p minus 6p initial premium cost) x 1,000 shares equals a profit of £140.

There are many combinations of puts and calls which you can use to take advantage of different views which you might have of the market trend at any one time. You might be strongly bullish, strongly bearish, mildly bullish, mildly bearish or just undecided.

To obtain more understanding and informed advice on the use and scope of the traded options market, you should contact the London International Financial Futures and Options Exchange (LIFFE), Cannon Bridge, London EC4R 3XX.

It is very dangerous to 'write' traded options and the ordinary investor should never be tempted to do so. You can lose a fortune if the market moves the wrong way against you, and many people have become bankrupt in this way

Futures

Futures are very similar to traded options and they are both traded on LIFFE.

Dealing in futures is akin to gambling at a casino, and it makes sense to 'write off' your investment at the outset. This is a market for experienced traders who are able to devote all day to monitoring their investments.

As far as the private investor is concerned the only futures market which may be of interest is the market in the future level of the FT-SE 100 Index.

It is possible to buy or sell an option on the level of the FT-SE 100 Index in exactly the same way as a traded option and in the same dealing parcels. The option time periods are similar and at the end of its life, the option dies without value

Nowadays the movement of the futures prices of the pound and its relationship with the US dollar and, to some extent, the German D-mark, taken together with the anticipated movement of interest rates in those countries, has a big impact on the FT-SE 100 futures price. This in turn can have considerable effect on the prices of ordinary shares whether the hopes or fears are real or imagined.

It is largely this factor which accounts for the volatility in market prices and quite often when there have been some fairly big rises or falls in the FT-SE 100 Index, the volume of trades recorded in equities is low. In the case of a significant fall, it does not necessarily mean that there has been any wholesale dumping of shares on the market, which makes forecasting short term market movement difficult.

Warrants

A warrant is a derivative and in many ways is similar to an option.

It is used by companies to raise money without having to pay the current rate of interest for loan stock.

- **It does not have any voting rights.**
- **It has a limited life, and if it is not converted into ordinary shares before the expiry date, it disappears at no value.**
- **It carries a coupon payable each year of its life.**
- **It is not redeemable by the company although, like a convertible, it can be exchanged for ordinary shares of the company at set dates each year according to a formula established at its creation.**

If the conversion rights are exercised before its expiry date and ordinary shares are exchanged for a warrant, its coupon will disappear but the holder will become eligible to receive dividends. If the warrant is not converted, the warrant will disappear at no value and its coupon will vanish.

A market is made in warrants in exactly the same way as for ordinary shares, and they can be bought and sold independently from the ordinary shares to which they are attached.

The price of a warrant will move much more closely with that of the underlying security.

Warrants are attached to ordinary shares only.

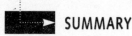

SUMMARY

In this part we have dealt with those investment instruments which have no intrinsic values, only a price.

They have a role to play in investment management but they can be extremely dangerous, and we have demonstrated that anyone considering buying such instruments should be prepared to consider the cost of such investments as having been written off at the outset.

In particular we have examined:

- **Traditional options**, their advantages and disadvantages. Very little trade is done nowadays in traditional options, with the result that they are expensive to deal in. Unless there is a particular reason for using them, they are best avoided because of the cost.

- **Traded options** and the role they have to play, whether for use as an aid to protecting existing shareholdings, or as a means to lock in a profit. In addition, we have shown how they can be used as an enhancement to a portfolio designed for trading. They are extremely dangerous for anyone who has not got the money to lose and the time to spend keeping constant watch over their progress. Also the fact that they have a limited life and expire without value makes them even less attractive for those with limited capital.

- **Futures** and their disadvantages for the private investor.

- **Warrants**. Their brief lives, coupled with the absence of any asset backing, does not make these instruments attractive investments unless it is for very short periods, and provided the share to which they are attached is likely to increase in price dramatically.

If you buy a share without doing enough homework, you stand a very good chance of losing money.

4

Gathering your share information

Share information

Share price information

Information from other sources

Speculative buying

Summary

It has been said that information is worth money. That may well be true, but it is certain that if you buy a share without doing enough homework you stand a very good chance of losing money.

You would be unlikely to buy a house without first finding out as much as you could about the local amenities, or whether there were plans to build a motorway through the garden, or indeed, whether the building was sound and safe. **So why not do the same with your investments because it is your money which is at risk.**

You can divide information into two categories:

- that which is, or may be, to your advantage; and
- that which poses a potential threat.

In this book, we tell you where to look for your data and what questions you should be asking.

Information comes in two forms: opinion; and facts.

The most meaningful information is derived from reading and analysing company reports and accounts, and we deal with this subject in the next chapter.

In this chapter we describe the other sources such as the financial Press, trade journals and general news items.

We discuss the importance of collecting as much published information about a company as possible concerning:

- management;
- products;
- markets;
- competition;
- share price history;
- dividends and dividend cover;
- price earnings ratios.

We explain how to read the financial Press and interpret the key indices which you need to make your investment decisions.

SHARE INFORMATION

The stock market is a dynamic entity and is constantly subject to a mass of different and frequently conflicting influences. Emotions such as fear and greed play a considerable part in creating or killing a demand for a particular share.

There is a great deal of information which is only available from firms who supply 'real time' data via terminals for which you have to subscribe, such as Reuters, Datastream, Micropal, Topic and others. The cost is considerable.

Examples using such sources are given in this book to illustrate various points, but most people would not find it economical to lease such equipment. You may be able to get some of the more detailed and historical information from a broker but you might have to pay a fee. Otherwise you will have to compile your own records from information which is published nationally.

Rumours or hard fact are discussed in the Press and the share price will move to reflect current opinion which may be 'bullish' or 'bearish'.

This is most evident in those shares which are actively traded, and the volatility can be such that certain share prices often move up and down by substantial amounts during one day's trading. The smaller and less appealing companies' share prices tend to remain fairly static. It is important to bear this in mind if you are considering buying into smaller companies.

The press

There is a huge amount of information published about companies, their management, markets, products and the possible effects on their future profits, of changes in legislation or such things as base rate and exchange rate alterations.

> The smaller and less appealing companies' share prices tend to remain fairly static.

Press speculation about a company will draw attention to the share and this can have a marked influence on the price which may last only for as long as the newspapers keep talking about it.

Management changes are very important

Remember that companies are run by people and people are fallible. You should be alerted when a successful chief executive retires or a merger or takeover happens, in case the control and dynamic of the company deteriorates.

Any change in the status quo means that investors, existing or otherwise, may well become nervous and watch to see whether the change is for better or worse.

In view of all this, and because you cannot spend all day and every day reading all that is printed, you have to select a few guidelines to use to make your decisions.

■ SHARE PRICE INFORMATION

The spread

Share prices are always quoted in the market showing two prices; the bid and offer. The difference between the two is called the spread. Unfortunately, share prices are given in the media using the midway figure between the two and you do not have any idea how wide the spread is either side of the middle.

Figures 4.1 and 4.2 show two companies at either end of the range.

```
SHEL.L                                                      10:21
SEAQ GBp SHELL TRNPT(REG)        Cls   708-711            REUTER
NMS 75    PL 225  SS 8                              GMT 10:24
                              Net -4          H 713    L 703
Vol 728.3                                      News   6SEY
Last ↓704    705    708    707    707                   10/8
```

WARB	LEHM	SGST	704-708		NWSL	UBS	JPMS
AITK	703-708	25+25	08:53	NMRA	704-709	100+100	10:22
BEST	704-709	100+100	10:16	NWSL	703-708	100+100	08:54
BZWE	703-708	100+100	09:45	RAML	703-708	25+25	08:53
GSCO	704-709	100x100	10:06	SALB	704-709	100x100	10:22
HOAE	704-709	100+100	10:15	SBCE	703-708	100x100	09:37
JPMS	703-708	100x100	09:19	SBRO	704-709	100+100	10:14
KLWT	704-709	100+100	10:13	SGST	704-709	100x100	09:16
LEHM	704-709	100x100	09:57	UBS.	703-708	100+100	09:16
MOST	703-708	100x100	09:24	WARB	704-709	100+100	10:02

Figure 4.1 Bid and offer prices for Shell on 18 July 1994
Source: Reuters

```
MTI.L         MTL  INSTRUMENTS        Cls   305-315      07:20
SEAQ GBp                                                  REUTER
NMS 0.5   PL       SS 0.5                          GMT 10:26
                              Net 0          H 310    L 310
Vol
                                                   News
Last  ↓310                                               2/2
        WINS   BZWE      305-315      BZWE   WINS
BZWE   305-315      1+1   07:20   WINS  305-315    1+1  07:25
```

Figure 4.2 Bid and offer prices for MTL Instruments on 18 July 1994
Source: Reuters

You will see that the best price at which you can sell Shell (the 'bid') is 704p, and the cheapest price to buy (the 'offer') is 708p. This is a difference of 4p or 0.56 per cent, whereas in the case of MTL Instruments the difference in the spread is 10p on a bid price of 305p or 3.27 per cent.

Does the percentage difference matter?

There are many people who hold the view that a 'penny' share only has to move up a few pence to produce a large percentage gain and so they prefer low-priced shares.

I would make two points here:

- First, in the examples given, and ignoring dealing costs, MTL has to move up 3.27 per cent before you break even, which is much more than is required in the case of Shell. If you have to get out of your investment in a hurry, you would lose less with Shell, assuming that both prices remained unaltered.

- Second, while most 'penny' shares are much cheaper to buy than MTL, the amounts in which you can deal at the price quoted do not make the investment economically attractive. If the price of the share is around 100p, and the market maker is quoting that price for 1,000 shares only, you would want to buy many more than 1,000 shares to make the investment worthwhile. You can see in the two examples given that the market makers are quoting firm prices for Shell for up to 100,000 shares in most cases, whereas in the case of MTL, they are only making firm prices for up to 1,000 shares. Whilst they will probably be happy to sell a larger amount to you, it will almost certainly be a different story when you want to sell more than 1,000 back into the market, and at a lower price than the mandatory quote shown on the screen.

Volume traded

One of the reasons for the difference is because Shell is widely traded and MTL Instruments is not. You can see this in two places in the examples. The abbreviation NMS stands for 'normal market size' (of bargain), and in the case of Shell it is 75,000 shares, whilst in the case of MTL Instruments it is 500 shares. Also, there are 18 market makers prepared to deal in Shell, and only two for MTL Instruments.

Price movement

The price of Shell is shown to be lower than the closing price in the market on the previous day (708–711) and the price of MTL Instruments has remained the same. The difference in the spread for Shell has widened by 1p, but it is still a low percentage.

Unless you can visit a broker's office you will not be able to see this data, but by asking for any items which are shown on the screen, you will not be stepping outside the rules governing 'execution only' service. Information is not advice.

You should ask how many market makers there are for any share in which you are interested, and what has been the volume traded that day. Any share with less than five market makers involved is one which you should treat with a great deal of caution. Otherwise you have rely on what is published. The *Financial Times* prints the closing prices daily of many more companies than do any of the other national papers, and if you want comprehensive coverage of the prices of smaller companies, then it will be essential to get the paper at least once a week.

'Highs' and 'lows'

After you have drawn up a shortlist of shares for consideration, the first thing to look at is the 'highs' and 'lows' of the prices. If the current price is at or near its high then you may want to research the price movement on a monthly basis, perhaps over the last three years.

What does it tell you?

Let us take some lessons from the share information shown in Figure 4.3. Details are shown for two of the larger companies in the food manufacturing sector, Associated British Foods and Cadbury Schweppes. You will see that A.B. Foods is standing at 582p compared with a high of 607p and a low of 499p. The current middle price is 25p off its high for the year.

Cadbury Schweppes, on the other hand, is standing at 453p compared with a high of 545p and a low of 407p. The current price is 92p off its high.

Name	Price	+ or −	1994 High	Low	Yield Gross	P/E
Associated British Foods	582	+1	607	499	3.2	11.6
Cadbury Schweppes	453	+12	545	407	4.0	15.3

Figure 4.3 **Share highs and lows**

Since they are both first-class companies you have to ask what has happened to depress the price of 'Cads', and whether there is anything fundamentally wrong with the company.

More research is therefore needed

If the reason seems to be trivial or temporary, the recovery in the price could capture a good profit for an investor. Also, subject to the findings of your research, if the share has been as high as 545p it is quite reasonable to expect it to get back to somewhere near that figure again. Beware of a previous 'high' being achieved as the result of a takeover rumour, because that would indicate that the price was not reached through fundamental value of the company's performance. However, in the absence of such a reason, you could expect to see an increase of 20 per cent from the current price level of Cadbury Schweppes, whereas to look for a similar percentage increase in the price of A. B. Foods would demand a share value which has never been achieved so far.

 If your subsequent research confirms that it is a share worth having then you can set a price limit at which to buy which is realistic and at which it has been available within the last 12 months.

The value of keeping records of price movements over a period of, say, three years can not be overstated.

You may find it more instructive to show the record graphically.

You will see from the record of the price of Dalgety in Figure 4.4 that the share could have been traded profitably several times during the period from January 1991 to January 1994. We shall return to this company in subsequent chapters to illustrate other points, but it is a good example of a share which can be regarded as a short-term trading opportunity. Also,

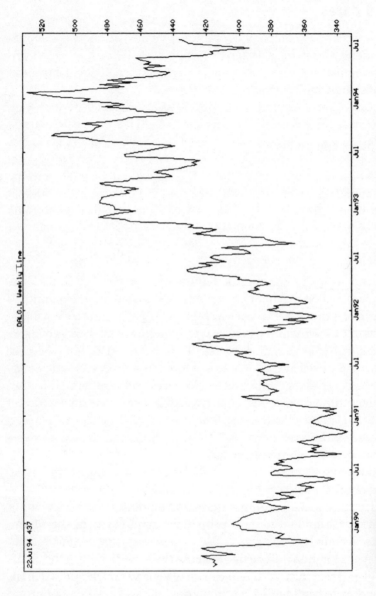

Figure 4.4 Graph of Dalgety share price movements from July 1989 to July 1994

Source: Reuters

by using some other techniques to safeguard your capital, it can qualify as a longer term investment.

Dividend dates

Some time before the company announces whether or not it is going to pay a dividend, the share is declared 'ex-dividend' in the market. A symbol indicating that the share has gone ex-dividend (or XD) will appear in the lists of shares published in the daily Press.

This means that a buyer is not entitled to receive any dividend on shares purchased from that time until the dividend has been paid to those who are on the register up to the date when the registrar 'closes his book'. That date, known as 'book-closing day', will always be later than X date. So if you buy a share which has gone XD, you will not be entitled to the dividend announced recently. If you buy a share which is not quoted XD, you will be entitled to the next dividend, so long as you have not sold the share before it has gone XD. If you sell the share *after* it has gone XD, you will be entitled to receive the dividend when it is paid.

Price movement at dividend date

When the share goes XD the price always falls. The reduction is usually about the same amount as the value of the dividend, although sometimes it can be less.

The decision to sell before the drop in price, or wait for the right to receive the dividend, can be influenced by an individual's tax position and whether the holding was bought for capital gain or income purposes. This aspect is examined later in Chapter 10.

However, if a dividend is reduced, the loss of faith in a share and, therefore, in the company's management, is enormous and, if the dividend is 'passed' (meaning no dividend paid), the effect on the share price can be catastrophic.

The share price will drop dramatically, and unless there is a very strong and creditable reason for full restoration of the dividend in the short term, the price is likely to remain depressed for a very long time to come. Unless there is a change of leadership fairly quickly, the share is likely to be 'rerated'. This means that you have to re-establish your parameters when monitoring the progress of that share in your portfolio and assessing its future contribution to your objectives.

✳ EXAMPLE ICI

In May 1994, it was widely rumoured in the Press that ICI figures due for the quarter would be considerably worse than expected, and the share price dropped by £1 (see Figure 4.5). When the results were announced, they were poor but not catastrophic, and the chairman was sufficiently encouraging about the future for confidence to be restored in a very short time.

Of course, if you had been keeping your intelligence systems up to date, you should have seen enough to start alarm bells ringing in plenty of time and sold long before incurring a loss. However, even the best managers can be caught unawares, so it is bound to happen at some stage.

Alternatively, the bold and brave might have reckoned that the market had over-reacted and that it was a risk worth taking to buy some shares as soon as the price started to recover. If you are tempted to have a gamble of this sort, you should back first class companies only if such a situation arises. Do not be tempted by any similar price drop in anything other than household names, and do make sure that the reason for a larger than expected drop in earnings is not a symptom of a major change in the company's longer-term future performance.

Dividend cover

This number is also published in the daily Press and is an important factor when judging whether or not to include a share in your shortlist. We shall examine earnings and dividends and the effect of inflation in more detail in the next chapter when considering company reports and accounts, but here we are concerned only with the concept of a quick appraisal of the company's strength. The figure denotes the number of times the last annual dividend was covered by the earnings available for each ordinary share, after allowing for prior charges such as preference dividends or loan stock interest, if any.

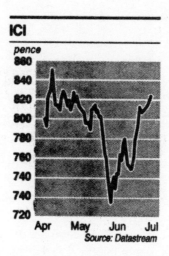

Figure 4.5 ICI share price movements from April to July 1994

Source: Datastream

You can set your own level of dividend cover with which you are happy, but a good general rule is that it should be at least a factor of two.

Very low cover should alert you as to whether the dividends can be maintained at the level last declared, or possibly whether any dividend can be paid at all.

Unless there is solid evidence to the contrary, the lack of adequate earnings indicates either rash management or poor progress.

Either way the share could easily lose support and you would expect to see the price drop

In Figure 4.6. the dividend cover for Cadbury Schweppes was 1.9 compared with that of A.B. Foods which was 3.2. However, in the case of Dalgety it was only 1.6.

Name	Dividend cover
Associated British Foods	3.2
Cadbury Schweppes	1.9
Dalgety	1.6

Figure 4.6 Share prices of food manufacturers showing dividend cover

Price earnings ratio (PER)

This is a number which is arrived at by expressing the price of a share as a ratio of the earnings per share.

By itself it is meaningless but it is generally used to compare one share with another **in the same sector.** You would compare a bank with a bank, not with a water company or a company in a different business.

In the example in Figure 4.3 above, the PER for Cadbury Schweppes is 15 whereas that for A. B. Foods is only 11.6.

Stock markets do not move in straight lines, rather more in a succession of peaks and troughs, sometimes erratically, but they do tend to follow a pattern. The best analogy is a bouncing ball and the trick is to anticipate the next upward or downward movement.

Another aspect which is useful is to compare the average PER of the UK market as a whole with that of another market such as the USA or Japan. If the market PER is reaching new heights it can often indicate an imminent reaction downwards and you should be alerted.

High PER

It is usually accepted that the higher the PER the more the share price is expected to rise further. Demand has usually outrun supply and the demand has been generated by belief that the company's earnings are set to grow even more than heretofore. Since, as has been indicated, emotion plays a large part in fuelling demand, you must be chary of the 'hope' factor if you are attracted to a share with a high PER, and satisfy yourself that the price has not reached an all-time high from which it is just about to retreat. This will almost certainly happen if the company's earnings are not as high as the market is expecting.

> Stock markets do not move in straight lines but they do tend to follow a pattern.

It is generally perceived that markets are driven by two things – fear and greed. There is an element of truth in this somewhat simple belief, because in general the public tend to miss the boat when buying a share that has started to rise in price, and they usually get in long after the greater part of the rise has taken place. The extra demand for the share pushes the price up even more, and by that time the PER is standing at a level which, if it is to be justified, means that the earnings have to rise by a very large percentage indeed.

More often than not the expected increase does not materialise and the late buyers are disappointed. Those who had bought the share when it started its upward run in price are happy to take their profit, so they sell their holding. This pushes the price off its peak, and others start to limit their potential losses by selling as well. Then fear sets

> **'Sell on a rumour and buy on an announcement'.**

in and more holders start to sell, which depresses the price even further. The market makers do not want to become overloaded with the stock, so they mark the price down savagely, and so the PER drops to a more realistic level.

Very often, of course, the market reaction is overdone and the price drops to a level below that justified by the earnings, and so the share becomes a 'buy' again, always assuming that there is no other reason to doubt the ability of the company to continue to increase its earnings at the same rate as heretofore.

There is an old saying – 'Sell on a rumour and buy on an announcement'.

Low PER

A low PER indicates lack of support, and justifies further investigation to see whether it is worth taking a risk and buying. It is always worth looking to see why a share has a low PER. Frequently you will discover sufficient reasons fairly early on in your research, which will confirm your

> **Apart from analysing the report and accounts, you can start digging for clues elsewhere.**

doubts about the share as a worthwhile investment, but occasionally you will not find any good reason, and it can simply be the case that the shares in the rest of the sector have become popular and this one has been overlooked.

No PER

There are some companies whose share prices are shown in the Press which do not have a PER indicated. This is either because the nature of their business makes such a measurement meaningless – insurance composites and investment companies are two examples – or because they may be foreign shares and the information would be irrelevant.

Apart from analysing the report and accounts, you can start digging for clues elsewhere.

INFORMATION FROM OTHER SOURCES

The areas to look at are the same for any share whether it has a low PER or not. The search for information applies just as much to people as it does to companies. Here are some guidelines and questions which you may want to answer before you are satisfied that you know enough about the company for your own satisfaction and peace of mind. Do try to be objective in evaluating your answers because, gathering share information is rather like reading your horoscope: it is only too easy to convince yourself that anomalies are unimportant.

Management

Who are the directors ?

Have you ever heard of them? Have they got good or bad records?

How long have they been in business?

Inexperience of managing people and business can be expensive however brilliant people may be technically.

What other directorships do they hold?

A lot of non-executives on the Board is not necessarily a good thing.

Is their pay disproportionate to those in other companies in the same sector of a similar size?

Consideration for shareholders, or lack of it, and greed, or lack of it could perhaps be indicated by the director's emoluments which they award to themselves.

Is the company effectively run by one person only?

Companies which are dominated by one man, or which are run on the lines of a dictatorship, very rarely have adequate successors-in-waiting. The departure of such individuals leads to a management vacuum and perhaps some in-fighting for the throne. Consequent lack of leadership will demoralise the rest of the employees and certainly the market opinion of the company will deteriorate.

Products

What is the range of products?

Avoid a single-product company unless there are very good reasons for it e.g., a gold mine.

Are the products out-of-date?

Companies which do not innovate will die, and it is their products or services which are their life-blood. The computer industry is an example of an area where new products and designs sprout like mushrooms almost every month.

Is there a threat of more effective competition from elsewhere, either at home or abroad?

If there is, you should be very wary of investing in their shares and give this deficiency a fairly heavy weighting in arriving at your conclusions. For example, China is becoming an even greater threat than Japan or Taiwan or Korea because of their cheap labour costs.

How much do they spend on R&D?

Pharmaceuticals, cars, electronics, aircraft, oil exploration companies, in particular, must invest heavily – but compare like with like.

I am a great believer in doing your own market research in a small way. A regular trip round the shops will tell you which products are popular and which are not. You can see for yourself which ones are in demand. However, you must beware of products which are selling fast because they are the latest fad. Whatever happened to hula hoops?

Markets

Is the market for the company's products expanding or contracting?

This is one of the most important questions to ask, and you should research it thoroughly until you are satisfied that you can make your decision from a knowledgeable base. There is no point in backing a company whose market is shrinking, unless it has got demonstrable and publicised plans to enter new markets. However, changing horses in mid-stream can be perilous.

What is the competition?

The brewing industry has been hit hard by the removal of restrictions on the amount of beer and spirits which can be imported by individuals for their own consumption. Thus a change in the law led to a considerable increase in competition and consequent loss of sales. Foreign competition for the booze business is strengthened by the much lower taxes imposed on alcoholic drink by countries abroad.

Are the main markets in politically and financially stable countries?

Recently several companies have gone bust through not getting paid for goods and services sold to East European countries. This was not necessarily brought about by a weak currency but more because of bad management.

Is the market one which is likely to be affected by rises in the cost of living?

So-called luxury goods are the first to suffer when the cost of living gets out of hand. In Japan until recently, the 'smart set' of young executives bought £300 platinum cigarette lighters and really expensive designer handbags for men. All this trade ceased when the cost of living suddenly exploded.

Is the market limited?

Weapons and electronic guidance systems are dependent on big orders from a small number of buyers. This means you either win a big order or lose altogether.

Is the company dependent on one or two big customers ?

Supermarkets or chain stores have a stranglehold over their suppliers because of the power that their ability to place very large orders confers. The motor car manufacturers used to have a bad reputation for driving smaller subcontractors to the wall by demanding ever lower prices from their suppliers.

Are the sales heavily dependent on advertising?

Such marketing tools are very expensive, and unless the volume of sales increases sufficiently and the company earnings even more so, the company could get into trouble.

What are the chances of opening up overseas markets ?

Beware of the cost of establishing a reasonable market share, and the time it will take. Earnings could suffer considerably in the meantime.

A great deal of information giving whole or partial answers to these questions can be obtained from reading, and, as has been stated above, since it is people who run companies, you should always be interested in announcements of changes in boards of directors, even if they are not related directly to companies in which you hold shares currently.

Nowadays, company reports are much more informative then they used to be. You can get a great deal more information about the company, its directors, its products and its markets. Also, the new accounting reporting standards ensure that a great deal more of the figures shown are analysed, so that you can get a more accurate picture of how the company is faring. The company secretary will be only too happy to send you a copy on request even though you are not a shareholder.

It is a very good place to start your research because, apart from the information given about their general activities, you will need the detailed figures in the accounts for your main analysis.

You never know when such knowledge might give you an edge and prove to be profitable. As they teach you in the Army, 'time spent on reconnaissance is seldom wasted'.

Directors' shareholdings

Another area which you should watch is changes in shareholding by directors. Although rules are very strict governing the times when directors can buy and sell shares, significant share deals by directors and large institutional shareholders are reported in the Press, and these should be noted.

There may be many reasons why a director sells his shares. Domestic needs, such as school fees, moving house, hospital bills, to name but a few. However, usually there is only one reason for buying them and that is because he expects the share price to go up.

Institutional buying is another point to note. Institutions employ analysts whose job is to find undervalued shares, so that the fund managers can get in at a price which they believe will show a profit.

> 'Time spent on reconnaissance is seldom wasted'.

When you see reports of large amounts of shares being bought in a company, either by directors or institutions, it should alert you to do more research. *It should not be the sole reason for your purchase.* Sometimes pension funds, (which translated usually means insurance companies), are so full of cash that they make an investment which looks to the outsider to be a fairly large one. It may actually be a fairly insignificant investment in money terms as far as they are concerned, so you should always calculate what percentage of the issued capital of the company is represented by their purchase. If it is around 2 per cent, it is not particularly remarkable because you don't know whether the amount of money invested is a significant percentage of the fund making the investment.

SPECULATIVE BUYING

No share should ever be bought on a speculative basis alone. It must stand up on its current performance. Any subsequent event such as the arrival of a bid for the company, or the discovery of a gold mine under the works canteen, should be regarded as a happy bonus, but the possibility of such an event occurring should never influence the decision to buy the share in the first place.

SUMMARY

In this chapter, we have looked at the kind of general and basic information which you should seek in order to satisfy yourself that you know as much as anyone about a particular company before you put your money into the shares.

These factors form only a part of the whole picture which you will require before making a final decision to invest any capital.

We have explained what sort of data you need to obtain in order to measure the strength (or weakness) of:

- **Dividend cover.** Ideally it should not be less than two times because anything below that figure means that not enough profit is being put to reserves to provide some 'fat' to be drawn upon to maintain the dividend if lean times occur.

- **Price Earnings Ratios (PER)** and the importance of comparison of PER for any individual company with others in the same sector. We have stressed the need to beware of historic PER which may be significantly out-of-line with others in the same sector whether they are too high or too low. We have emphasised the need for further research in depth should you find such a situation.

We have also emphasised the importance of finding out all you can about the company's:

- **Products and their competition**, particularly from overseas manufacturers. Also their design and long-term future, and whether they are a 'fashion fad' or whether they will form part of the essential requirements in everyday life.

- **Markets and their stability** from the point of view of both political and currency threats.

- **Management and their track record and reputation in the market place.** We have pointed out the dangers of a board of directors consisting of one strong character surrounded by a lot of 'yes' men.

Finally, Table 4.1 shows the chief characteristics of different classes of investment instruments, the main factors which influence their prices and the reasons for buying them.

Table 4.1 **Different types of investment instruments**

Type of share	Purpose for holding	Reasons for price change
Ordinary	Growth	Company results
Gilts	Income and safety	Change in interest rate
Preference	Income	Change in interest rate
Convertibles	Income and growth	Change in interest rate and ordinary share price
Warrants	Growth	Change in ordinary share price
Traded options	Growth and protection	Change in ordinary share price

It is important to separate fact from opinion ... It is too easy to be convinced by rumour which turns out to be fallible and without foundation.

5

Interpreting share information

Market data and how to use it

Charts

The IC/Coppock Indicator

Forecasting future PER

Summary

In this chapter we shall look at some of the most widely used sources of data and suggest some ways in which you can use the information. We shall explain:

- Where to get the information on a regular basis.
- How you interpret the facts and forecasts.
- How to apply the formulae to alert you when to buy and when to sell.

MARKET DATA AND HOW TO USE IT

Sources and types of information

As we have said earlier on in this book, there are two distinct types of information to the serious investor, namely, fact and opinion.

If you were to read the financial columns of every newspaper and journal published, not only would you end up cross-eyed and exhausted, but you would be unable to make any rational decisions because of the conflicting opinions which abound.

So it is important to separate fact from opinion, and form a view of both the current situation, whether by country, sector, or individual share, and get a feel for the forecasts of future achievements either by the gross national product (GNP) for a country, the estimated rise in earnings for a sector or an individual share.

Analysts' reports

Analysts are employed by large firms of stockbrokers, merchant banks, investment houses and financial journals and quality newspapers. They make frequent visits to companies and keep extensive records of their findings in order to compare company forecasts with the factual information which they have discovered during their visits.

They pore over the entrails of the data which they have collected and question the boards of directors to justify their forecasts for individual companies and compare these with the perceived overall trends of the relevant sector for the industry. They make their own forecasts for the future achievements of the companies concerned which may or may not agree with those of the chairmen.

> Historic performance will enable you to establish benchmarks from which you can judge what goals are both achievable and realistic.

Whilst they are not infallible, they provide a useful and ongoing watching brief on markets, sectors and companies, and they have the time to analyse information, both past and present, to see if the claims which are being made are realistic. Over the years some have gained reputations for being more accurate in their forecasts than others, and the same goes for the economists who take an overall view of markets and currencies rather than individual companies.

The journals and newspapers are also jealous of their reputation, and would frown on wild and unsubstantiated claims made by their employees, so you are likely to get a realistic picture of forecasts of earnings, profits, turnover and market share from such publications as the *Financial Times*, *The Times*, the *Telegraph*, the *Daily Mail* and the Sunday editions of the latter three papers, as well as the *Investors Chronicle* which is published weekly.

Specialist data services

Other sources of information regarding individual company share performance or market movements are available from such firms as Reuters, Extel and Datastream, but the machinery on which their information is published is not usually available to the public. This is because the cost for each terminal and the services provided is too high for public information centres such as libraries.

However, as we have said, stockbrokers have access to these sources and you can ask them for a copy of the data which we describe below.

Nevertheless, it is important to start with data about what the market or share has done in the past and to find reasons for variations in trends, because this historic performance will enable you to establish benchmarks from which you can judge what goals are both achievable and realistic.

Interpreting information

Let us start by looking at what investment has achieved on the London Stock Exchange over the period 1935 to 1992.

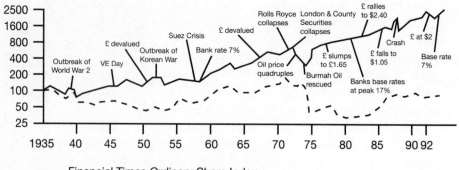

─────── Financial Times Ordinary Share Index

- - - Adjustment for inflation (annual average)

Figure 5.1 **Graph of the FT Ordinary Share Index showing adjustment for inflation**

Source: Investors Chronicle

The FT All Share Index has risen from a starting point of 100 to a figure of 2,500 over a period of 57 years.

Because the scale is very small, the illustration does not show how violent were the fluctuations at the time of outbreaks of various wars, large-scale changes in the bank rate, devaluation of sterling, etc. It is very interesting to note, in spite of the smallness of the scale, how steep and prolonged was the fall in market prices brought about by the fourfold increase in oil prices lasting from 1972 to 1975. This coincided with the miners' strike ending with the fall of the Heath government.

At first sight, it would seem that money invested in 1935 in the ordinary shares on the market would have shown a reasonable increase in value, until you look at the line on the chart showing the same index adjusted for inflation. Then you will see that the real value of capital invested in that way is actually worth less in 1992 than it was in 1935.

So let us look at the various methods which are available to the investor, or trader, to enable him to start to make individual selections.

Because these methods need to be explained in detail if they are to be fully understood, we shall show suggested practical examples of utilising them in the next chapter.

The methods which we examine here are:

- charts;
- the IC/Coppock indicator;
- forecasting potential rises in the PER of individual shares.

None of these methods are infallible. If they were, then you would simply be able to programme a computer to analyse large quantities of data, and leave it to machinery to make your fortune while you have a splendid time going fishing. There is an art to successful investing, and it requires a certain perception, feel, nose for a bargain – call it what you will – together with a little bit of luck.

However, you can increase the odds in your favour by adopting a system of analysis of trends, whether it be for the market as a whole or an individual share, because the systems impose a certain amount of discipline on your interpretation of historical data. Also they will reduce the area of the unknown, when you come to forecasting future earnings and share prices.

CHARTS

To be a pure chartist, you have to ignore any reasons for past performance. The chart is everything and you follow its signals with blind and total faith.

It always reminds me of the disciples of the Delphic Oracle in the times of the ancient Greeks. The pronouncements of the Oracle were accepted without question and they had a widespread effect on a great many people. Students of history of that time will recall that the replies emanating from this Hellenic soothsayer were always ambivalent. They were able to be interpreted in many different ways and, to some extent, the conclusions which were drawn were probably those which the supplicant wanted to hear in order to reinforce a half-held belief.

It is certainly true that charts will present a visual record of performance to date, and to that extent they are invaluable. But you must make up your own mind as to whether you are prepared to ignore any other data in formulating your decisions, or whether you use them as a tool in conjunction with other information.

> **To be a pure chartist, you have to ignore any reasons for past performance.**

I recommend that you include the use of charts as part of your equipment.

This is how you can draw some useful points to consider when looking at a chart.

In the graph shown in Figure 5.2, there are two lines shown, apart from the plot of the share price of Dalgety.

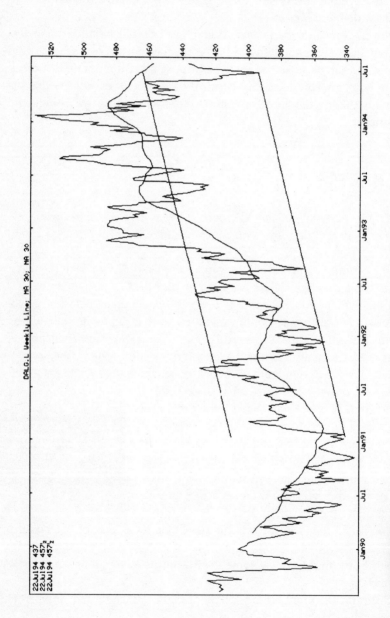

Figure 5.2 Graph of Dalgety share price movements showing 30-day moving average, lows and highs

Source: Reuters

The graph runs from January 1990 to July 1994, and the 30-day moving average has been superimposed on to the share price record. In addition, parallel lines connecting the 'lows' from January 1991 to July 1994, as well as the 'highs', from the most recent in June 1994 back to June 1992. Remember the lines must be parallel. This area within the parallel lines establishes the 'trading range' of the share price.

If you consider the graph from the period January 1991 until August 1992, and assume that you are now in August 1992, you could predict with some confidence that, providing the share price did not penetrate the lower parallel line, after it had turned upwards, the price should go from a level of about 365p to somewhere between 420p and 440p within 12 months.

Provided a share price stays within its normal trading range, you can select the price at which you buy to maximise your profit, and you will be right more often than you will be wrong.

The next point to remember is this. If the share price breaks through its trading range, **in either direction**, then you must expect it to establish a new trading range. The limits in which the new trading range will be established will be unknown at that point, and so if the breakthrough is downwards, you should get out of the share immediately, because the fall in price could be considerable. It will only be when the new trading range has been established, and with it a change in all the other indices such as the PER and general opinion of the share in the market, that you should consider whether the share is worth buying again.

The probability is that you will want some substantial reassurance that the reason for the bigger than normal drop in share price is not the manifestation of a deeper sickness in the company.

However, back to the example. In November 1992 the price broke through the upper trading level significantly, and within 12 months a new trading range had been established. This is represented on the graph by a pair of parallel broken lines.

The share price broke downwards dramatically in June 1994, and it remains to be seen where the new trading levels will establish themselves.

If we just concentrate on the trading levels for the time being, it will be useful to consider what an investor (as opposed to a trader) might have done.

Depending upon when the investor had bought the shares, he would expect to see an increase in the value of his holding of about 7.8 per cent between January 1991 and January 1993, excluding dividends. The increase in share price between January 1993 and January 1994 amounted to 10.4 per cent, again excluding dividend income.

Thus a realistic expectation of capital growth in this share at the beginning of 1991 would have been not less than 8 per cent per annum. In fact an investor who was watching the share and keeping himself well-informed about the company's affairs would probably have made a great deal more profit, particularly if he had been operating a stop-loss control in his management techniques. We shall demonstrate this mechanism in Chapter 10.

Now let us look at the lessons which can be learned from the 30-day moving average of the share price shown in Figure 5.2.

- Whenever the plot of the share price cuts significantly through the moving average line, in either direction, you can expect the share price to continue in the same direction.

- The picture is reinforced if you plot both the 30-day and the 200-day moving average on the same graph superimposed on the share price history.

If you look at the graph prior to January 1991 you will see that the share price did not penetrate the 30-day average for at least nine months.

In January 1991 the share price began a rapid climb and although it penetrated the average in July the same year, the fall in price below the average was neither significant nor was it sustained. The next significant movement downwards occurred in November/December 1991 and you can see that the price remained below the average until March/April 1992.

Although the price moved up and down through the 30-day average line, it still kept within its established trading range from January 1991 until January 1993. In fact, during that period it cut through the 30-day moving average line no fewer than five times.

A trader could have bought and sold twice over between January 1991 and July 1992, and made profits before costs of anything from 10 to 22 per cent on each occasion.

If the trader had bought put and call traded options as well, he would probably have enhanced his capital quite considerably.

You can see how the same situation existed between July 1992 and January 1994.

A trader needs a share whose price fluctuates considerably within a fairly wide trading range, whilst an investor is not so much interested in short-term movement as a share price with a steadily rising trend.

Do not forget that the information and indications produced from looking at graphs is historical. In the market today, there is much more volatility than there used to be, and so you have to combine the indications which graphs show with current figures released in the accounts, as well as any reports from analysts on internal or outside events which might affect market sentiment towards the share.

THE IC/COPPOCK INDICATOR

The original Coppock Indicator was invented in 1962 by an American. He believed that people who bought shares, whether for a short or long term, acted with a herd instinct and usually at the same time. His theory was based upon observation of behavioural patterns of people during death or serious illness. His conclusions can be summed up as follows:

- The herd instinct makes people all follow each other.
- Emotion rather than rational thought is the prime factor which triggers people's actions.
- The main motivating factors are greed and fear.

The results of his studies led him to the conclusion that the effects of their combined actions would alter the price of a share out of all proportion to the fundamental value of that share, whether they were buying or selling it. They would create a demand for a share to such an extent that it would push the price up to levels which were unjustifiable under any rational economic analysis of the company's accounts or its potential earnings performance. Similarly, when the sentiment towards a given share turned into reverse, the concerted selling which resulted would depress the share price to a level which was far below that which could be justified on economic grounds.

> Coppock's theory was based upon observation of behavioural patterns of people during death or serious illness.

The weakness in his thinking is demonstrated by the fact that he never thought that any of the funds which had bought a share at an advantageous price would want to sell it because such institutions receive a constant inflow of cash and are therefore always looking for suitable investments to buy. His indicator was designed for use by the investment managers of pension funds and companies operating regular savings schemes.

In March 1963 the *Investors Chronicle* decided to adopt the principles and apply them to the Financial Times index, but with a modification of the original formula.

In essence the percentage changes are computed in the current monthly average of the Financial Times index, and the monthly average of that index 12 months ago. The same computations were applied to world markets as well as sectors, and these tables were added to those of the Dow Jones and the FT indicators.

How do you interpret the indicators and spot buying and selling signals?

Figure 5.3 demonstrates how the indicators are shown each month in the *Investors Chronicle*:

IC/Coppock Indicators

Index/Market	Average index Dec 1991	Indicators Dec	Indicators Nov	Indicators Oct	Signal
UK Govt. Secs	86.69	+43.7	+47.5	+48.7	WAIT
FT30	1,828.93	+83.4	+88.5	+80.6	SELL
FT All Share	1,155.60	+84.3	+84.6	+72.4	SELL
FT Gold Mines	153.80	−35.4	−59.4	−82.5	HOLD
Amsterdam	190.07	+51.8	+43.5	+27.7	HOLD
Dow Jones	2,962.84	+73.6	+70.6	+60.5	HOLD
Hang Seng	4,172.75	+168.4	+159.1	+141.5	HOLD
Tokyo New S.E.	1,692.44	−31.3	−40.4	−60.8	HOLD

Figure 5.3 **IC/Coppock Indicator: Technical analysis**
Source: Investors Chronicle

Official BUY signal – When the indicator rises after a downward trend.
SELL signal – When the indicator falls after an upward trend.

When the indicators turn upwards whilst in the negative phase, you get a BUY signal. The indictors rise from the negative through zero and into the positive phase. When the indicators begin to fall whilst in the positive, you get a SELL signal.

Apart from BUY and SELL, the other two signals shown in the last column are WAIT and HOLD. WAIT means that you have sold and are now waiting until a BUY signal is given. HOLD means that you have bought at the last

BUY signal and are sitting tight until there is a forthcoming SELL signal.

By keeping a note of the monthly indicators a graph may be drawn similar to 'Graph A' shown in Figure 5.4. This will show you exactly when the signals were given, and by inserting the index on to the graph as in 'Graph B of Figure 5.5', you can see how accurate it has been.

The graph shown in Figure 5.6 (Graph C) demonstrates the principle applied to the FT All Share price index over the period between 1974 and 1985, and illustrates the results which would have been achieved by acting on the official and unofficial BUY signals together with the SELL signals.

What are the aims of the indicators?

You can construct and maintain your own IC/Coppock indicator. Comprehensive details as to how to set about it can be obtained from the *Investors Chronicle*, who publish the last three indicators once a month.

> The value of this indicator should be seen more as a way of confirming or contradicting your own conclusions.

You cannot rely on the indicator to be infallible. An upward movement in the indicator does not necessarily signal the start of a 'bull market'. The aim of the indicator is to alert the investor to the change in trend of the market and it should only be used as an indicator. It should be the trigger to start doing some 'in-depth' research rather than something which alone calls for investment action.

It is probably true to say that an investor should give more attention to the indicator when it signals a 'sell'. Graph C (Figure 5.6) shows that sometimes the indicator has proved very accurate in predicting a substantial downturn in the market. Protection of your capital is just as important as finding winners and you should make use of whatever tools there are to minimise risk. Successful investors are those who analyse market data *regularly* and learn to read the signals correctly so as to be forewarned, and thus forearmed.

Bear in mind that the data which is used to plot the movement of the indicators is at least one month old by the time you see the figures. At best they are giving you a bird's eye view of the market as a whole, rather than alerting you to the trend of any one share price or market sector in particular, and so the value of this indicator should be seen more as a way of confirming or contradicting your own conclusions.

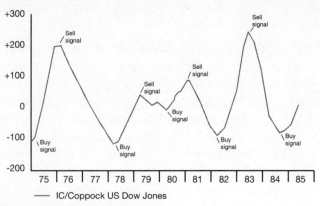

Figure 5.4 IC/Coppock Indicator: Graph A

Source: Investors Chronicle

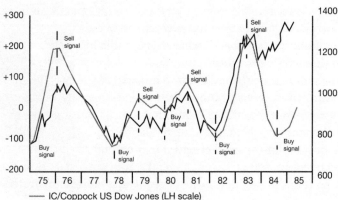

Figure 5.5 IC/Coppock Indicator: Graph B

Source: Investors Chronicle

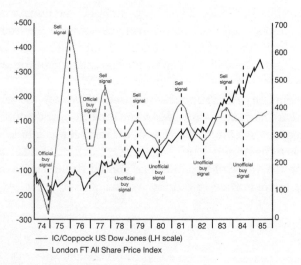

Figure 5.6 IC/Coppock Indicator: Graph C

Source: Investors Chronicle

FORECASTING FUTURE PER

Earlier in this book, we have described what a PER is and how it is calculated. As we said, it is a useful device to measure the market opinion of one share compared with another in the same sector. Those with a high PER are generally considered to be shares whose earnings in the future are expected to accelerate at a rate which is above average. However, in times of recession, sometimes when the results of the company are announced, the share price may drop back even though the earnings are in line with market expectation. It is very difficult to explain this reaction by the market when this situation occurs, but it is a sure sign of a weak market and general lack of confidence. Frequently there is nothing wrong with the company concerned and so one is driven to the conclusion that perhaps the share price was over-valued to start with.

Nevertheless, when the market is operating under normal conditions, it is always worth looking at shares with a low PER and finding out why they are out of favour. Sometimes, but by no means always, you can find a company whose earnings are perfectly sound and with adequate management, but where the share price has simply been left behind because the market has overlooked this particular share.

Essentially what we are looking for is a company whose earnings are accelerating at a rate which is faster than average, or faster than other shares in the same sector, and where it can be demonstrated that the growth rate will continue as fast or even faster than before.

In order to understand how the PER can increase, it is important to realise how it is arrived at in the first place.

Let us break down the PER into its component parts. The first one is price. That is listed. The second one is earnings. The historic earnings are a matter of record. The third part is the ratio of one to the other. Forecasting a future PER is where you move away from fact and into the realms of arbitrary judgement. If a share has earnings of 20p, and the share price is 200p, then the PER would be 10 (20 x 10 = 200).

If the earnings were to increase during the year by 40 per cent, it is assumed that the ratio would increase, from 10 to maybe 15. Therefore you will see that if the ratio increases and the earnings increase the resulting price must grow at a faster rate than 40 per cent in this case. It is this assumption that the market will re-rate the share wherein lies the basis for the theory for using the PER, both historic and forecast, to pick shares which are likely to out-perform the rest of the sector.

In order to find such a share, you need to have access to the earnings records over the last three years, and you have to calculate the **rate of increase** of the earnings from one year to the next. If the rate of increase is constant, or better still accelerating, and provided that the market for its products is not being affected by any adverse aspects, then it is reasonable to assume that the earnings will continue to grow at a rate which is similar to that achieved so far. However, what is somewhat arbitrary is the degree to which the market will increase the factor by which the earnings are multiplied in order for the forecaster to arrive at a price, and so there must be an element of 'hope' or 'presumption' in revising this factor upwards. After all, who is to say whether it would go from 10 to 15, or even 20, with any real degree of accuracy.

It is certainly true to say that given the rate of increase of earnings, as described above, the price will certainly increase but precisely to what extent is unknown. To get a more accurate picture, you would have to do the same calculations for each of the other shares in the sector, and choosing only those which had produced a steady increase in earnings, compare each one's subsequent rise in price to the percentage earnings increase, to get an idea of the comparative rise in the value of the multiplying factor. Nevertheless, it is certainly true to say that an undervalued share within a sector, whose earnings are showing a persistent and steady rise, will reward the investor with a corresponding increase in the share price.

As a rule of thumb, you should be looking for an earnings growth with a minimum level of 30 per cent per annum and a rate of growth of not less than 50 per cent.

For example, if the earnings growth before was 20 per cent, it must now be at least 30 per cent (i.e. a 50 per cent increase on 20 per cent equals 30 per cent).

A word of warning at this stage. The earnings growth must be generated organically from within the company, not simply by acquisition and subsequent asset stripping. If, during the company's trading year, an extraordinary profit arises from the sale of assets, and inflates the earnings of its core business, the enhanced level of earnings may not be sustainable in the future.

The best example of this has been Hanson, which has been considered in the past as requiring an endless stream of acquisitions to continue to produce above average growth in earnings. On the other hand, a company like Tomkins has managed to generate an increase of approximately 20 per cent per annum from those companies which it has acquired, and thus market sentiment towards this company and its share price has been much more favourable.

Using PER as a basis for finding potentially successful investments requires good tangible reasons as to why you expect the earnings to increase in the future at a steady and substantial rate. This will only come from a great deal of research. Unless you have access to the necessary data to carry out this research yourself, you will probably

> **The earnings growth must be generated organically from within the company, not simply by acquisition and subsequent asset stripping.**

have to rely upon forecasts from analysts which can be found at frequent intervals in the financial Press. However, they tend to be concentrated on the larger companies listed in the market. It is usually among the smaller ones that the potential lies for above average profit growth, and these do not get examined or written about as often as do the larger companies.

How important are these aids?

The ability to see the historic patterns of the market as a whole, and individual share price movements in particular, is extremely useful. Depending on whether the market is rising or falling, these aids can provide the following benefits:

> **A constant revision of the market as a whole will modify your judgement or expectation of a particular share.**

- They indicate whether to buy, sell, or hold your investments. If the market has established a firm downward trend, for example, you would not expect to find many opportunities to buy for growth. On the other hand, you might consider coming out of some investments and holding cash until the market had demonstrated that it had definitely reversed its trend and was set to climb.

- They provide an easier way of seeing the picture. Graphic representations of past performance usually have more impact than looking at a set of figures, and you can more easily assess the chances of your expectations being met.

- They provide assistance in setting your targets. If the market is falling, and you have found a share which is bucking the trend and rising, the chances of that share price continuing on upwards are less likely than if the market was in a strongly positive phase. Thus you would probably set a lower target for growth for that particular share at that time than you would otherwise.

- They can alert you to potential threat. It is all too easy to become lulled into a false sense of security when markets have been on a rising trend for some time. When the market or sector PER gets too high there is bound to be a reaction, and very often the imminence of such a downturn can be seen more easily from a graphic record of progress.

However, it is important to keep such aids or systems in perspective. They will not by themselves tell you everything you need to know, whether you are building a portfolio or managing an established one. In the final analysis it is you who has to make the final judgement as to what action you take, and such decisions are always based upon common sense. What these aids do at best is to help to refine your thinking and to set the background scene so that you are better equipped to make decisions.

As with any logical argument, you should start by describing the general truths before advancing to the particular in order to prove your theory. Thus a constant revision of the market as a whole will modify your judgement or expectation of a particular share, and may even save you from disastrous losses.

 SUMMARY

In this chapter we have looked at the sources of data. In particular we have examined:

- The essential need to separate fact from opinion. It is too easy to be convinced by rumour which turns out to be fallible and without foundation.
- The usefulness of analysts' reports, always bearing in mind the fact that forecasting involves a human factor and therefore the existence of fallibility.
- The buy/sell signals which are to be found in the IC/Coppock Indicator with regard to the market as a whole. Remember that they are a guide, not an inflexible dictator of your investment management.
- The use of charts with reference to the price history of a particular share as supplied by specialist data services such as Reuters, Extel and Datastream. Make sure that you get agreement from your stockbroker that he will supply you with information from these sources on request,

because without all the historic performance figures you cannot do your analysis. If he is unwilling to provide you with such data, find one who will.

- The ways in which to interpret such historic information and their uses for forecasting the probable future movement in the share price for individual companies.

> The ability to analyse the information so that you get an understanding of the company's progression is essential if you are going to achieve your investment objectives.

6

Company reports and accounts

New issues

Reading a set of accounts

Factors affecting the company

Indices

Summary

In this chapter we show how to analyse key parts of company accounts and describe the way to extract the essential information needed to make investment decisions about both buying and selling shares.

In particular we look at:

- how to read accounts;
- the influence of interest rates;
- the effect of inflation;
- the key indices.

The list of items for analysis described here is not as comprehensive as the one that would be used by an accountant or an analyst, because we are concerned only as a potential investor who is seeking to find ways to safeguard his capital as well as to protect his income.

The Press draws attention to company rumours which, in their opinion, are exciting or dangerous (whether real or imagined), and you would be foolish to ignore such reports. However, the basis for any purchase or sale of a share must include an analysis of the report and accounts over a period of five years if possible; three at the very least.

The ability to analyse the information so that you get an understanding of the company's progression is essential if you are going to achieve your investment objectives.

Obviously this does not apply to a decision to sell in a hurry if there is extremely bad news, whether it be about the company or its products or its market.

This is the most important source of information to be used when you are deciding whether to invest in a particular share and whether to retain it in your portfolio. The information contained in a company's report and accounts is fact, not someone's opinion.

NEW ISSUES

The information contained in a prospectus for a new issue will not go back five years, so obviously you have less data to work with. The decision to invest becomes a bit more speculative, and the 'hope' factor must not be ignored.

A prospectus for a new issue should show details of the company's products, markets and a full description of the history and experience of the directors, among other things. This is all important information and is factual.

If it is a small company, you should read about the background of each of the directors carefully to see whether any of them are known to you or anyone of your aquaintance. It is always possible that you might hear some information which is not published and which could influence your decision to invest. I remember on one occasion a client of mine took exception to the suit which the chief executive was wearing in the photograph of the members of the board of a new company. She said she would not trust someone who wore such clothes. A year later he left the company somewhat under a cloud, and the company nearly foundered. The share price has not recovered two years after this débâcle!

The prospectus will show the increase in earnings which is expected after flotation. Sometimes these forecast levels are considerably higher than has been achieved to date, and you have to question the likelihood of such growth being achieved. Nevertheless there have been some very successful new issues, but unless the company is well capitalised to begin with (£150 million or more), or is a privatisation of a state monopoly other than British Rail, you should regard such investments as being speculative.

READING A SET OF ACCOUNTS

There are some tried and tested adages which are worth remembering before we get into the detail and you may find it worthwhile to follow them.

What do you look at first?

You should always read a set of accounts starting from the back and work towards the front.

Contingent liabilities

These appear at the end of the balance sheet (sometimes the consolidated balance sheets) usually just before the chairman's statement.

Look for any contingent liabilities and if they are large, either stop then, or treat the potential investment with a great deal of caution. There have been cases when the contingent liabilities have come home to roost and wiped out the company. If, for example, the company has given guarantees to a subsidiary and the guarantee is called, the company itself might end up in liquidation.

Chairman's report

This appears after the figures in the accounts and is clearly marked. An ability to 'read between the lines' is an art which you must develop for yourself. In some cases in the past the descriptive terms used by chairmen have been compared to that of estate agents. Press criticism has made much of the duty chairmen have to report the progress of their companies, warts and all. However not all of them do so and you must always be on the look out for platitudinous phrases. It would be impossible to list all the types of generalities which may be used but if *you* feel that the chairman is padding out his statement with waffle, then you should mark this fact with a big red star.

You should count the number of times the words 'should' or 'would' appear in the chairman's report. Bear in mind the tendency of management to put the best possible face on their forecasts for the coming trading period, and so you should expect positive factual statements. Beware of statements such as 'the expenditure on a new £X million extension to the computerised warehouse should bring substantial benefits and if interest rates remain at present levels the additional capacity would add considerably to profits'.

Doesn't really inspire confidence that the chairman has a good grip on his company, does it?

Do you feel that the chairman is in control?

The chairman's report should be expressed in clear unequivocal language which is understandable to the layman and it should be positive. If there is bad news to report, it ought to be stated honestly. There should be clear explanations for any calamities and an evaluation of the effect on the company, its profits and the length of time it will take to overcome such setbacks.

Any claims for future growth in earnings should be accompanied with reasons which do not conflict with common sense in the mind of the reader.

Auditor's statement

You will find this in the report and accounts which you will have to get from the company secretary or the registrar. The information issued by Extel covering the company's results for the last five years does not include the auditor's statement. You should read the auditor's statement carefully to see if it is qualified in any way. If the statement says anything other than 'the accounts represent a true and fair picture' without any 'ifs', 'buts' or reservations, then alarms bells should start ringing!

> **If you feel that the chairman is padding out his statement with waffle, then you should mark this fact.**

Sometimes auditors state that they are unable to obtain certain information, such as the value of stock for example, and that such figures have been put in 'at the directors' valuation'. If this is the case, your level of scepticism should rise a few notches.

Worse still is a statement saying that the auditors were 'unable to form an opinion' about an aspect of the accounts.

In the latter case, you should avoid the share like the plague, or if you are unfortunate enough to own any, sell them as fast as you can.

Notes to the accounts

These are most important and you should read them carefully. Either they will explain anomalous figures shown in the accounts and produce satisfactory answers to your concerns, or they will raise further doubts in your mind. They are shown only in the report and accounts issued by the company which is available on request from the company secretary or registrar. They are not included in the Extel company reports.

Companies are required by law to file a set of accounts every year with Companies House, and most companies must present audited accounts. Certainly any companies whose shares are traded on the Stock Exchange must do so.

A set of accounts is similar to a photograph of a company's affairs at a particular date. Although one set will tell you a lot about the business, its assets and liabilities, its profits and its profit margins and many other pieces of useful data, it will not tell you how the company is progressing.

For this information you need several consecutive years of accounts.

All companies show comparative figures for each item in the accounts for last year as well as the current period and while this is useful, you really need the figures for the last five years.

Companies are not static. A company, like the economy and the stock market, is dynamic and constantly changing. Thus one still photograph on its own will not tell you whether the patient is recovering or dying, thriving or sick.

A company is subject to influences which are altering all the time. So when you analyse a company's history, it is essential that you take into consideration the effects of those influences at each stage and not whether they have increased or decreased subsequently.

For example, have they bought or sold subsidiary companies or changed their markets or products?

 EXAMPLE **The brewery industry**

This has changed its direction several times in the last few years. There was a threat of EEC legislation hanging over the beer trade for a long time which was not clearly defined, but very real nonetheless.

The brewers decided to diversify as a defensive measure and most of the larger ones started to build up investments in chains of hotels and restaurants.

When the EEC restrictions emerged eventually, the brewers decided that there was no need to retain the hotels and so they sold them off. Both the build up of the investments and the subsequent disposal took many months and these activities had substantial effects on the performance of the companies concerned.

FACTORS AFFECTING THE COMPANY

Some of the items which affect the company will be within the control of the management, others will not.

Interest rates

One of the most important and obvious items is the rate of interest. For any company a high interest rate is damaging. It affects profit margins on contracts which have been won with a fixed price and which take several months to complete. It can easily lead to uncompetitive product prices and thus make the anticipated sales and profits deteriorate. It puts up delivery costs and leads to increased wage demands, and so on.

The trouble is that interest rate is a blunt weapon and it is also about the only tool left in the hands of the government. It affects everyone and everything without exception. Whilst it changes the cost of borrowing and the return on saving immediately, it takes time to filter down to other aspects of life.

This breeds uncertainty throughout the economy and the biggest single factor which knocks the stock market for six is uncertainty. Bad news can be absorbed when it has been quantified and the full extent of the damage is known but otherwise it breeds jitters and fear.

Above all, it is inflationary.

There is, however, one benefit which is brought about in times of high interest rates. Normally when interest rates go up, the price of fixed interest stock such as gilts goes down. Thus you will get much better annuity rates from insurance companies if you contract for a pension in times of high interest rates. The insurance company buys gilts with the money saved into your pension fund to provide you with your pension income, and if the gilts are cheaper to buy at the time when you enter into the contract, they will get more stock for the money and you will get a bigger income.

If you have arrived at the point when you are in a position to arrange your pension, and you have enough time to spare before you must enter into the contract, it will pay you to wait for a period of high interest rates before you conclude your pension deal. When the time comes, do shop around because you will be surprised at the wide variety of pension rates on offer.

Inflation

Sustained inflation at a high rate erodes the purchasing power of your capital and therefore its value, so its negative effect must occupy a position of high priority both in your selection of shares for income and medium- to long-term capital growth.

Market confidence, or lack of it, stems largely from the perceived ability of government to be in control of the nation's 'housekeeping' and economic well-being. In 1993, in spite of an upward movement in stock market prices in the first quarter of the year, and in spite of constant claims by government ministers that industrial recovery was firmly established, very few investors believed in any of it. As a result, the FT-SE 100 index fell back from an all-time high of over 3,500 to around 2,800 in two months – a drop of 20 per cent. It started to recover early in August when widespread fears of an imminent rise in interest rates faded, although the Bank of England indicated the likelihood of an interest rate hike before the end of the year. This duly appeared in September with a rise of 0.5 per cent to 5.75 per cent, and the market lost its momentum and sense of direction.

The volatility that resulted in wild fluctuations in share prices produced some good opportunities for both traders and longer-term investors. This is illustrated in Chapter 10.

INDICES

There are several analyses of different parts of the accounts which you should carry out if you want to understand the full implications of how the company is being managed, and even when you have carried out a great deal of detailed work, you will have several questions to which you would like answers. The subject is covered comprehensively in 'Interpreting Companies Reports and Accounts' by A. Holmes and G. Sugden (published by Woodhead-Faulkner).

When analysing the accounts of a company there are two essential indices which an investor must establish, preferably for each of the last five years, and these are the earnings per share and the return on capital employed.

We shall describe briefly some of the others for those who want to get a broader picture, without going into greater detail.

Earnings per share (EPS)

The earnings per share is the amount of profit which is available to the ordinary shareholder after paying tax, preference share and loan stock interest. Part of the EPS is used to pay a dividend to the ordinary shareholders and the remainder is put to reserves.

If a company is paying out everything it earns in a given year in order to maintain its dividend rate, then apart from the fact that there is nothing left to put to reserves, its ability to maintain the dividend level is questionable. As we explained in Chapter 4, the dividend cover will show this up.

However the earnings per share are expressed in the value of money pertaining at the time when they were generated, and so it is vital to calculate whether the progression of EPS is either beating inflation or being eroded by it. To assess this you have to adjust past EPS by the average retail price index ('RPI') for each of the years under review. The EPS is usually shown in the company report, and copies can be obtained at any time either from the company secretary or from the Extel Financial Companies Service to which stockbrokers subscribe.

If the EPS is not shown then you can calculate it yourself by dividing the profit after tax by the number of ordinary shares in issue at the time.

Unless the report separates the ordinary share capital from the preference shares in issue, you must subtract the amount of issued preference capital from the amount of issued capital in total and then multiply the result by the denomination of the ordinary share.

For example, if the ordinary share capital in issue is £220,000,000 and the ordinary shares are 25p, then there are 220,000,000 x 4 = 880 million ordinary shares in issue.

EPS adjusted for inflation

Table 6.1 shows how you calculate the adjusted EPS of Dalgety allowing for inflation.

Table 6.1   Adjusted EPS of Dalgety

	1993	1992	1991	1990	1989
Earnings per share	35.7p	36.3p	5.9p	0.5p	30.1p
Average RPI for year	141.3	138.9	134.1	128.1	115.8
Adjusted EPS	35.7p	36.9p	6.21p	1.65p	36.72p

The RPI used is the figure for the month in which the company's financial year ends. In this case, Dalgety ends its year on 30 June.

If you can not get the average RPI figure for the year, the figure for the month in which the year-end falls will suffice.

There was a disastrous fall in earnings in 1990, and although the company has recovered since, the EPS in 1993 are less than they were in 1989 in real terms because of inflation, even though the opposite would appear to be the case.

High inflation wreaks havoc with EPS so much so that if a company is producing what may appear to be static earnings, your income is in fact reducing in real terms.

The EPS, both historic and anticipated, are the main factors which, when combined with the price of the share, form the basis for calculating the PER. So you will see how important it is for a company to have a record of steadily increasing EPS in order to forecast what the PER might become if the earnings of the company were expected to increase by an even larger percentage than had been the case to date. At the very least you would be able to make a reasoned judgement as to whether you thought the increase being suggested was within the realms of common sense in the light of the company's historic performance.

Why should earnings increase?

The earnings can be expected to increase for a variety of reasons. For example, the company might announce that it has landed a major contract which will provide employment and increased sales for a number of years ahead, or it might have produced a new product or design which is a world beater. It might have discovered large deposits of raw materials in land which it owns or leases, e.g. gold, oil, minerals, or it might have bid successfully for a major competitor.

What factors should be treated with caution?

Any increase in earnings which are not due to expansion of the normal business should be discounted. For example, the sale of a subsidiary or extraordinary profits, such as the settlement of a law suit in the company's favour should be excluded from any estimation of possible future earnings.

> It is of paramount importance that you look at the cash flow element of the accounts.

You should be very chary of sizeable debt shown in the accounts. A company which borrows heavily to finance expanding turnover may well be able to show increasing EPS while interest rates are low, but it could find itself in dire straits if interest rates rise to a point where they reduce profitability.

Cash flow

One of the essential factors in the recipe for success of any company is proper control and management of cash flow. It is perfectly possible for a company to go bust, even though its order book is increasing. In fact, if the order book increases dramatically, which can often happen as the country comes out of a period of recession, any problems inherent in their cash flow management will exacerbate the difficulties and push the company into bankruptcy even faster. It is, therefore, of paramount importance that you look at the cash flow element of the accounts whenever you are researching a company as a potential candidate for investment.

Company Report	EXTEL FINANCIAL COMPANIES SERVICE	December 7, 1994

WHITBREAD PLC

CONSOLIDATED STATEMENT OF CASH FLOWS

	Mar 02 1991 £m	Feb 29 1992 £m	Feb 27 1993 £m	Feb 26 1994 £m
OPERATING ACTIVITIES	284.2	319.1	275.1	351.5
INVESTMENT RETURN AND SERVICING OF FINANCE				
Other divs received	11.0	12.1	13.0	12.9
Assoc cos divs recd	2.2	2.1	1.6	1.9
Interest received	35.3	22.7	22.9	16.3
Interest paid	(55.5)	(62.2)	(63.8)	(42.5)
Dividends paid	(72.9)	(79.3)	(82.8)	(86.8)
	(79.9)	(104.6)	(109.1)	(98.2)
TAXATION				
UK corpn tax paid	(52.3)	(47.5)	(28.8)	(41.3)
Overseas tax paid	(2.8)	(0.5)	(0.3)	(0.3)
	(55.1)	(48.0)	(29.1)	(41.6)
INVESTING ACTIVITIES				
Securities net	–	53.4	–	–
Businesses acquired	(81.6)	(155.8)	(37.1)	(6.6)
Invests acquired	(73.7)	(53.0)	(89.1)	(73.8)
Tangibles acquired	(267.8)	(244.2)	(160.2)	(179.3)
Businesses sold	–	21.2	21.8	–
Investments sold	66.3	39.5	75.5	129.1
Tangibles sold	57.7	73.5	94.1	39.4
S/T investments	–	–	(9.1)	(225.3)
Trade loans net	–	–	15.1	14.7
	(299.1)	(245.4)	(89.0)	(301.8)
NET CASH FLOW BEFORE FINANCING	(149.9)	(78.9)	47.9	(90.1)
FINANCING				
S/T debt raised	–	33.8	–	–
Loan capital issued	164.7	107.1	94.9	200.5
Share capital issued	6.9	6.1	3.4	7.0
S/T loans repaid	–	(28.6)	(5.5)	–
Loan capital repaid	(33.6)	(30.3)	(107.5)	(207.3)
Minority contribn	4.7	2.3	0.9	0.5
	142.7	90.4	(13.8)	0.7
CASH INCR (DECR)	(7.2)	11.5	34.1	(89.4)
Currency appreciation	1.2	(0.8)	1.8	(1.2)
B/S CASH INCR (DECR)	(6.0)	10.7	35.9	(90.6)

Figure 6.1 Extract from the Whitbread accounts Extel card

Source: Extel Financial Limited

```
┌─────────────────────────────────────────────────────────────────────────────┐
│                                                                               │
```

NOTES TO CONSOLIDATED STATEMENT OF CASH FLOWS

	Mar 02 1991 £ m	Feb 29 1992 £ m	Feb 27 1993 £ m	Feb 26 1994 £ m
OPERATING ACTIVITIES				
Trading profit	245.5	186.1	229.3	226.1
Depreciation	7.17	82.8	86.9	84.8
Other tdg adj incr	(9.2)	32.9	(15.6)	10.2
Decrease in stocks	(3.9)	(2.1)	5.0	34.2
Increase in creditors	8.8	13.6	(22.8)	(8.3)
	284.2	319.1	275.1	351.8

CONSOLIDATED BALANCE SHEETS

	Mar 03 1990 £ m	Mar 02 1991 £ m	Feb 29 1992 £ m	Feb 27 1993 £ m	Feb 26 1994 £ m
FIXED ASSETS					
Tangible assets	2,703.6	2,929.2	3,001.8	2,318.4	2,356.2
Financial assets	307.0	294.4	283.9	334.6	340.1
	3,010.6	3,223.6	3,285.7	2,653.0	2,696.3
CURRENT ASSETS					
Stocks	113.6	118.4	153.6	147.7	113.3
Rcble-eqty A/c cos	2.8	1.6	0.9	0.7	0.7
Trade debtors	88.1	91.2	85.2	79.0	77.8
Prepays/accrued inc	17.8	36.5	38.8	41.2	30.3
ACT recoverable	16.2	17.8	–	–	–
Tax recoverable	14.8	28.4	32.3	25.3	17.8
Misc debtors	53.9	55.8	61.2	40.6	40.1
Cash & equivalents	126.1	127.9	100.1	119.7	157.1
Properties to be sold˙	–	34.6	–	–	–
	433.3	512.2	472.1	454.2	437.1
CREDS due within 1 yr					
Short term debt	52.3	66.9	63.5	195.4	84.1
Pble-equity A/c cos	17.0	7.9	2.3	3.5	1.4
Trade creditors	127.2	141.6	172.3	138.6	136.4
Accruals & defd inc	54.8	63.3	88.7	98.5	103.9
Corporation tax	59.3	59.7	33.0	51.6	61.4
Tax & social security	36.7	38.3	50.4	52.2	53.8
Dividends	48.6	53.6	55.7	58.7	66.0
Misc creditors	86.7	146.5	89.5	78.1	71.9
	482.6	577.8	555.4	676.6	578.9
NET CURRENT LIABS	(49.3)	(65.6)	(83.3)	(222.4)	(141.8)
TOTAL ASSETS LESS CURRENT LIABILITIES	2,961.3	3,158.0	3,202.4	2,430.6	2,554.5

Figure 6.1 continued

CREDS due after 1 yr					
Long term debt	261.0	390.9	489.9	332.2	339.0
PROVISIONS	81.8	106.8	113.4	26.2	10.5
NET ASSETS	2,618.5	2,660.3	2,591.1	2,072.2	2,205.0
SHARE CAPITAL	120.2	121.2	122.0	122.6	129.3
Share premium	76.0	86.3	97.6	105.4	108.4
Revaluation reserves	1,083.2	1,067.1	1,307.3	673.8	706.1
Oth non-dist reserves	25.8	36.2	35.0	61.9	219.6
Profit & loss account	1,253.0	1,286.4	971.2	1,039.5	1,037.3
SHAREHOLDERS' FUNDS	2,558.2	2,597.2	2,533.1	2,003.2	2,200.7
Minority interests	60.3	63.1	66.0	69.0	4.3
NET ASSETS	2,618.5	2,660.3	2,599.1	2,072.2	2,205.0

NOTES TO CONSOLIDATED BALANCE SHEETS

	Mar 03 1990 £ m	Mar 02 1991 £ m	Feb 29 1992 £ m	Feb 27 1993 £ m	Feb 26 1994 £ m
TANGIBLE ASSETS					
Property – costs	229.1	461.3	631.6	59.2	141.5
Property – vain	2,184.7	2,154.6	2,037.4	1,926.5	1,887.7
Property depreciation	(29.9)	(36.5)	(47.6)	(10.7)	(19.8)
Property NBV	2,383.9	2,579.4	2,621.4	1,975.0	2,009.4
Oth tangible FA-cost	598.4	667.9	741.9	705.3	727.0
Oth tangible FA depn	(278.7)	(318.1)	(361.5)	(361.9)	(380.2)
Oth tangible FA NBV	319.7	349.8	380.4	343.4	346.8
Tangible assets	2,703.6	2,929.2	3,001.8	2,318.4	2,356.2
FINANCIAL ASSETS					
Assoc company loans	52.8	38.9	38.9	34.9	30.9
Invs in assoc cos	65.5	42.5	26.6	26.4	31.1
Other trade invs	188.7	213.0	218.4	273.3	278.1
Trade investments	307.0	294.4	283.9	334.6	340.1
Mkt valn-trade invs	714.3	698.5	727.3	736.1	435.6
STOCKS					
Land	3.7	3.9	–	–	–
Raw materials etc	18.9	15.7	14.4	12.6	11.3
Work in progress	20.8	21.5	25.7	33.3	7.6
Finished goods	70.2	77.3	113.5	101.8	94.4
	113.6	118.4	153.6	147.7	113.3

Figure 6.1 continued

DEBTORS includes					
Due after one year	–	–	–	30.9	30.6
DEBT BY TYPE					
Loan capital	282.2	418.9	495.3	500.1	369.0
Bank overdrafts	31.3	38.9	58.1	27.5	54.1
	313.3	457.8	553.4	527.6	423.1
DEBT BY MATURITY					
Short term loans	31.1	38.9	58.1	27.5	54.1
Debt due within 1 yr	21.2	28.0	5.4	167.9	30.0
Short term debt	52.3	66.9	63.5	195.4	84.1
Due within 2 to 5 yrs	–	–	–	70.6	2.7
Due after 5 years	–	–	–	261.6	336.3
Due after 1 year	261.0	390.9	489.9	–	–
	313.3	457.8	553.4	527.6	423.1
DEBT BY SECURITY					
Secured	36.9	173.8	166.8	220.1	217.5
Unsecured	245.3	245.1	328.5	280.0	151.5
Misc debt by backing	31.1	38.9	58.1	27.5	54.1
	313.3	457.8	553.4	527.6	423.1
PROVISIONS					
Deferred taxation	–	–	–	–	2.0
Misc provisions	81.8	106.8	113.4	26.2	8.5
	81.8	106.8	113.4	26.2	10.5
SHARE CAPITAL					
Ordinary shares	110.4	111.4	112.2	112.8	119.5
Preference shares	9.8	9.8	9.8	9.8	9.8
	120.2	121.2	122.0	122.6	129.3
SHAREHOLDERS' FUNDS					
Eqty s/holders funds	–	–	–	1,993.4	2,190.9
Non eqty s/holder fds	–	–	–	9.8	9.8
	2,558.2	2,597.2	2,533.1	2,003.2	2,200.7
MINORITY INTERESTS					
Eqty minority int	–	–	–	(69.0)	(4.3)
COMMITMENTS AND CONTINGENCIES					
Bank guarantees	–	–	–	25.0	11.6
Other guarantees	–	–	–	32.1	54.6
12.4	17.6	16.3			
Cap not contracted	56.7	45.0	29.5	20.1	69.9

Figure 6.1 continued

In the extract from the accounts of Whitbreads shown in Figure 6.1, you will see that over the last five years, the cash flow item was negative to the tune of £6 million in 1991, positive to the value of £10.7 million in 1992, positive to the value of £35.9 million in 1993 and negative to the value of £90.6 million in 1994. If you look back in the same section of the accounts, you will find that in 1991 the corporation tax payment was £52.3 million, and this probably accounted for the negative cash flow in that year. In 1994, there was an abnormal increase in the short-term investment item of £225.3 million and at first sight this would seem to be the reason for the negative cash flow amount in the current set of accounts.

Whilst there is no cause for alarm in a company the size of Whitbread, if you are considering making an investment into the shares of this company it would be as well to ask your stockbroker to obtain confirmation that this indeed was the reason for such a negative item, particularly in view of the size of the deficiency.

Return on capital employed ('ROCE')

This index measures the profitability of a company and is expressed as a percentage.

$$\frac{\text{Operating (or Trading) Profit} \times 100}{\text{Capital Employed.}} = \text{ROCE \%}$$

In the same way that a history of EPS adjusted for inflation over a five-year period will show you whether the real earnings are growing or not, the return on capital employed calculated over a similar term will show you whether the company is prospering.

The definition of precisely what is included in arriving at the capital employed can vary. Some argue that share capital plus reserves plus all borrowing including leasing and other forms of financing should be included, but excluding associates and investments and government grants.

We shall adopt all items in our definition, with one major caveat: **Be extra careful when considering a property company.**

This will be explained after describing how to calculate ROCE.

You can calculate the ROCE for individual component parts of a company, particularly when it has a number of different products or when it trades in different countries or has a number of subsidiaries, but for the average investor we shall use the rather less precise figure of total capital.

CONSOLIDATED BALANCE SHEETS (£m) DALGETY					
	Jun 30 1989	Jun 30 1990	Jun 30 1991	Jun 30 1992	Jun 30 1993
TANGIBLE ASSETS					
Tangibles	458.0	483.5	434	415	447
Investments	38.5	40.7	13	10	9
	496.5	524.2	447	425	456
CURRENT ASSETS					
Stocks	408.7	235.0	198	181	214
Trade Debtors	452.6	277.3	231	228	243
Other Debtors	73.1	71.7	41	32	28
Pension Prepayments	0.1	3.7	4	2	4
Prepayments &c	23.2	19.3	11	13	11
ACT Recoverable	–	–	–	11	13
Investments	4.5	0.3	3	3	2
Loan Notes & Bonds	a	1.0	16	10	11
Deposits	46.3	39.0	8	5	1
Cash	11.4	11.0	10	12	32
	1,019.9	658.2	522	497	559
CREDITORS (due within one year)					
Bankers	219.6	69.2	25	51	38
Other Loans	–	24.5	–	1	1
Finance Leases	9.1	7.2	2	2	1
Bills of Exchange	0.5	0.6	–	–	–
Trade Creditors	350.3	325.8	280	286	327
Taxation	33.1	34.6	30	34	31
Other Creditors	209.5	66.6	52	46	45
Accruals &c	52.1	42.1	51	50	49
Dividend	36.6	40.4	41	43	46
	910.8	611.0	481	513	538
NET CURRENT ASSETS	109.1	47.2	41	(16)	21
TOTAL ASSETS LESS CURRENT LIABILITIES	605.6	571.4	488	409	477
CREDITORS (due after one year)					
Bankers & Other Loans	114.8	99.7	74	17	40
Finance Leases	9.4	6.5	3	2	2
Taxation	1.3	0.1	–	–	–
Other Creditors	0.4	0.4	–	–	–
PROVISIONS FOR LIABILITIES & CHARGES					
Deferred Taxation	6.0	1.1	1	2	2
Acquisition	–	27.9	13	8	4
Other	15.0	17.5	11	10	15
	146.9	153.2	102	39	64
NET ASSETS	458.7	418.2	386	370	413

Figure 6.2 continues over

CAPITAL	230.6	231.5	233	234	235
SHARE PREMIUM ACCOUNT	2.9	4.4	7	9	13
REVALUATION RESERVE	77.4	70.6	63	48	51
OTHER RESERVES	(82.1)	(132.7)	(128)	(181)	(177)
PROFIT & LOSS ACCOUNT	217.5	229.7	211	260	291
SHAREHOLDERS' FUNDS	446.3	403.5	386	370	413
MINORITY INTERESTS	12.4	14.7	–	–	–
	458.7	418.2	386	370	413

Figure 6.2 **Extract from the Dalgety accounts Extel card showing consolidated balance sheets**
Source: Extel Financial Limited

To calculate the capital employed add together the issued ordinary share capital and the reserves.

In the case of Dalgety, this value is shown in Figure 6.2. You will see that it consists of capital (including preference capital), share premium account, revaluation reserve, other reserves, and profit and loss account.

Divide this figure into the operating profit including continuing business and acquisitions. This is shown under the heading 'Consolidated Profit and Loss Account' in Figure 6.3.

Express the result as a percentage to find the ROCE (See Table 6.2).

Table 6.2 **Finding the ROCE**

	1989	1990	1991	1992	1993
Operating Profit	130.0	128.5	117.1	122.8	130.4
Capital Employed	458.7	418.2	386.0	370.0	413.0
ROCE %	30.3	30.72	30.33	33.18	31.57

The immediate conclusion to be drawn from the trend shown in Table 6.2 is that it is pretty flat, and you might make some assumptions.

Either the management is not making the best use of the capital employed, or the profit margins are being squeezed (operating costs too high or lower product prices to meet competition, or both).

The chairman states in his report at the interim stage in February 1993, that 'trading conditions were generally tough', and although he goes on to say that 'operating companies succeeded in maintaining or improving

CONSOLIDATED PROFIT AND LOSS ACCOUNT (£m)					
	Jun 30 1989	Jun 30 1990	Jun 30 1991	Jun 30 b1992	Jun 30 1993
Continuing				3,982.4	4,467.5
Acquisitions				–	2.8
TURNOVER	4,757.7	4,634.2	3,659.4	3,982.4	4,470.3
Changes in Stocks	2.0	7.7	(6.4)	(9.1)	(8.9)
Own Work Capitalised	(0.2)	(0.8)	(1.4)	(0.5)	(2.6)
Other Operating Income	(24.4)	(24.6)	(12.8)	(7.9)	(6.5)
Raw Materials	3,942.3	3,795.3	2,976.8	3,262.6	3,703.9
Staff Costs	293.6	312.1	272.7	279.0	310.3
Depreciation	47.4	49.6	43.6	45.6	50.0
Other Optg Charges	–	1.8	–	–	–
OPERATING PROFIT	139.0	128.5	117.1	122.8	130.4
Continuing				122.8	130.3
Acquisitions				–	0.1
OPERATING PROFIT				122.8	130.4
Continuing Operations:					
Business Disposal &c	–	–	–	(5.9)	–
Asset Disposal	–	–	–	5.6	–
Discontd Operations					
Business Disposal &c	–	–	–	1.8	–
Disposal Provision	–	–	–	–	9.0
Property Disposal	–	(7.7)	(2.5)	–	–
Associated Companies	(2.1)	(4.4)	–	–	–
Investment Income	(2.9)	(2.2)	–	–	–
Interest Receivable &c	(23.9)	(14.8)	(5.3)	(2.3)	(1.8)
Interest Payable	57.5	39.5	14.0	12.0	11.0
PROFIT (LOSS) BEF TAX	110.4	118.1	110.9	111.6	112.2
Corporation Tax	18.0	22.8	23.7	28.7	27.5
ACT	(0.5)	(3.2)	(5.0)	(16.9)	(9.8)
Deferred Tax	–	0.7	–	0.8	1.9

Figure 6.3 **Extract from the Dalgety accounts Extel card showing consolidated profit and loss account**

Source: Extel Financial Limited

their market share', the ROCE shows that over a period of five years the real return on capital has been dropping when you take inflation into account.

However, a more detailed examination of Figure 6.2 shows that the negative figure under the heading 'Other Reserves' has been increasing at a considerable rate.

ROCE is a very useful indicator of profitability for a number of reasons.

A low return can easily turn into a negative figure if there is a slump in the business in which the company is engaged.

If the figure is lower than the cost of borrowing money, increased bank loans will reduce the earnings per share.

A persistently low return compared with others in its sector could attract the interest of a predator. In other words it could become a takeover target.

Property companies would be regarded differently.

Earlier we said that one should beware of assessing the figure for capital employed in property companies. The reason is that if property is revalued upwards in a rising property market, the figure shown in one of the reserve items will distort the overall capital employed, with the result that the ROCE will drop, sometimes by quite a lot.

If the property company is one which relies on 'letting' income rather than property trading, this can be disconcerting.

Net asset value (NAV)

This figure shows the asset value of each ordinary share. It does depend very much on the asset values shown in the balance sheet being realistic.

As we have shown, a part of the earnings is normally put to reserves, and thus the figure shows not only whether the company is able to make profits but also the extent to which the share price reflects this, as well as the asset backing per share.

You calculate the NAV by dividing the ordinary shareholders funds (ordinary capital plus reserves) by the number of ordinary shares in issue.

Thus for Dalgety the NAV figures are as shown in Table 6.3.

Table 6.3	**NAV figures for Dalgety**				
	1989	**1990**	**1991**	**1992**	**1993**
Shareholders Funds (a)	458.7	418.2	386.0	370.0	413.0
Ordinary Shares (b)	223.3	224.2	225.5	226.5	227.9
NAV (a/b)	205p	186p	171p	163p	181p

So we have a poor NAV record over five years which corresponds with the historic ROCE.

Market capitalisation

The market capitalisation of a share is obtained by multiplying the current ordinary share price by the number of ordinary shares in issue. This figure is given once a week in some daily papers.

It is a useful measurement for comparing the relative size of a company in the same sector. Size alone does not equate with safety necessarily.

To repeat what has been said at the beginning of this chapter, the picture that emerges about a company and the way in which it is changing does depend upon your extracting essential information from past company accounts and applying the necessary adjustments to allow for inflation.

A share which you have selected for investment, whether for capital growth or income purposes, and which meets all the criteria of EPS and ROCE, may subsequently begin to look a bit sick. Unless you monitor its performance using the indices described above, you could be looking at both a reduction in income in real terms and an erosion of the value of your capital without realising it.

 SUMMARY

In this chapter we have described the way to read company reports and accounts from the point of view of an investor.

We emphasise that the analytical exercises contained in this chapter are by no means exhaustive but they will suffice to give you enough of an understanding to make investment decisions.

They will, in addition, enable you to monitor the real returns of your investment if you keep your records up to date.

In particular we have looked at:

- **Contingent Liabilities.** The potential time bomb that these could represent, and their importance as far as your decision on whether to invest or not, or whether to sell immediately if you hold the share already.

- **Chairman's Reports.** How to read between the lines and the danger signals which should alert you if there is a lot of waffle and platitude.

- **Auditors' Statements.** The essential need to check to see whether the accounts have been qualified in any way. If so, avoid the share or get out of your holding fast.

- **The effect of interest rates.** Their negative influences on companies' future earnings, and their immense contribution to generating inflation.

Their positive effects which enable you to buy annuities for pension contracts to enhance pension income.

- **The effect of inflation.** The corrosive effect which can erode your capital values. ('Rust and moth doth corrupt'; so does inflation.)
- **Key indices** including earnings per share, return on capital employed and net asset values. The vital need to calculate these figures before you commit yourself to investing in a share. Probably the most important data needed in all your analyses.

► Every layer of management between you, the owner of the capital, and the individual share or security purchased will cost you money.

7

Making the most of managed funds

Investment trusts

Unit trusts

Other managed funds

Personal Equity Plans (PEPs)

Summary

So far we have looked at individual stocks and shares and explained the different characteristics which each type has. There are occasions when you will want to make use of managed funds for reasons which will be made clear in this chapter, and these include:

- investment trusts;
- unit trusts;
- other managed funds;
- personal equity plans ('PEPs').

In this chapter we shall examine in particular the fundamental differences between investment trusts and unit trusts.

We shall consider the advantages and disadvantages of both from the point of view of the investor, as well as explaining the rules by which they are governed and the effect these have on their potential performance.

Above all, we shall compare the cost of acquisition and administration of these funds.

Before we get down to details, there is one basic truth which many people ignore although it is so obvious that it may appear to be trite to repeat it.

Whatever capital is placed in any fund, whether investment trust, unit trust, pension, life assurance policy or managed investment, it will end up in stock, shares, bricks and mortar or cash. So every layer of management between you, the owner of the capital, and the individual share or security purchased will cost you money.

You have to decide whether you think that the investment expertise being offered by the fund managers is so much better than making your own selections that the cost of their services is worthwhile. The costs, when analysed, vary considerably between various types of managed funds and you must make your own decisions as to whether you think they are reasonable.

INVESTMENT TRUSTS

An investment trust is a company whose shares are listed and traded on the Stock Exchange.

Each investment trust will have its investment objectives published in a prospectus at the time when the shares are issued. Some will be general trusts investing in leading UK industrial shares and will attempt to provide a mixture of capital growth with a fairly low income commensurate with safety. Others will aim specifically to provide a higher than average income, probably at the expense of capital growth, whilst others will aim to produce above average growth with little income.

Some will specialise in certain sectors of the investment spectrum such as emerging markets, smaller companies, or convertible shares for example. Yet others will invest in geographical areas such as the USA, South America or the Far East.

All will have different degrees of risk and it behoves the investor to assess this aspect before making a commitment.

Ways of assessing risk

Net asset value ('NAV')

This figure shows the value of the company's assets applicable to one ordinary share. It is calculated by dividing 'shareholders' funds' by the number of shares in issue. Shareholders' funds are calculated as the total assets minus all prior charges such as preference shares, debentures and loan stocks at their par or asset value.

For example, if shareholders' funds are worth £2 million and there are one million ordinary shares in existence, the NAV would be 200p.

Discount/premium

Investment trust shares can frequently be bought at a discount. This occurs when the share price is less than the NAV and investors are, therefore, paying less than the value attributable to the underlying assets. The discount is the difference between the share price and the NAV, expressed as a percentage of NAV. If the share price is 90p and the NAV is 101p, the discount is about 12 per cent.

A premium occurs when the share price is above the NAV and investors are paying more than the value attributable to the underlying assets. If the share price is 100p and the NAV is 80p, the premium is 25 per cent.

Investment trust share prices move in the market in line with the usual forces of supply and demand.

Gearing

An investment trust is able to borrow money like any other company.

All the money raised by the issue of shares, together with any money borrowed by way of loan or debentures is invested in listed securities or held in cash pending such investment. Such borrowings are known as prior charges because they rank before the ordinary shares in their entitlement to capital and/or income. However, they have a fixed repayment value, and it is this which provides the gearing, in the following way:

If a company has £10 million of assets and £1.3 million of prior charges, shareholders' funds are worth £8.7 million. Say the assets then grow by 10 per cent to £11 million. Because the prior charges remain fixed in value at £1.3 million, shareholders' funds grow proportionately more – to £9.7 million, which is an increase of 11.5 per cent.

Split capital trusts

Split capital trusts have different classes of shares, each of which have different characteristics and entitlements. They also have a limited life span. When they are wound up, the different classes of share are repaid in a predetermined order of priority. During the life of a split capital trust, the shares can be bought or sold in the normal way at the prevailing market price. The different classes of share are as follows.

(a) Zero dividend preference shares

These shares are designed to offer a low-risk investment, as they are usually the first class of share to be repaid on the wind-up date, with a predetermined capital return. When you buy zero dividend preference shares, you know how much you can expect to receive when the company eventually comes to be wound up, provided that there are sufficient funds available. Zero dividend preference shares have no entitlement to dividends.

The NAV shown in the financial Press against these shares applies to this class of share only. In the case of zero dividend preference shares, the NAV is a predetermined amount which is fixed at the start and then increases by a certain percentage over the life of the company to a final value, the redemption price, determined when the company was formed.

The asset cover indicates the progress the company is making in providing sufficient assets to cover the redemption price at the wind-up date. If, for example, the asset cover is 0.7, this means that the company currently has only 70 per cent of the assets necessary to repay the redemption price of the zero dividend preference shares.

The hurdle rate

This shows how much the company's assets must grow year-on-year (i.e., compound growth rate) if they are to be sufficient to pay the predetermined redemption price of the zero dividend preference shares at the wind-up date. A hurdle rate of 2.0, for example, means that the company's assets must grow by 2 per cent each year in order to pay the redemption price at wind-up. A minus hurdle rate (–2.0 for example) means that there are surplus assets and that the total assets can decline by that amount each year and still leave enough to pay the redemption price at wind-up.

After the redemption price has been paid to zero dividend preference shareholders, any surplus assets form the capital entitlement of the next class of share in priority, and so on.

Some companies have a class or classes of share or loans which rank for repayment before the zero dividend preference shares. Where this is the case, the obligation to repay those shares (or stocks) is taken into account when calculating the hurdle rate and asset cover.

(b) Stepped preference shares

Stepped preference shares are designed to offer a low risk investment with a predetermined growth in dividends and capital. When you buy stepped preference shares, you know what dividends you can expect to receive each year and how much you can expect to receive when the company is wound up, provided there are sufficient assets available.

Gross redemption yield

This measures the capital and income return on your investment until wind-up, expressed as an annual percentage so that it can be compared with the return from other forms of investment such as building society accounts or gilts.

A gross redemption yield of 8 per cent, for example, means that the money invested at the price shown will grow by 8 per cent per annum compound interest, until the company is wound up. This includes all your dividends during that time and finally the redemption value of the shares.

Annual step

This is the predetermined percentage rate at which the dividends and net asset value are set to increase each year.

(c) Income shares

These shares are designed to produce high income. Once a company has met its expenses and the income requirements of any higher-ranking classes of shares, income shareholders are entitled to all the surplus income.

Most income shares have a predetermined redemption price when the company comes to be wound up. However, because the main purpose of these shares is to provide income during the life of the company, the redemption price is often the same as the issue price, or sometimes less. In these cases there is no increase in capital and sometimes even a capital loss, but the terms and conditions will be clearly set out and must be considered carefully.

The gross redemption yield is the same as for stepped preference shares described above.

(d) Capital shares

Capital shares have no predetermined redemption price, and therefore have the potential to produce a high capital return since they are entitled to all the remaining assets of the company at winding-up, once all the other classes of share have received their redemption entitlements. The success of the capital shares, therefore, depends on the growth of the company's assets. There is always the possibility that there may be insufficient assets to make any return at all to capital shareholders.

Hurdle rate

Because capital shares have no predetermined redemption price, this indicates the necessary compound growth of total assets until the wind-up date if the assets are to be sufficient to repay the current share price.

(e) Highly geared ordinary shares

These shares offer high income as well as an entitlement to any assets remaining at the wind-up date, but only after any prior charges – in most cases zero dividend preference shares and/or stepped preference shares –

have been repaid. Highly geared ordinary shares
have no predetermined redemption price.

Investment trusts sometimes have warrants
attached, and they enjoy all the same characteristics as the warrants described in Chapter 3.

> There is always the
> possibility that there
> may be insufficient
> assets to make any
> return at all to capital
> shareholders.

Costs

We shall divide the costs into two parts: costs of administration, and costs
of dealing.

Costs of administration of investment trusts

The costs of administration vary from one investment trust to another,
between 0.75 per cent to 2 per cent per annum. This charge is levied on the
value of the total assets of the fund and is usually charged at half-yearly
intervals. The charge covers management fees and the cost of all administration other than dealing. Because investment trusts deal in substantial
amounts of money with each transaction, they are frequently able to negotiate stockbroking commissions down to 0.2 per cent per bargain within
the fund.

Investment trusts do not normally pay commissions when business is
introduced to them. There is no need to do so since their shares are listed
and dealt on the Stock Exchange, so anyone who wants to buy shares does
so through a stockbroker and pays whatever commission the broker
charges. Since an investment trust has a finite number of shares in issue, it
is called a 'closed-ended' fund. This means that whatever the demand
may be for its shares, no more are issued, and consequently the administration costs are limited to investment activity within the fund. It has no
concern with the volume of trading in its own shares.

Costs of dealing in investment trusts

This is one of the fundamental differences between an investment trust
and a unit trust.

The costs of dealing in the shares of an investment trust are exactly the
same as those incurred in buying or selling any other share through a
stockbroker.

Let us consider the cost of investing, say, £5,000 in one of the oldest and
best-regarded investment trusts, Foreign & Colonial (see Table 7.1).

We shall take the price of the share as 247p bid, 250p offered. The spread is 3p or 1.21 per cent on the bid price.

| **Table 7.1** | **Example of costs of dealing in shares of an investment trust** |

	£
2,000 shares @ 2.50p	5,000.00p
Commission @ 1.85%	92.50p
Government Stamp Duty at 0.5%	25.00p
Total Cost	**5,117.50p**

The cost of acquisition of this investment trust is £117.50p which, expressed as a percentage of the sum invested, amounts to 2.35 per cent.

Since the bid price of the share is 1.21 per cent lower than the offer price, you are immediately 3.56 per cent worse off than before you made the purchase. Or, to put it another way, the bid price has got to rise by 3.56 per cent (9p) before you start to show a profit.

In fact, since it is likely that you will have to pay another commission on the sale amounting to a further 1.85 per cent, it is more true to say that the bid price has got to rise by 5.41 per cent (13.5p) before you break even.

Obviously you will have checked the recent 'high' and 'low' to see whether it is realistic to expect the share to perform to this minimum level required before you commit yourself, but you will be well advised to bear this calculation in mind when comparing costs of dealing with unit trusts and other managed funds.

How should you regard investment trusts in planning your investment strategy?

By their very nature, investment trusts are not given to much volatility in their prices. This, of course, excludes any warrants whose prices do move about much more frequently.

In general, though, they are to be regarded as a longer-term investment. The reason is obvious. When you buy a share in an investment trust, you are buying a very small proportion of a fund which is spread over a large number of industrial or mercantile company shares. If the portfolio consists of, say, 75 companies out of the FT-SE 100 Index, and if five of those company shares increase by 20 per cent whilst the remainder stay largely unchanged, the overall performance of the fund is hardly going to be affected. On the other hand, if there is a dramatic and sustained fall in the price of a few of the underlying investments, the fund will not be damaged substantially either. Thus you would not expect an investment trust to outperform the sector in which it is invested by any substantial margin.

Investing overseas

This is an area where investment trusts, like unit trusts have a positive advantage for the average UK-based investor. By using an investment trust to obtain an interest in foreign shares, in particular Chinese, Indian, Pacific Rim countries and South America you will save yourself a vast amount of aggravation and risk.

Not only are you able to buy and sell in sterling, thereby eliminating the problems of obtaining foreign exchange, but you have none of the difficulties of delivering stock or share certificates to an overseas market.

Also, since many of the markets are functioning when it is night time in Britain (and frequently in foreign languages, making negotiating prices well nigh impossible), an agent who is acting for you in this country to buy shares in a foreign country has to deal via another agent abroad and there is very little feeling of being in control.

Most of the big firms of investment trusts have their own representatives living in the countries concerned whose job is not only to deal in the local market, but also to keep themselves *au fait* with resident company developments as well as the political climate. As a stockbroker, I can get rapid and accurate information for my clients from the London offices of investment trusts who operate in overseas markets with much greater confidence than if I had to check up on individual companies.

Regular monthly savings plans

There is another aspect which is attractive, particularly for the investor who is unable to make purchases in reasonable amounts of money at any one time, and that is using regular saving plans. Such arrangements are available from most investment trust managers and they will accept monthly investments from as little as £20 per month.

Pound cost averaging

By using this form of saving, the investor is able to benefit from what is called pound cost averaging. This means that since the amount of money being invested each month is fixed, the number of shares which that sum buys will vary according to the price of the share at the time of purchase.

If the share price is fluctuating throughout the year, the investor will get more or fewer shares purchased on his behalf each month during the course of the savings plan so that the overall cost per share will average out to a mean figure. The managers tend to charge less in commission for this type of arrangement so there is an advantage to the regular saver.

There is no penalty for interrupting the monthly savings plan, and the investor can sell all or part of his accumulated holding at any time.

The computation of liability to CGT and indexation of purchase prices under a monthly savings plan is described in Chapter 8.

UNIT TRUSTS

A unit trust differs from an investment trust in the following fundamental ways:

- Unit trusts are not allowed to borrow money so there is no element of gearing.
- There are no shares issued which can be traded on the Stock Exchange.
- The number of units which can be issued to buyers is unlimited.
- The only 'market' wherein you can buy or sell a unit trust is made by the managers of their own fund.

This last aspect raises some contentious points.

First, since there is no competition in the 'market' for the units, there is no way in which the buyer or seller (or his agent) can negotiate the price. If there is only one source of supply, you have to take the price or leave it; you have nowhere else to go.

Second, the argument that the price fully reflects the net asset value, neither more nor less, is irrelevant. The NAV for an investment trust is published daily, and yet you can buy such shares at a discount to NAV. Also, the prices which are made by different market makers for the same share will vary, sometimes by several pence per share. It is, as we have said, an essential part of the role of a stockbroker to negotiate the best price that he can on behalf of his client, but it is impossible so to do when buying or selling unit trusts. It does not seem to me that it is correct to claim that there is a proper market in unit trusts in the conventional sense, if they are to be compared with stocks or shares or investment trusts, from the point of view of the investing public.

> If there is only one source of supply, you have to take the price or leave it.

Areas of investment

Each unit trust has specified areas where it invests in the same way as investment trusts.

When you buy a unit, the money is invested in a fund which is itself invested in shares in companies which come within the scope of the declared parameters of the individual unit trust. For example, there are unit trusts which range from a general fund to specific areas such as North American, Far East, Emerging Markets, Smaller Companies, etc, so the choice is wide and varied. The success or otherwise of the individual performance of each fund will depend entirely on the ability of the investment manager in every case.

Types of fund

Most unit trust funds will be split into separate classes offering predominantly either capital growth or income.

Some funds offer a subdivision within the fund called an accumulator and these units do not pay any dividend, but reinvest all earnings in order to maximise capital growth.

Unit trusts do not have a limited life, so there is no redemption date, nor is there any class of unit which takes precedence over another within a fund.

Each fund is valued daily using the mid-market price of the underlying assets and this total value is divided by the number of units in issue to establish the unit prices. Since there are no instruments in issue which constitute prior charges, there is no NAV published because it should be the same as the published price of the units.

Unit trusts are not allowed to put any profit generated from trading into reserves so there is no cushion against falling income.

Costs

We shall again divide costs of dealing into two parts: costs of administration, and costs of dealing.

Costs of administration of unit trusts

The cost of administration will vary in a way similar to that of investment trusts, and ranges between 0.75 and 2 per cent per annum. Unit trust managers are responsible for all records including registration of unit holders, cancelling units sold and issuing new units to buyers, as well as carrying out daily valuations of each fund. Whilst these costs may be considered reasonable, the investor must not forget them when measuring the performance of the fund.

Unit trusts pay commissions to introducers of business. The usual amount is 3 per cent of the sum invested. In addition, some fund managers pay what is called a 'trailing commission' to the introducer if the buyer keeps his money invested in the fund. This extra payment can amount to 0.75 per cent per annum and is paid for each complete year after the first for which the investment remains in place.

It is very difficult to see how this commission can be justified. Either there has been no work involved on the part of the introducer or agent because the client has not expressed any desire to sell the units, or the suspicion arises that the intermediary could be influencing the client against getting out of his investment for reasons other than best advice.

There is nothing to stop you, as a potential investor, asking the intermediary if he is being offered a trailing commission by the fund which he is recommending, and if so, that you would like such extra commission to be reimbursed to you, perhaps in the form of additional units. Since there is often quite a high turnover of staff among firms of agents, it will pay you to get such arrangements confirmed in writing.

Alternatively, it is possible to buy units directly from the management company, thus avoiding the charges.

Costs of dealing in unit trusts

When you look at the price spreads of unit trusts published in the daily Press, you will see that they vary between 5 and sometimes 7 per cent. The bulk of those advertised show a spread of 6 per cent.

The difference between the bid and offer prices is used to pay commissions on new business amounting to 3 per cent, as well as covering set-up costs incurred with every new registered holder. In addition, although the buyer of units does not have to pay Government Stamp Duty when he makes his purchase, such duty has to be paid by the fund managers when they invest the money into the underlying securities. Also, there is no commission levied on a seller of unit trust units. Naturally, the fund managers will have negotiated dealing commissions for their market activities down to the same levels as their investment trust counterparts, but, as we have said already, there is no chance of negotiation over the bid or offer price.

THE FIVE WAYS TO REDUCE YOUR COSTS WHEN YOU BUY UNIT TRUSTS

1. Save on commission payments.
Remember that if a unit trust fund manager makes a sale direct to an investor, he does not have to pay away any introductory commission to an intermediary.

2. Buy direct and get the commission paid to you.
In such cases the fund manager has managed to 'save' 3 per cent of the money invested. Since this money saved does not go to increase the assets of the fund you should ask for the commission which would be otherwise payable, to be used to increase your holding in the fund by increasing the number of units allocated to you at the time of your purchase.

3. If you buy through a stockbroker make sure you get a rebate.
If you buy units through the offices of a stockbroker, he will issue a contract note and will show his usual charges therein. These charges are payable to the stockbroker and have nothing to do with the unit trust fund manager. However, since the stockbroker will be entitled to receive introductory commission from the fund manager, you should make sure that you receive a reimbursement in cash from the stockbroker for the introductory commission, or you get an increased allocation of units to the same value.

Most firms of stockbrokers will make this arrangement for you without being asked, but it is always worth your while to confirm that you will benefit in this way at the time of placing your order. It is very difficult to re-arrange such a transaction at a later date when the bid/offer prices may have moved against you.

4. Do not buy through a bank.
Do not let your friendly bank manager buy any units for you, however persuasive he may be. His branch will be credited with the introductory commission, and there is no reason for you to make gratuitous gifts to such organisations who never miss an opportunity to pile on charges.

5. Make your rebate arrangements before you commit yourself.
If you are going to make special arrangements for extra allocation of units for reasons described above, you must conclude such agreements before you commit yourself to making a payment. It is too late to negotiate any alterations subsequently, and it really is important to confirm any such treatment in writing.

Table 7.2 Comparison of costs of buying a unit trust v. an investment trust	
	% cost of the sum invested
Unit Trust (incl. purchase and sale)	6
Investment Trust (incl. purchase and sale as described above)	5.41

Table 7.2 compares the cost of buying a unit trust and an investment trust, and shows that you can be 6 per cent worse off immediately when you purchase a unit trust, and the bid price will have to rise by that amount before you break even.

However, there are some things you can do to alleviate the costs, and these are shown in the box on page 141.

Unit trust managers, like those running investment trusts, will operate regular savings plans within their funds in most cases. The minimum amount acceptable is usually £20 per month, and you can stop contributing at any time, or restart after a lapse, without penalty. You are at liberty to sell all or part of your holding whenever you please, also without incurring any costs.

The calculation showing any potential liability for CGT which might arise on the sale of all or part of a holding constructed under a monthly savings plan is shown in Chapter 8.

OTHER MANAGED FUNDS

There are several managed funds in existence which are neither investment trusts nor unit trusts, but which run funds which invest in several of them. Most of them appear in the *Financial Times* under the heading 'Management Services'.

The justification of their own costs on top of those already being incurred by the underlying layer of fund managers is hard to comprehend.

To the unit trust fund managers whose units they buy, they are simply introducing new business and are therefore eligible for commission of 3 per cent.

The fund of funds is then unitised, and an initial charge of 5 per cent, is frequently made when someone buys the new units.

In addition to this added cost, there will probably be a spread between the bid and offer prices which they publish.

The problem is that you cannot analyse the costs or commissions receivable which apply throughout the layers of managements involved. The unit which you buy is invested in a fund (with its own management making initial and annual charges), which is itself invested in one or more funds (each making their own annual administration charges), and with around 6 per cent bid/offer spreads at each layer. The spread will be less if the underlying investments are investment trusts, but the administration charges will remain.

You must make your own decisions as to whether you believe that the fund managers who operate managed services funds are able to outperform the sector of the market in which they are engaged when you consider the costs involved.

Table 7.3 gives a comparison between investment trusts, unit trusts and other managed funds for you to see at a glance how their costs and ease of dealing compares.

Earlier on in this chapter we explained the advantages of using investment trusts particularly for investing in overseas markets as well as for the monthly saver who does not have significant sums of money to invest at any one time. You will realise that, apart from the size of individual funds which is easily quantifiable, past performance is the only other yardstick available to help you to choose which one to entrust with your capital.

There are over 300 registered investment trusts whose shares are dealt with on the London Stock Exchange, many of which have subdivisions of different classes of shares. Each fund has a fund manager.

There are more than 1500 authorised unit trusts, and in addition about one and a half times that number which are managed either by life assurance companies or offshore managers resident in Eire, the Channel Islands and the Isle of Man.

They cannot all be above average fund managers who consistently out-perform the market.

| Table 7.3 | Comparison between investment trusts, unit trusts and other managed funds |

Item	Investment Trust	Unit Trust	Other Managed Funds
Bid/Offer Price Spread	1–2%	6–7%	min.5–8%
No. of market makers per instrument	several	one	one
Ability to negotiate buying and selling prices	yes	no	no
Price changes	minute by minute	once a day	once a day
Published NAV	yes	no	no
Ability to buy at a discount to NAV	yes	no	no
Commission: Purchase Sale	1.5%–1.85% 1.5%–1.85%	none none	none none
Govt. Stamp Duty on purchase	yes	no	no
Introductory commission payable	no	3%	3%
Annual administration charge	0.75–1.5%	0.75–1.5%	0.75–1.5%
Specialist funds available: e.g.,.by country or commodity	yes	yes	yes

PERSONAL EQUITY PLANS (PEPs)

What you really want to know about PEPs

What is a PEP?

The PEP consists of a portfolio of one or more shares which are granted special concessions both for income tax and CGT purposes. It is a separate fund which has to be approved by the Inland Revenue in every case *before* you start. You cannot buy a share and then apply for approval later. In order to get approval, you have to complete an application form, and the most important items to be included are your national insurance or pension number, and the address of your tax office. Without these items you will not get approval.

Who manages a PEP?

Strictly speaking, a PEP can be self-administered or managed on the PEP holder's behalf, but since the majority are invested in investment or unit trusts we are including them in this chapter. However the actual split of management responsibility falls into two parts. There is an administration manager, who has to have Inland Revenue approval, and an investment manager who has to be authorised to deal in securities. All firms of investment and unit trusts and other managed funds who offer PEPs in their own names combine the two functions in one firm, as well as some firms of stockbrokers.

Can I choose what shares go into my PEP?

It is possible to arrange to have the administration dealt with in one firm and the dealing done by another, usually your own stockbroker. This arrangement is called a 'self select' fund. In this way you can decide what instruments are bought for your PEP and when to change them if you wish. You have no control over the underlying investments selected by managed fund PEPs.

The best way to understand what you can and cannot do within the current legislation is to regard a PEP as a fund with its own identity. Each new PEP that you start in a different financial year should be regarded as a separate fund, even if you increase your investment in the same shares as are already held in a previous one.

How do I start a PEP?

In order to enjoy the benefits allowed to a PEP holder, you must buy any shares which are to be held in the PEP with money which is in the PEP account at the outset. Thus you have to put enough money into the PEP account to to enable it to make the purchases. PEP accounts are not allowed to be in debit.

Can I transfer shares I own into a PEP rather than put up cash to begin with ?

If you hold shares in your own name, and you wish to transfer them into a PEP, they have to be sold first and repurchased by the PEP. This generates dealing costs.

How much can I put into a PEP?

You are limited as to the amount of money which you can transfer into a PEP each financial year. At present the maximum allowed is £6,000 per person over the age of 18. In addition you are permitted to invest a further £3,000 into a single company PEP each year. You are restricted to investing all or part of this extra cash into the share of one company which has Revenue approval for this purpose. Not all companies have this facility.

What are the concessions?

The first concession is that all income arising from investments held in a PEP is totally free of income tax, and further that any tax which has been deducted at source from a dividend due to the PEP holder is reclaimable in full from the Inland Revenue. This applies whether the dividend is paid out in cash to the PEP holder or retained within the portfolio for further investment.

The second concession is that any profit which is made on the sale of investments within the PEP is completely free from CGT and does not form part of the annual CGT-free allowance of £6,300.

What are the restrictions?

Naturally there are restrictions imposed by legislation as to what type of share you can hold within a PEP, and there are some financial disadvantages also of which it is as well to be aware.

Restrictions

You cannot include any investment in gilts or any form of derivative in a PEP. In his Budget in November 1994, the Chancellor announced that some fixed interest securities other than gilts will be allowed to be held in a PEP from 6 April 1995 onwards, and this concession will open up many opportunities, particularly as far as using high yielding investments to provide capital growth is concerned.

> All income arising from investments held in a PEP is totally free of income tax.

You cannot include any share of a company which is registered outside the EEC in a PEP, unless the value of the investment at the time of purchase amounts to less than 50 per cent of the total amount invested in the PEP in that financial year, with a maximum of £1,500 in non-qualifying shares. A qualifying share is one issued by a company whose registered office is resident within the European Union.

You may only invest up to a maximum of £6,000 in a general fund in a PEP (although this can all be invested in one qualifying share), and up to a maximum of £3,000 in a single-company PEP in addition in any one financial year.

Disadvantages

If you sell any of the investments in a PEP and remove the money from the PEP, you cannot reinstate the money at a later date.

You cannot take up rights issues for shares held within a PEP, should they arise, unless they occur within the financial year that the PEP is created, **and** you have got sufficient investment room unused within the PEP to accommodate the cost of taking up the rights without exceeding the limits described above.

You cannot offset any profits or losses arising from sales of investments within a PEP either inside or outside the PEP.

You can invest up to a maximum allowed individually each year but you cannot transfer any part to another person without selling the shares first and withdrawing the cash from the PEP.

Advantages

There are a great deal of advantages if you use a PEP as part of a long-term plan.

What are the advantages apart from the concessions?

The main advantage of using PEPs in portfolio planning is that provided you can ensure that you are able to invest the maximum amount each year for, say, seven years and that you are not going to withdraw any of the capital during that time, you will end up with a tax-free fund of a reasonable size. Also, if your investment management has been successful during that period, the concessions allowed for CGT should enable you to achieve a growth rate which is considerably in excess of that which would have been possible otherwise, even if you had matched investments outside the PEP.

By using high-yielding fixed-interest stocks in your PEP and reinvesting the yields (which have had tax reclaimed so that you receive the interest gross), you will be able to increase the value of your PEP at a much faster rate.

You are able to convert income into capital without suffering any tax on the money either on the way in or on the way out.

If any or all of your investments were to be the beneficiaries of scrip or bonus shares, or receive cash as a result of a takeover, there is no limit to the amount which can be retained in a PEP.

Using a PEP for mortgage repayments

A PEP is a cost-effective way of repaying a mortgage loan if a building society will accept this method, and more and more are prepared so to do.

If you use a PEP to repay the capital element of a mortgage, the amount of monthly or annual contribution which you will have to make is considerably less than if you use a with-profits endowment insurance scheme or other form of repayment. Whilst it is only common sense to cover your mortgage risk with a term assurance policy which is the cheapest form of life assurance, it means that you can shop round for the best rates for your life cover, rather than being tied to the policies produced by the life assurance company who may be providing the loan.

Not only is the growth rate likely to be better than most other forms of saving over an extended period, for the reasons explained above, but if your circumstances change and you are able to dispose of your property without loss before the period of the mortgage has elapsed, you can liquidate your PEP at any time without penalty.

Compare this, for example, with an endowment policy taken out with a life assurance company. At the time of the sale of the property, the policy may have a number of years to run until maturity, and regular premiums will still have to be paid before you can get your hands on the money, unless you are prepared to suffer considerable financial penalties for early surrender. Even if you make the policy 'paid up' you will not get any further growth in the capital subscribed and you will have to wait until the policy matures before you get paid out.

What are the costs involved in running a PEP ?

Unfortunately there are some costs to be taken into consideration and unless you do your sums the rewards may fall below your expectations.

Every PEP has to be registered with the Inland Revenue and since all the reclamation of tax deducted at source has to be made from each company's tax vouchers, a recognised and approved administrator has to be employed to carry out this work on your behalf. To give them their due, the work involved is considerable and very time consuming.

However, as you would expect, their costs vary.
Sometimes by quite a lot. If you read the terms
and conditions of various PEP managers you will
find that an average charge is 1.5 per cent per
annum of the value of the fund. Your fund. Thus if
your PEP fund is yielding 6 per cent gross, i.e., 4.8
per cent net after deduction of tax at 20 per cent

> ....Do not forget that as
> your capital invested
> in the PEP grows, so
> will the administration
> charge in money
> terms. ....

rate of tax which is what the situation would be if the investment were
outside the PEP, you will actually not be benefiting from the PEP's tax-free
status if the administration charge is more than 1.2 per cent.

Share dealing costs are extra if you choose a self-select PEP and use a
stockbroker.

Is investing in a PEP a good way to achieve capital growth ?

If your objective in building up a PEP fund is to maximise capital growth,
and really that is all that it should be, then you should not expect to
change your investments within the PEP very often. In fact, if your objective is to achieve a sizeable fund over a seven-year period as described
above, then you should buy one share each year for £6,000, and invest
£3,000 in addition in a single-company PEP, so that you keep your dealing
costs to a minimum. Now that you can put fixed interest stocks into your
PEP, if you reinvest the yield and pay your administration charges from
money outside the PEP, you will be able to build up your capital fund at a
faster rate than can be achieved by any other investment.

Do not forget that as your capital invested in the PEP grows, so will the
administration charge in money terms. This will
have to come out of your dividends receivable
within the PEP although you can pay them separately from outside the PEP. If you choose to pay
them from within, the amount which is theoretically building up both from tax reclaimed on the
dividends, as well as the retained dividends themselves, will not be anything like so large as you
might have expected.

> ...... If your objective in
> building up a PEP fund
> is to maximise growth
> then you should not
> expect to change your
> investments within the
> PEP very often. ....

The use of unit trusts as the investment portfolio within a PEP will
never produce the kind of growth which is achievable by managing your
own share selection, for reasons explained in the previous section of this
chapter.

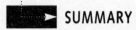 SUMMARY

In this chapter we have examined the advantages and disadvantages of managed funds. We have discussed in particular:

- **Investment Trusts.** Their particular advantages when investing in overseas markets. We have also looked at dealing costs and protection against exchange rate fluctuations when dealing in foreign stocks. We have covered price spreads and administration expenses.

- **Unit Trusts.** We have demonstrated the five ways to save money when you buy unit trusts. We have compared the relative expenses of dealing in unit trusts and other managed funds including investment trusts.

- **PEPs.** We have described all you really want to know about PEPs and why you should use high-yielding fixed interest stocks in a PEP to achieve maximum capital growth faster and free of tax.

It is not difficult to work out your own computations so that you can complete your return to the Inland Revenue. It just takes a methodical approach to the analysis of your dealing records throughout the last financial year, and some time.

8

Capital gains tax – a voluntary tax

CGT – the basics

Rights issues

More ways of reducing your liability to CGT

CGT computation for monthly savings in investment and unit trusts

Summary

In this chapter we shall examine the ways in which you can:

- compute your taxable capital gains;
- use indexation to reduce your liability to capital gains tax CGT;
- reduce your liability to pay by using B&B transactions.

We shall explain:

- who is liable to CGT;
- what CGT is;
- how you calculate CGT;
- what indexation is and how it is applied;
- what the rates of CG are.

CGT – THE BASICS

Who is liable to CGT?

Anyone resident in the UK who makes a profit on the sale of shares in a financial year is liable to pay CGT with the exception of those domiciled in the Isle of Man or the Channel Islands.

A trust which is properly registered with the Inland Revenue is regarded as a person and treated as such. The trustees are liable for payment of any liabilities.

What is CGT?

CGT was introduced on 6 April 1965. Up to that date you could make as much profit as you liked without having to pay any tax on it.

If you make a gain from selling a share at a higher price than you paid for it, you may be liable to pay tax on the amount of the net gain after allowing for costs of dealing and any charges involved such as government stamp duty. The computation of possible liability is much more complicated and one of the purposes of this book is to try to make it understandable to everyone. Because the Inland Revenue seems unable to draft rules which are straightforward and comprehensible, you will have to persevere with what appears to be rather long-winded and pedantic examples of computation. Do not be deterred, because it is very much to your advantage to master how it is done.

How do you calculate CGT?

In order to calculate any liability, a 'base date' had to be established. The date adopted was 6 April 1965, and it remained so until a new base date – 31 March 1982 – was set under the 1988 Finance Act. As of March 1995 it remains unchanged. The important thing to remember at this stage is that you need to record all shares *held in your portfolio currently* which were acquired *before* 31 March 1982, and are shares *held in your portfolio currently* which were acquired *after* 31 March 1982. You must record the cost of each shareholding in each section, those acquired before 31 March 1982, and those acquired after the date. Don't forget that the cost of each shareholding is obtained by dividing the total charge for the purchase, including all incidental costs, by the number of shares bought in that transaction.

If you hold a share which was bought after 1965 you can choose, as its base, the value as at 6 April 1965 or the purchase price whichever is the greater. But you must make your choice (or election as it is called) in writing to the Inspector of Taxes within two years of selling the share *and* if you make such an election, it must apply to *all* the shares still held in your portfolio which were purchased between 6 April 1965 and 31 March 1982. You cannot elect to select one or two shares only out of the list. The only reason why you would make such an election would be because the original purchase price was higher than the share price on 31 March 1982.

If you do not make an election for original cost values for shares purchased before 31 March 1982, then the base price for valuation purposes will be the price at that date. Subsequent scrip and rights issues will be treated similarly as the main asset to which the shares relate. (In the case of 'rights' issues, the money paid for the new shares will be treated, for the purpose of calculating the indexation relief, as being incurred at the time of the issue and not when the expenditure for the original shares was incurred.) This is known as *rebasing to March 1982* and it only applies to shares purchased prior to that date.

Pooling

Now we come to the other significant factor which you have to remember, and this is called 'pooling'. Let us call all the shares currently in your portfolio, your 'active' portfolio. We are not concerned at this stage with any shares which you may have sold in the past for the purpose of calculating CGT liability. Your active portfolio is now divided into two pools – those shares acquired before 31 March 1982, and those shares acquired after 6 April 1982. The pre-31 March pool is called the 'frozen' pool.

The rule which you have to remember is that when you come to dispose of a shareholding where there are holdings in both 'pools' *in the same company*, it is deemed that the disposals take place on a last-in first-out basis.

Let us take an example of purchases and sale to demonstrate the pooling system, and then subsequently apply indexation rules to the same transactions.

✳ EXAMPLE Holding at March 31 1982

- 100,000 Ordinary shares of X Company – value on 31.3.82 £25,000
- Adjustable only for scrips, 'rights' and takeovers

Post March 31 1982 purchases

(a) December 1982 – purchase of 50,000 Ordinary shares of X Company
   @ £3 per share = 150,000

(b) July 1985 – purchase of 100,000 Ordinary shares of X Company
   @ £3.50 per share = £350,000

(c) October 1989 – purchase of 100,000 Ordinary shares of X Company
   @ £4.50 per share = £450,000

Frozen pool (Unindexed)	100,000 ordinary shares in X Company = £250,000
Total unindexed pool	250,000 Ordinary shares in X Company = £950,000

Indexation calculations

The method of calculating the indexation factor is explained later in this chapter. For the moment we are concerned with demonstrating the indexation of the share values in a composite holding.

(1) Indexed cost of December 1982 purchase (frozen pool) (*a*) up to and including July 1985, using the indexation factor 1.154 (1.00 representing the original holding plus 0.154 indexation allowance for the period December 1982 to July

1985); then add the cost of the July 1985 purchase (*b*):

$$£150,000 \times 1.154 = £173,100$$

New pooled holding (*a* and *b*) = 150,000 Ordinary shares
(50,000 (*a*) + 100,000 (*b*) at a cost of £523,100 (173,100 (*a*) + £350,000 (*b*))

(2) Index cost of new holding (*a* + *b*) for period July 1985 to October 1989
(using the indexation factor 1.234 for this period);
then add October 1989 purchase (*c*):

$$£523,100 \times 1.234 + £645,505$$

New pooled holding:
(*a*, *b* and *c*) = 250,000 Ordinary shares (150,000 (*a* and *b*) + 100,000 (*c*)) at a
cost of:
£1,095,505 (£645,505 (*a* and *b*) + £450,000 (*c*)) – **Indexed pool at October 1989**.

Holding at October 1989

March 1982 – 100,000 Ordinary shares of X Company = £250,000 (unindexed
frozen pool)

Pool – 250,000 Ordinary shares of X Company = £1,095,505 (indexed to
Oct. 1989).

Note: If, subsequent to October 1989, X Company made a scrip issue, for example on a one-for-one basis, the above holding would be adjusted accordingly, i.e. the 31 March 1982 Holding (Frozen pool) would then comprise 200,000 Ordinary shares and the Pool 500,000 Ordinary shares.

Similarly, if X Company effected a 'rights' issue the 31 March 1982 Holding and the Pool would be adjusted proportionately.

In the above example, if the 'rights' were taken up in full, the 31 March 1982 Holding would be indexed up to the payment date of the 'rights' and the Pool from October 1989 to the payment date for the 'rights' shares.

Subsequent disposal ('last in – first out')

If a subsequent sale of, say 100,000 Ordinary shares in X Company was made, for example in November 1989 at an aggregate net price of £500,000, the 'last-in first-out' rule would apply. In other words, the 100,000 Ordinary shares would come out of the Pool as follows:

£1,095,505 x 1.009 (indexation factor) = £1,105,365 for period October to November 1989

$$\frac{£1,105,365}{250,000} = £4.42146 \text{ (unit cost)}$$

£4.42146 x 100,000 = £442,146

Capital Gains Tax liability: £500,000 (sale proceeds) minus £442,146 (cost of 100,000 Ordinary shares indexed to November 1989) = £57,854 gain.

Balance of Pool: 150,000 Ordinary at £4.42146 (unit cost) = £663,219 (indexed to November 1989).

- If the acquisition dates of shares held in your current portfolio create a 'frozen pool' and a pool (post 6 March 1982 purchases), all subsequent disposals must come from the pool first on a 'last-in first-out' basis until the pool is exhausted. Only then do you start to subtract shares held in the 'frozen pool'.

- If you do not own any shares which were acquired prior to 31 March 1982, and you create a pool of shares in your portfolio which were all purchased after 6 March 1982 then you index the holdings in exactly the same way as has been demonstrated above, and you dispose of them on a 'last-in first-out' basis also.

What is indexation and how do you apply it?

The first thing to remember is that the retail price index (RPI) is *not* the same thing as the indexation factor.

The RPI figure is calculated each month and is announced in the press around the middle of the month. Don't forget that the figure which is declared relates to the previous month so you can only get an approximation of the capital gain or loss at the time when a disposal takes place. You may have to wait for up to six weeks after a sale before you can get an accurate picture.

The second thing to bear in mind is that if there should be a decrease in the retail price index from the purchase month to the disposal month, there cannot be any allowance.

There is no indexation allowance where assets are bought and sold in the same month, nor is there any allowance where shares are disposed of in a particular month but were bought within the previous nine days, which happened to be in the month before.

RIGHTS ISSUES

In an ordinary 'rights' issue, with a call or all calls payable within 12 months of the application date, *indexation applies to the total amount paid as from the original application date*. However, if there should be a call payable more than 12 months from the application date, this call money receives the indexation allowance only from that date when it is paid.

If, for example an investor takes up a rights entitlement in May 1990 and the total cost is £3,000, payable as to £1,000 on application, £1,000 in December 1990 and the balance of £1,000 in July 1991, indexation is received on £2,000 from May 1990 and on £1,000 from June 1991.

Most privatisation issues are allowed to receive the indexation allowance on the total amount to be paid, from the initial payment date, irrespective of whether the instalments are payable within 12 months or over a longer period. However, it is advisable to check this for each one and you can do so from your local Inspector of Taxes.

Whenever you take up shares in a rights issue, or elect to take shares in lieu of dividend, you will receive a voucher stating the value per share for use as acquisition cost. There are no commissions or Government Stamp Duties involved and this amount is known as the *ex. cap. price*. The same applies to scrip or bonus issues of ordinary shares.

The golden rule is that you cannot 'create a loss' or increase an actual loss by using indexation allowances.

What are the rates of Captain Gains Tax?

The rates applicable are directly related to the level of income tax payable by the individual in the financial year in which the gain is made. Thus if your income is within the 25 per cent tax bracket, and the value of all the net gains achieved in that financial year does not increase your overall monetary receipts sufficiently to put you into a higher tax band, the CGT rate will be 25 per cent.

You will see that it can be to your advantage to transfer shares to your spouse if you have used up your own CGT-free allowance before the end of the tax year and you are considering taking a gain on some more sales.

Concessions

The rules allow two quite simple concessions and one restriction:

- You can make profits of up to £6,300 per person per annum for the financial year starting 6 April 1996 before you are liable to any CGT assessment.

- Trusts are allowed to make profits of up to £3,150 per annum before becoming liable to CGT. If there is more than one beneficiary then the concession is divided by the number of beneficiaries within the trust but the total concession must not exceed £3,150. This is an area akin to a minefield and I do not recommend anyone to attempt to cope with the management of trust tax accounting without professional advice.

- However, the affect of the indexation factor on the acquisition cost can go a long way towards reducing the apparent gain, so that you may be able to keep your taxable gains within the £6,300 limit, and thereby avoid having to pay any CGT.

'Carry-forward' losses

In addition, you can 'carry forward' any actual losses incurred from previous years and you can use them to offset against any gains arising in subsequent years.

It is vital that when you are faced with a gain, you use up the annual allowance of £6,300 *first*, before you eat into any 'losses carried forward'. The reason is that you can not 'carry forward' any unused annual tax free allowance, whilst previous actual losses can be carried forward for as long as you like.

Such actual losses can be added to, or entirely created from, the use of Bed and Breakfast dealing which we shall explain later in this chapter. **It is particularly important to keep records of any shares taken in lieu of dividends, new issues or rights issues which you have taken up, because you will not receive any contract notes for these items.**

There is no quick way to carry out your calculations but you can do them yourself quite easily.

MORE WAYS OF REDUCING YOUR LIABILITY TO CGT

In addition to using indexation to reduce the book cost of the gain arising from the sale of investments, you can store up benefit against future liability to CGT. The price of using this device is far less than the amount of tax which you would have to pay otherwise. It is called 'Bed and Breakfasting' and it will appeal particularly to those who wish to save money.

Bed and breakfasting ('B&B')

Bed and Breakfasting is a very useful tool in managing your portfolio so that you reduce your liability to Capital Gains Tax as far as possible. It can be effective in reducing liability in the current tax year as well as in future years. The cost of establishing such 'losses' far outweighs the amount of tax which you would have to pay otherwise. It is for this reason that many people describe CGT as being a voluntary tax. If you enjoy making unnecessary donations to the Inland Revenue then the practice of B&B transactions is not for you.

> 'Bed and Breakfasting' will appeal particularly to those who wish to save money.

What is a B&B?

This is a term given to a transaction which involves selling a share on one working day and buying it back on the next. The purpose is to establish a new base price for a share in your portfolio.

How is it done?

You have to agree both transactions with the same market maker and you must also arrange for them to be settled on the same day.

You can not spread the two parts over a weekend; the sale can not be made on a Friday for a repurchase on the following Monday.

Is it expensive?

Dealing costs will vary from firm to firm, but you may be able to agree on normal costs on the sale with a handling charge of say, £25, on the repurchase plus Government Stamp Duty.

What are the risks?

Whilst you agree the repurchase price, in principle with the market maker on the day you make the sale, he is not bound by an indicated price, and if some disaster struck the company overnight, he might not be prepared to complete the other part of the transaction at the price arranged. Thus there is a risk involved, but it is small if you stick to companies with a substantial market capitalisation.

Are there any advantages?

There are two separate advantages to consider. The first is to establish a 'book' loss which can have an immediate value, and the second is to establish a new acquisition cost for a share which has risen in price considerably since you bought it and consequently represents a potential liability to CGT when you come to sell it.

It is very useful to take a 'book' loss, if you have one, on a share which you want to retain, but which for some acceptable reason is standing well below the price at which you bought it. For example, the whole sector could be depressed temporarily or the market as a whole could have taken a dive.

To justify the costs involved the loss should be several hundred pounds.

Is it worth doing?

If, because of market volatility, you are looking at worthwhile losses in your portfolio from time to time, it would be a false economy not to 'bank' such losses by the use of B&B because of cost.

✳ EXAMPLE Table 8.1 assumes that you have got two good shares which are showing losses in your portfolio.

Table 8.1

	Purchase Price	Current Bid Price	'Loss'
1,000 Royal Bank of Scotland	420p	318p	£1,020.00
1,000 Zeneca	828p	701p	£1,270.00
Total loss			**£2,290.00**

The purchase price includes acquisition costs and is indexed. You have every reason to want to continue to hold these shares, and yet here is an opportunity to file away some useful ammunition.

Table 8.2 shows the cost of B&B for the Royal Bank of Scotland shares.

Table 8.2

	£	£
1,000 Royal Bank of Scotland sold @ 318p		3,180.00
less commission @ 1.85%	58.83	
administration	6.00	
		3,115.17
1,000 Royal Bank of Scotland bought at 320p		3,200.00
Add commission	25.00	
stamp duty (0.5%)	16.00	
administration	6.00	
		3,247.00
Total cost of B&B		**131.83**

The same B&B exercise calculated for Zeneca, assuming a current offer price of 703p, shows a total cost of £250.26.

So for a total outlay of £382.09 you have 'booked' a loss of £2,290.00 which represents 16.7 per cent. This loss can be carried forward indefinitely.

The tax which you would otherwise pay on a profit of £2,290.00, if it was in excess of your CGT-free allowance of £6,300.00, would be as follows:

At 25% tax rate	£572.50
At 40% tax rate	£916.00

The use of B&B to reduce future liability to CGT

If there are shares in your portfolio which are showing a good profit, and you have every reason to want to keep them and no reason to sell them, you are building up a liability in the future to CGT when you do come to sell.

Bear in mind that sometimes this liability may be forced upon you when you least want it. This can come about if the company receives a bid which is accepted at a price well above the current level of the share price.

The Inland Revenue deems that, under these circumstances, there has been a disposal and therefore you could have the problem described above.

The way to mitigate this potential tax burden is to apply any unused portion of your CGT free allowance to mop up as much of the 'paper gain' as you can. You establish a new base acquisition cost at a higher level so that eventually you have a smaller gain for tax purposes.

If you do this as near to the end of the tax year as possible, then if a bid does materialise there is more of a chance of it arriving in another tax year, and you will have a new tax-free amount to help to reduce the liability further.

Utilising husband's/wife's spare tax-free allowance

With good forward planning you can utilise any spare tax-free allowance belonging to your spouse by making a gift of sufficient shares to the other person and doing a B&B transaction.

You cannot index the original acquisition price in calculating how many shares to give to your spouse, because that transaction does not constitute a disposal, but he or she can when carrying out the B&B.

CGT COMPUTATION FOR MONTHLY SAVINGS IN INVESTMENT AND UNIT TRUSTS

Statutory basis

If you buy shares in an investment trust or units in a unit trust on a monthly savings scheme, should you sell the whole holding after five years, under the statutory basis for calculating the liability to CGT, there would be 60 separate calculations needed to find the inflation adjustment.

The Inland Revenue have introduced an optional alternative basis for calculating the inflation adjustment which will reduce substantially the number of calculations required.

The optional basis

The optional basis is simply this: the cost of shares or units bought through a monthly savings scheme during the company's accounting year will be aggregated and treated as if they were a single investment made in the seventh month of that year.

Operation of the optional basis

The questions and answers given below show how this optional alternative will work in practice.

Can I use the optional basis?

Yes, if you have invested regular monthly amounts for at least seven consecutive months in the monthly savings scheme of a company approved by the Inland Revenue.

How can I apply?

You must write to your tax office within two years of the end of the tax year in which you sell the shares or units invested through a monthly savings scheme. There will be no point in applying unless:

- your capital gains are above the CGT annual exemption in the year in which you make the sale (£5,800 for 1993/94, £6,000 for 1994/95 and £6,300 for 1995/96);

- or the proceeds of all your sales of assets in that year exceed the reporting exemption laid down by the Revenue for the year (and hence have to be reported to the Revenue) (£11,600 for 1992/93 onwards);

- or you have made other disposals in the year which, taken together, produce overall losses.

If the sale is of only part of your holding, an election to operate the optional scheme will apply to subsequent sales subject to your right to revert to the statutory basis.

If you have a monthly savings scheme in more than one fund, a separate application will be needed for each scheme.

How does it work?

The cost of each of your monthly investments bought through a monthly savings scheme during the accounting year of the investment trust company or unit trust fund will be aggregated and treated for the purpose of calculating liability to Capital Gains Tax as a single investment made on the day on which the seventh monthly contribution in that year was due. This is particularly relevant for calculating the indexation allowance.

Note that the relevant period is the accounting year for the investment trust company or unit trust, *not* the tax year. You will normally be notified annually which is the relevant date in the seventh month of the accounting period.

What about partial sales?

If you sell part of your holding purchased through a monthly savings scheme, the sale will not be treated as a disposal for tax purposes if the proceeds of all the sales made in the accounting year are less than one-quarter of the total regular contributions for that year. In addition, if the trust's accounting period differs from the tax year, any sales in the part of the accounting year before 6 April must not exceed total savings in that part of the accounting year.

If the sale (or sales) is within this limit, all the sale or sales in the accounting year will be treated as being made in the seventh month of that year and deducted from the amount invested in that year.

If the proceeds of the sale (or sales) exceed the limit, not only will the sale be treated as a disposal for CGT purposes, but all the investments made in the accounting year will be excluded from the optional basis.

However, if you have a holding of the same shares or units acquired outside the monthly savings scheme, any sales will be treated as far as possible as coming from that holding first, and only after that holding is exhausted, from your scheme share or units.

What happens if I make my own arrangements to sell?

If you make your own arrangements to sell shares or units acquired via your monthly savings scheme, rather than using a facility provided by the scheme operators, any sale will be treated as far as possible as being of a holding of any of the same shares or units you acquired outside the scheme.

Can I revert to the statutory basis?

Yes. But if you do revert, you cannot normally use the optional basis again in respect of the same scheme. You can, however, elect for the optional basis on any other scheme(s) you may have now or in the future.

What happens in the first year of contributions?

If you start a regular monthly savings scheme part way through the trust's accounting year, your investments will be treated as an investment made on the last monthly contribution date in that accounting year.

What happens in the last year of contributions?

When you stop contributing to a monthly savings scheme, your investments in the final year will be treated as one investment made on the last contribution date or in the seventh month, whichever is the earlier.

The optional basis will still be applied if only one month's contributions are missed in any accounting year. If more than one month's contributions are missed, the statutory basis will apply for all the investments made in that accounting year.

What happens if I increase my monthly contributions?

If you make your first increase in your monthly contributions after the seventh month of the trust's accounting year, the additional amounts invested in that year will be carried forward and treated as invested in the first month of the following accounting year, with indexation running from the seventh month of that year.

What if I miss any of my regular payments?

The optional basis will be applied if only one months contributions are missed in an accounting year. If more than one months contributions are missed, the statutory basis will apply for all the investments made in that accounting year.

Are dividend reinvestment schemes included ?

If the dividends paid on the shares or units you buy through a monthly savings scheme are automatically reinvested, they will be included under the optional basis. The cost of shares or units bought with dividends credited to you during the accounting year will then be aggregated with your monthly investment and treated as investments made in the seventh month of that year.

Note that the dividends will be treated as invested in the year in which they are credited to your scheme, where this differs from the year in which they are paid; thus a final dividend paid in respect of one accounting year will be treated as invested in the seventh month of the next accounting year.

Dividend reinvestment schemes not linked to a regular monthly savings scheme will not be eligible for the optional basis and must, therefore, be treated under the statutory basis.

What about lump sum investments?

Lump sum investments will, like shares or units acquired in other ways, normally be treated as separate purchases under the statutory basis and cannot be aggregated with your monthly contributions. However, if you have a monthly savings scheme and decide to top it up with an additional lump sum, it will be aggregated with the monthly investment for the purposes of the optional basis, provided the additional amount invested as a lump sum in this scheme is no more than twice the regular monthly contribution under the scheme. If it is more than this amount, the whole of the lump sum will be treated as a separate purchase on the date it was made. If the lump sum is treated by the trust separately from the monthly savings scheme, it will be outside the optional basis.

What if I have shares or units acquired outside the monthly savings scheme also?

The optional basis will not apply to shares or units acquitted outside the monthly savings scheme.

What happens if the trust's accounting period is not 12 months?

If the accounting period is less or more than 12 months, either because the trust has just started or because of a change in the accounting date, the following rules apply:

- If the period is less than seven months, your investments in that period will be treated as made on the last contribution date in that period.
- If the period is between six and 12 months, your investments will be treated as made in the seventh month of that period.
- If the period is more than 12 months, it will be split into two. The first period of 12 months will be treated as a normal accounting year, and your investments will be taken as made in the seventh month of that year. Your contributions made after the 12th month's will be treated as invested on the last contribution date in the period. Variations in the length of the accounting period by a few days will be ignored.

What should I do in my annual tax return if the trust's year does not coincide with the tax year?

If you applied, or intend to apply, to use the optional basis for calculating your tax liability on the sale of shares or units in a monthly savings scheme during a tax year, and do not know if the conditions will be met at the time you complete your tax return, you can assume that the monthly savings will continue to be invested for the rest of the trust's current accounting year and that no further disposals will be made in that year.

If it turns out that the conditions for the optional basis are not satisfied in the period between the end of the tax year and the trust's next year-end, the treatment of any investments or disposals made before the end of the tax year will not be disturbed.

What happens if the trust ceases to be approved by the Inland Revenue?

In the unlikely event that the trust whose share or units you are buying through the monthly savings scheme does not receive approved status for any accounting year, your contributions for that year would not be eligible to be included in the optional basis, but would have to be treated as separate purchases under the statutory basis. It is, however, understood that if you had made an election and tax had been levied on the optional basis, the Inland Revenue would in practice be likely only to seek to levy additional tax if the optional basis had produced a significant benefit to you.

The rules summarised above were issued as a Statement of Practice by the Inland Revenue in March 1989, under the heading 'Unit Trust and Investment Trust Monthly Savings Scheme' (Ref. SP 3/89). Copies may be obtained either by writing (enclosing a stamped addressed envelope) to The Inland Revenue, The Public Enquiry Room, West Wing, Strand, London WC2R 1LB, or by calling personally at the Public Enquiry Room.

 SUMMARY

In this chapter we have looked at the way in which CGT is calculated and we have described ways in which the liability can be reduced or, sometimes, eliminated altogether. We have demonstrated how to establish acquisition costs and compute indexed gains or losses and how to revalue share prices within a portfolio. This has been achieved by:

- **Indexation of acquisition costs.** Computing your own tax returns and demonstrating how to make big savings on professional fees.

- **Bed and Breakfasting.** Storing up tax benefit for future use to offset and reduce liability to CGT. This tax has often been referred to as being a voluntary tax, and we have explained in detail how you can opt to avoid paying more than you have to, should you so wish.

- **Carrying forward** losses for future use to offset gains in excess of the concessionary £6,300 annual tax free allowance.

- **Resating upwards acquisition costs** for those shares which have grown in value considerably, and which are likely to continue the upward trend in order to minimise future liability to CGT.

- We have described the Inland Revenue's rules for calculating CGT liability on the sale of a holding in investment trust and unit trust companies acquired through a monthly savings scheme.

There is no magic formula which will enable you to make some investments, and then sit back and leave the portfolio to grow of its own accord, until you wake up one fine morning to find that you have become a millionaire.

9

Build your own strategy

Part 1: Overall factors to consider

Summary

Part 2: Personal strategic planning

Summary

It is essential to establish what you are trying to achieve at the outset and then consider subsequently what tactics to use to reach your goals.

Since this subject requires a great deal of thought, and covers a wide variety of items for consideration, it will be split into two parts.

First, the need to understand the overall factors which have an effect on stock markets and why they must be given consideration when you are planning your strategy.

Second, and stemming from such consideration, how to construct your own particular strategy which is both realistic and achievable.

It always amazes me how few clients really think through their investment philosophy and simply leave their shareholding to its own devices. Shares are products and if they are not doing the job for which they were bought originally, they should be abandoned and exchanged for others which are producing the goods. The trouble is that too few shareholders have formulated any clear idea of what they can reasonably expect from their investments.

PART 1

Overall factors to consider

This part of the book shows you how to establish your strategy and then, by using the data which you have unearthed in your research, how to set targets for your capital to achieve.

In order to satisfy yourself that you have arrived at a conclusion which makes sense you should start by considering the whole picture.

Establish the facts governing the world markets, whether it be by country, sector, currency or commodity and work from that database.

The items which you must consider include:

- Why are individual markets up or down?
- Why are some markets 'in' or 'out' of favour?
- What are the reasons for financial interdependency and how might they affect any investment which you might contemplate?

As we have said before, and repeat again, the value of research and records cannot be stressed too strongly. There is no magic formula which will enable you to make some investments, and then sit back and leave the portfolio to grow of its own accord, until you wake up one fine morning to find that you have become a millionaire. If there were, not only would this book have remained unwritten, but the formula would be a closely guarded secret.

It matters not whether you have £500 or £500,000 to invest, you must have an objective, whether it is to achieve a certain amount of capital growth, or a level of income, or a mixture of both.

You should establish at the outset what performance you expect for each year during the life of the investment.

Your strategy must be:

- **achievable, and**

- **realistic.**

This means that you have to have a benchmark against which you can measure the performance so that you are constantly in control of your investments.

Such benchmarks can and should be established for markets as a whole, whether in the UK or overseas; sectors; individual shares; currencies or rates of inflation.

Before getting into the details of how to establish your benchmarks, it is important to repeat the necessity for realism.

As a stockbroker, I am asked frequently to produce an investment recommendation which is impossible to fulfil. Do not be impressed by stories about people making several hundred per cent profit in the space of a few weeks. It is just the same as being told that someone backed six winners at a race meeting and won a fortune. You never hear about the number of losing bets they have made, or how much money they have wasted as a result.

How do you establish what is realistic and achievable?

Use common sense, and above all, have an awareness of what is possible and what is not. Records will tell you that if the market as a whole is rising at an annual rate of, say, 4 per cent per you should be able to beat the growth rate by 25 per cent to 30 per cent with safety. To expect to double your money in the same period with little or no risk would be unrealistic.

If you reinvested the yield, even bearing in mind the erosion in value from inflation, you would increase the annual growth rate.

The figure that you would end up with would be both realistic and achievable. Your benchmark would be whatever index you have chosen, together with the average yield for that market or sector.

Naturally everyone wants to make as much profit in as short a time as possible but it is foolish to expect too much unless you are prepared to gamble and risk heavy losses.

You must quantify your targets for growth and income, and remember to allow for the costs of dealing. If you choose to invest in managed funds then you must allow for administration charges.

No index, whether it be the FT-SE 100, 250, 350 or the All-Share, includes dealing costs in its statistics.

Strategic planning

How do you start, and what factors should be taken into consideration?

It is important to look at the whole picture to begin with, and the elements which are beyond control, in order to set the scene. This will help you to understand what elements are exerting pressures on the markets both from within the UK and overseas.

Certain aspects such as exchange rates, interest rates in other countries and political stability both at home and abroad will affect all or part of the British stock market. Such appreciation will help to explain what might appear to be anomalous in the behaviour of the London market in general, or individual stocks in particular.

Interest rates

Interest rates can affect both the economy and exchange rates of a country. Sometimes the pressure to alter or even maintain high rates may be wholly external.

It is often said in the Press that Britain may have to increase or reduce interest rates if America or Germany move theirs. Many people do not understand why there should be such a close relationship between the economies of these countries.

To illustrate the point, let us take an imaginary situation, but one that is both typical and familiar.

Germany

The German federal bank, the Bundesbank, has one overriding concern and that is to keep inflation under control at a level around 3 per cent per annum. The Bundesbank is not subject to control by the German government and therefore is not obliged to make expedient changes to interest rates which might help the politicians.

> Remember that a downward movement in the exchange rate is a *de facto* devaluation of the currency.

The unification of East and West Germany has produced what is potentially a very powerful industrial country with tremendous earnings power in the future. But the immediate cost of this expansion of domestic responsibility is enormous and if it had to be met out of current resources would threaten the inflation control programme.

The only way to accommodate the costs of the unification and absorption of a large and relatively untrained labour force, with all the attendant social security demands on the one hand, and enable inflation to be contained on the other, is to borrow large sums of money for reasonably long periods.

This requires two things. First, interest rates must be high enough to attract deposits from foreign sources and they must remain sufficiently attractive to keep the deposits in place, even if the rates are higher than domestic industry requires.

Second, the gross national product ('GNP') must be sufficient to demonstrate that the country can earn enough money to pay the interest on the loans without there being any fear of devaluation of the exchange rate. Remember that a downward movement in the exchange rate is a *de facto* devaluation of the currency.

For this situation to be maintained, the country needs a strong and stable political regime which can demonstrate to the world at large its integrity and control of the economy.

Nevertheless, it must not be forgotten that although high interest rates will assist in attracting overseas loans, they will penalise domestic companies, making manufactured goods more expensive in foreign markets and thus less competitive for export.

The USA

In the same imaginary situation, the United States of America has a weak administration, which is unable to get legislation enacted to carry out health care and welfare programmes in line with its election promises.

The Federal Bank, which is independent of the government, like the Bundesbank, has reduced interest rates to very low figures in order to assist the domestic economy to come out of a recession. This has enabled industry to borrow cheaply and increased employment and production. It has encouraged capital investment by industry and the GNP has risen faster than at any time since the war. It has encouraged consumer spending which has benefited foreign importers, particularly Japan.

Wall Street and mutual fund managers begin to get scared of rising inflation and the world at large regards the American economy as being out of control. The US dollar/£ sterling exchange rate weakens in the space of nine months from US$1.42 to 1.65. This represents a loss in value of 16 per cent.

The chief executive of the Federal Bank raises interest rates but the effect on the exchange rate is minimal. The world at large thinks that the remedial action has been too little and too late.

Thus the other ingredient, confidence, has not been restored and so foreign capital remains anxious about the US dollar.

Japan is a big exporter of goods to the United States and the main products include motor cars, domestic appliances, electronic equipment such as radios, televisions, VDUs, cameras, etc.

Over the years, as a result of political and economic pressures from successive US administrations, a large part of this balance of payment surplus has been reinvested in American treasury bonds. However, the Japanese economy is weakening and there is a resistance to further investment in US government stock. This is partly due to the drop in value, because of the lower exchange rate, of the investments which are already in place, and partly due to the need for Japan to repatriate balance of payment surpluses for its own domestic requirements.

The US T-Bond, or long bond as it is often called, which is regarded as the benchmark of the American economy, is yielding over 8 per cent, well above the level at which economists get the jitters.

The presidential elections are two years away, and traditionally no US president introduces fiscal legislation which is likely to be unpopular with the electorate in the year before the election takes place.

The chief executive of the Federal Bank is under tremendous pressure to raise interest rates to cool down the economy using the only weapon left available to him, and to raise them by a significant amount.

The United Kingdom

In the middle of this is Britain. A severe recession lasting several years appears to be over but the growth in orders and the reduction in unemployment is desperately slow and the confidence among investors is shattered.

Napoleon once described Britain as a nation of shopkeepers, and the small company has been the backbone of British industry for decades. Retail sales are increasing slowly and sporadically.

Any increase in manufacturing output is coming from the larger industrial groups, particularly those with developed overseas markets.

The government has managed to get inflation rates down to levels unseen for many years, and has reduced interest rates from over 10 per cent to under 6 per cent. However, there is very little evidence of any upturn in the small retail or manufacturing business returns.

One of the effects of the recession has been to remove confidence in job security with the result that there is a reluctance to increase debt on the part of the population. In fact, the emphasis has become more directed to saving money and reducing borrowings rather than spending.

Nevertheless, Britain also needs to keep foreign money invested in government stocks because the cost of the welfare state is huge, and ministries have over-spent over the years with the result that the cupboard is bare.

Any rise in domestic interest rates is thought to be likely to kill the hesitant recovery, whilst at the same time an increase will be essential to keep the foreign money in Britain if either the Germans or the Americans, or both, raise their rates.

It is rather like being in a poker game where you can't afford to ante up, but if you don't you will be bankrupt.

So what does all this mean to the private investor who is trying to formulate a strategy for his portfolio?

It demonstrates the need to examine and be aware of the possible and probable economic and political developments of the major industrial countries in the world, because their fortunes will dictate the movement and direction of the stock markets overall.

The stock market will move inexorably and the wise investor will realise that fact. There is no possibility of swimming against the tide or bucking the trend.

You do not buy for growth in a falling market unless you are as sure as you can be that the underlying trend is about to turn upwards and sustain its new direction. So the tea leaves must indicate that the tide is about to turn; not just pause before continuing to recede even further.

Naturally there will be unexpected events, and these tend to result in danger signals rather than causes for celebration.

A local war may threaten to escalate into a much bigger conflict and involve many other countries. Sanctions could be imposed which may include trade embargoes and these could last for a very long time. This could have a shattering effect on individual companies' markets and earnings.

> **The stock market will move inexorably and the wise investor will realise that fact.**

When the invasion of Kuwait by Iraq took place, several major companies in Britain who were involved in the manufacture of weapons and communication systems lost a great deal because they were never paid for goods which they had delivered, and they never will be paid.

You will recall that earlier on in this book we alerted you to the dangers of buying shares in companies which depended for their existence upon few but very large orders. Where are Ferranti and Marconi now, to name but two?

Where should the investor look to achieve growth when the UK market is falling?

There will always be areas in the world where the economy is growing and these are where research is needed. As an example, you would probably look at the Pacific Rim including India, South East Asia, China, South America, and for future consideration, South Africa.

The starting point for research into any of these economies is exactly the same as for the developed western world:

- the stability of the currency;
- the stability of the government;
- the amount of national debt and the ability to pay the cost.

Most of the under-developed world will be operating with wage rates which are considerably less than those paid in the developed world, and whilst this is a considerable factor in their favour from an investment point of view, it should not be the only criterion in making a decision to invest.

Also, it is *sine qua non* that any investment which you may be considering must be able to be liquidated at any time and at minimal cost to yourself. You must satisfy yourself about the ability to liquidate and the costs involved before committing any capital.

We have explained earlier in this book that many of these Far Eastern markets are at work when the London Stock Exchange is shut.

Also, and most important, the liquidity in many of these other stock markets is much less than exists in London. This means that it may be difficult to unload a large parcel of shares at the price quoted.

Thus direct investment into individual foreign shares by a UK-based investor is risky. Couple that aspect with the fact that many of the Far

Eastern markets, in particular, can be extremely volatile, and the risks and problems of liquidating investments are compounded.

Nevertheless, there can be good opportunities for investments in these markets and the safest way to exploit them is via investment trusts (see Chapter 7).

So the strategy for investing in less developed countries which are nonetheless attractive must be as follows:

- Do your homework, starting with satisfying yourself that the economy is sound and the government is stable.

- Decide upon an annual growth rate which is achievable in the light of the actual growth rate and that which is projected in the GNP of the country concerned.

- Plan to leave your investment in place for two or three years unless circumstances change.

- Select an investment trust which has a proven track record in the countries concerned.

- Monitor the performance at monthly intervals at the very least. Do not be afraid to communicate with the fund manager and to ask questions if the results appear to vary from a historical pattern.

Analysis of the UK market

From the point of view of the British domestic investor, this is the market where there is more information available than any other.

Earlier in this book we stressed the need to differentiate between fact and opinion, and the statistics which are available in Britain about British firms are voluminous. You could end up reading reams and reams of facts and figures which would not only damage your eyesight, but which would occupy you for every waking hour.

Let us extract some of the indices which are probably the best ones on which to concentrate your research and which will not take up too much of your time in compiling records.

Remember two points.

- We are looking at the behaviour of the constituent parts of the London stock market as a whole rather than any individual share.

- Any analysis is carried out on historical data and so what you are looking at is history. Admittedly recent history, but markets are dynamic and they can move rapidly on occasions.

Historic patterns

History, as they say, has a habit of repeating itself. But there is usually a reason for this and it is very often because the underlying natural laws have not changed, people have simply forgotten them. Memory is notoriously fallible.

One of the basic tenets which establishes a price range for a share is the PER value and, as we have said, it forms a useful yardstick against which to measure whether a share is cheap or otherwise within the same sector. If the PER is high, unless the company can produce earnings in the near future which are sufficiently enhanced **and** higher dividends, (and sometimes the demands of the market are unrealistically high), the next movement in the price is likely to be downwards.

I often think that the market behaves like a greedy bitch; frequently alluring, but when balked of her excessive demands goes into a sulk and ostracises what was recently the object of her desires.

> **Another market truism is that the swing in share prices is always overdone – in both directions.**

You can adopt exactly the same critical approach to the overall level of the price of the market as a whole and perhaps be better equipped to look into the future.

Figure 9.1 shows the ratio of the PER to the earnings of the All-Share Index minus some constituent parts such as property and financials. When the ratio is high, it shows that the market prices relative to earnings are expensive, and vice versa.

Now the market prices are reflecting expectations of earnings 12 to 18 months ahead. The reason for discounting future performance so far ahead is because the accounting periods of all the companies range from one year's end to the next, and if you are looking at the market as a whole, movement in either direction is normally slower than would be the case for any one particular share or sector.

Another market truism is that the swing in share prices is always overdone – in both directions. So when you see warning lights, particularly when the prices look expensive, you should be forewarned and start to take appropriate action to safeguard your capital.

There is no hard and fast rule as to what the average PER for the market as a whole should be, but the reality is that a range of between 12 times and 15 times is probably about right.

Lessons

You will see from the graph shown in Figure 9.1 that before 1993 there have only been only three occasions since 1966 when the ratio broke above the 50 mark.

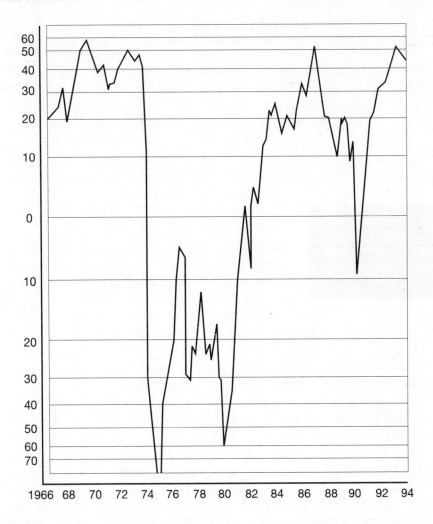

Figure 9.1 Ratio of the PER to the FT Non-Financial Index from 1966–94

Since there is a reason for everything, you have to start to find out why the prices got so far out of line as to make the picture look dangerous. There will not be one single factor alone which is responsible, that is for sure, unless it is something like a war.

In 1994 the politicians managed to achieve the lowest rate of inflation almost within living memory.

Interest rates came down to levels which had not been seen for very many years, which meant that industry could look forward to borrowing money extremely cheaply.

The combination of these two factors should mean that earnings ought to grow at a steady rate, since company managers can plan their expansion programmes knowing that the two biggest threats to profitability have disappeared, namely inflation-driven wage demands and expensive money which requires servicing. Both of these cancers have been the cause of industrial uncompetitiveness for so long in British industry.

But unfortunately the earnings which were reported, from the market as a whole during the latter half of 1994, did not match expectations. It is, of course, perfectly possible that they will rise above the levels achieved by the end of 1994, but it is more likely that they will not rise fast enough or far enough to justify the prices.

> ... Very often the market is pointing the way, and you ignore such indications at your peril. ....

An analysis of the increase in earnings showed that a large proportion of the reported increases was attributable to cost cutting, rather than from organic growth within the companies. There is a limit to the ability to continue to produce substantial savings, and thus increased profits, from such economies. An example of this is the 'pension contribution holiday' which a lot of companies enjoyed at the start of the decade. It was discovered that the money subscribed into their employees' pension funds was well in excess of what would be required to meet their obligations and so further contributions were not necessary for some years.

In addition, fears were constantly voiced concerning the strong possibility of a rise in interest rates in the USA. Whilst such an event has a marginal effect on British industry (beneficial to those companies exporting to North America since it makes British goods less expensive), the fear was that Britain would follow suit and increase interest rates in the UK.

Whatever the other reasons being promoted at such times, the lesson to be learned from this simple analysis is that very often the market is pointing the way, and you ignore such indications at your peril.

The second lesson is to be obtained by studying the records of dividend cover applicable to the same all share list of companies to which the graph refers.

We have said that good husbandry dictates the need to keep adequate reserves in companies and the build-up can only come from retained profits. If too high a proportion of the annual profits are distributed by way of dividend then the cushion against reduced profits starts to wear thin. The earnings per share record is shown in Figure 9.2.

	Average EPS
January 1991	100.19
January 1992	85.13
January 1993	83.48
January 1994	76.50
January 1995	86.56 (adj)
January 1996	110.00 (adj)

Figure 9.2 **Earnings per share record of companies in the FT Non-Financial Index from January 1991 to January 1994**

So the investor would not commit any further funds into the UK market until he has seen either a drop in share prices or a substantial and sustainable increase in company earnings.

However, as we have said before, there will always be individual shares which are worth further investigation. It may well be worth looking at UK companies whose earnings are generated outside the UK and therefore you need to analyse the markets in the countries in which they are trading.

Table 9.1 gives just such a list of companies whose earnings are generated in the USA to a greater or lesser extent. The figures are taken from the latest accounts.

Now at first sight this list looks attractive.

The shares are all traded in London, there is no problem with regard to liquidity – you can sell your holdings at any time – and as we have said earlier, the American domestic markets are expanding fast.

However, the US dollar/£ sterling exchange rate remains as the fly in the ointment.

Since the pound is strong compared with the dollar, the companies listed in Table 9.1 will have to keep the prices of their products as low as possible to compete in American markets, and you have to watch out for the possibility of maintaining turnover at the expense of profits.

Refer to Chapter 6 and plot the return on capital employed for any company which fires your interest.

Remember that earnings generated in US dollars will have to be translated into pounds sterling and at the time of writing the dollar is at a very low rate of exchange.

Table 9.1	Table 9.1 'Companies' earnings generated in the USA as a percentage of sales.

	% of sales		% of sales
Willis Corroon	61	Dalgety	58
Grand Metropolitan	57	Cookson	54
Sedgwick	51	SmithKline	50
Wolsely	49	Wellcome	48
Siebe	47	Hanson	46
Lonrho	45	Carlton Comms.	44
Glaxo	43	Tomkins	43
Tate & Lyle	41	TI Group	38
Pearson	37	Reed Elsevier	37
Rolls Royce	37	United Biscuits	35
General Accident	34	Zeneca	33
British Airways	31	Pilkington	31
Racal Electronics	31	British Petroleum	30
Hillsdown	30	P & O	29
Body Shop	27	Commercial Union	27
Rank Organisation	27	United Newspapers	27
BTR	26	Arjo Wiggins	25
British Aerospace	25	BET	25

Source: Annual reports 1993/4

At this point you will have to make a decision about your timescale in terms of your desired investment returns.

The reason is that the weak dollar exchange rate to the pound is unlikely to last for ever, and when the dollar strengthens, the profits of those companies listed in Table 9.1 will increase in sterling terms without any action on their part, assuming that the volume of sales remains the same in each case, or better still, the volumes increase.

The unknown element is, of course, how long is it likely to be before the dollar becomes popular again?

This begs the political question described above and here is the crux of the matter – timing.

The second factor to be examined is the share price relative to its 'highs' and 'lows' and we shall be considering this aspect when we come to looking at tactics later on in the book.

 SUMMARY

So far we have concentrated on the need to start by establishing the overall direction in which the market is going for two main reasons:

- You cannot expect to get general growth from making investments in a falling market, although there will be individual exceptions.
- The overall view will alert you to factors which will have an influence on the market as a whole, such as:
  - (a) changes in interest rates in the major developed countries;
  - (b) external pressures which may dictate changes in UK domestic interest rates and the consequences;
  - (c) changes and trends in exchange rates in the major currencies and the possible effects on export markets and the prices of imported goods and raw materials;
  - (d) political stability, or lack of it, in the countries in the world which represent either the major currencies or the markets for goods and services in which you may be considering investing.
- The essential need is to remember the corrosive effect which inflation can have on the real returns both from an income and a capital growth point of view.

 PART 2

Personal strategic planning

In this part we examine the ways in which to formulate your own strategic planning.

It is essential that you establish clearly at the outset what your financial requirements are now, and what they are likely to be in the future.

You will need to itemise all calls on your income for your daily, monthly and annual living expenses.

You will need to itemise all amounts of income, their sources and frequency and see whether there is a surplus or deficiency.

Next, you must list your capital, irrespective of where it is placed just now. This exercise will show you how much income your capital has to generate to meet your day-to-day expenses if your sources of income do not match outgoings, at the very least.

What we are concerned to do is to establish your vital needs before deciding how they are to be met. Also, by doing this exercise, you will be able to evaluate the degree of risk that you can afford to contemplate for some or any of your capital.

I do not advocate taking risk for the sake of it. A senior partner in a firm with whom I was formerly associated once said, 'If you cannot afford to take risks, you should not do so. If you can afford to take risks, why do so?'

Nevertheless, all investments carry a degree of risk, and it is generally accepted that the higher the return the greater the risk.

Figure 9.3 shows a simple sketch which you can draw to help you to allot your capital into areas of investment with varying degrees of risk and return which you can expect.

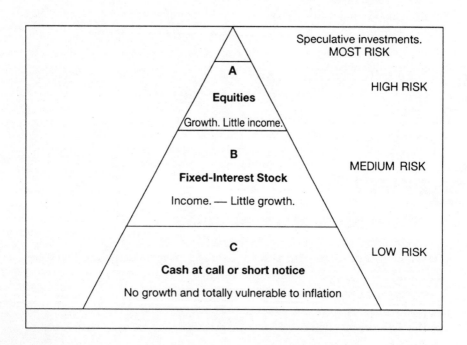

Figure 9.3 Areas of investment: degrees of risk and return

An investor will probably put more cash into category 'A' whereas a trader will speculate to a much greater extent.

The categories shown above can be used to do several things, such as to decide what degree of risk you might be prepared to run, or to apportion investments between income and capital growth, for example. The most common use is to start with category 'C' as being the safest, with category 'B' being slightly less so, and category 'A' representing the more speculative investments.

> '**If you cannot afford to take risks, you should not do so. If you can afford to take risks, why do so?'**

You start by allocating capital to the categories shown above. In broad terms, you would probably use the categories as follows.

Category C: Cash which is available at call, or very short notice

This money is to cover unexpected or emergency requirements, sometimes referred to as 'rainy day money'. Each individual will have different ideas as to how much should be allocated to this depository, and only you, the investor, can quantify the amount necessary.

Such capital should be deposited in a building society or bank account bearing interest. Naturally, you will have to make a judgement as to how much interest rate you are prepared to forgo, depending on the degree of notice of withdrawal which you feel you can live with.

Whilst you have rapid access to your capital and safety in this category, there is no protection against erosion by inflation. Thus it will pay you to keep the minimum amount of money invested in this manner, commensurate with your perceived possible needs.

A word of warning at this point. Do make sure that you read and understand precisely what are the penalties for early withdrawal of funds before the deposit time has elapsed in the unfortunate event that you are forced to get at your money in a hurry. There are some term deposit accounts offered by some building societies which impose what appear to me to be extremely onerous penalties in the event of early withdrawal. I have seen some where the penalty for removing funds in the first three months after the initial deposit means that you get back less capital than you put in originally, quite apart from loss of interest.

However, such deposits will generate interest, and this will form a part of the 'income' to be expected from your capital.

Category B: Fixed-income investments

These instruments will carry more risk than cash on deposit, and certainly should produce a much higher return if interest rates are relatively low. In addition, and depending on the current rate of inflation, the underlying price of such investments should at least match inflation rates providing they are not out of control.

The amount of capital to be allocated to this category will depend upon the shortfall, if any, between your outgoings and income from other sources such as salary, wages, pension and interest generated from money on deposit in category C.

The question of what sort of fixed-interest instrument(s) to select and the mix of the different types of stock or share will depend on the circumstances of each individual and the differences will be considerable. Also the emphasis will differ depending upon whether your strategy demands income or capital growth from your portfolio. Examples of different approaches will be given in Chapter 10.

Category A: Equities

This is the category into which you invest capital for growth purposes. As we have explained earlier, you will not expect to obtain as much income from equity investments as you can get from fixed interest stocks, so the objective for the capital invested in this category is twofold:

- to compensate for the relative lack of capital growth from the money invested in categories B and C so that your overall capital is not being eroded by inflation in real terms, and
- to make a profit.

The amount of risk which you are prepared to take with some or any of the capital invested in this category will depend entirely on the circumstances of each individual, and there is no hard and fast rule which can be applied to the degree of risk which you might contemplate.

What do you do next to crystallise your strategy, after you have analysed your 'budget' in the manner described above?

The first thing you have to decide is whether you are going to be:

(a) a trader, or
(b) an investor.

The second thing to be established is the meaning of the words 'short term', 'medium term' and 'long term'.

There are people who trade in the market to whom 'short term' means four or five hours, 'medium term' means up to one week, and 'long term' means within a month.

An investor would normally consider 'short term' up to six to 12 months, 'medium term' to be 12 to 18 months and 'long term' would probably be two years or more.

If you are going to discuss individual investments with your stockbroker it is most important that you establish at the outset that you both mean the same thing when you talk about how much time you expect to elapse before an investment is likely to achieve its objective.

A trader

Essentially a trader is a risk taker. Whilst we shall examine ways to keep the risks to a minimum in Chapter 10, we are concerned here to explain the difference in approach to investment between a trader and an investor.

When I am asked to recommend a share for a 'short-term' punt, and having established how short is 'short-term' in the mind of my client, I always ask how much money is he prepared to lose. The situation is not quite analogous to backing a horse at a race meeting, because usually you can cut your losses if a share does not perform as expected or, worse still, the price goes into rapid decline. Occasionally, of course, the share gets suspended and the company goes bust, and then there is a total loss, so that under those circumstances there is no difference between such a punt on the market and backing a loser on the race course.

Although there are many people who trade in the market every day, it is not something which the average person should contemplate unless he or she is prepared to lose money.

However, for those who are prepared to take risks, which can be considerable, here are some points to remember.

Investment income
Generally traders ignore any expectations of income arising from their trading activities because they do not anticipate holding a share for sufficient time to qualify for dividends.

Account trading

Rolling settlement demands that the cost of a purchase is paid ten days (soon to become five days) after the bargain is executed. However, it is possible to negotiate a delayed settlement date for up to 28 days from the purchase date, provided that you make such arrangements at the time of purchase.

Because this arrangement is specifically contracted with one market maker, you will have to 'close out' the purchase with the same market maker if you do not want to pay for the shares 'Closing' a bargain is the term used when you sell shares which you have bought before you have to make a payment for the purchase.

The market maker may well demand a higher price for the shares at the time of the purchase, since he has to agree to the deferred settlement of this account. Also, since he will anticipate being asked to buy the shares back at some date in the future to coincide with the settlement date of the purchase, he can crucify you over the price which he is prepared to bid you for your sale to him. In other words, he will probably do his best to ensure that he keeps his losses to a minimum, particularly if the price of the share has gone up in the meantime.

Financing your trading

We have said that you must settle your account on the due date, and increasingly stockbroking firms will demand that they are in possession of cleared funds on settlement day. So if you want to trade in a number of shares within a few days, you cannot use the anticipated proceeds of a recent sale to finance subsequent purchases, unless the revenue from the sales equals or exceeds the cost of purchases **and** such revenue receivable is certain to be in the hands of your stockbroker in the form of cleared funds on or before settlement day due for the purchases. Thus you will probably find that you will only be able to trade in this fashion if you use the stockbroker's nominee company.

It will be essential to check the costs of such a facility and to add them to the dealing costs when you are calculating the price which the share has to reach before you break even.

Access to share price information

If you are going to be a trader, you will need frequent reports of share prices. This is particularly the case if you are going to invest in traded options. On average you should expect to obtain the price of each share twice a day at the least, and traded option prices hourly during market hours for as long as you hold the option. Market volatility is a fact of life and is here to stay, so if you are going to be a trader, you cannot expect to be successful if you are not in control of your investments.

Profit objectives

A trader can afford to be much more limited in his profit objectives because he is intending to make the same amount of capital work much harder. Naturally the risks are greater, particularly if he has to cut losses several times within a short time, but he can afford to set relatively low limits of profit to be achieved in a limited period. If a trader can make a net profit (after all dealing costs and any losses) of 3 per cent per month, every month in the year, he will have achieved a profit of 36 per cent on his capital employed and the first £6,300 of that profit each year will be free of tax.

When we deal with tactics, we shall demonstrate how to trade in a falling market as well as in a rising one. It is true to say, and well worth remembering, that the market rate of fall tends to be faster than its rate of rise. We shall discuss the ways in which you can establish market trends in Chapter 10, and show how you can use its momentum to assist in reaching your profit objectives, rather than try to achieve them against the flow.

If you are going to allocate some capital to be used solely for trading, you should still set targets to be achieved within a defined timescale because the profit which you are aiming to achieve will have to contribute to your overall projected return on capital employed. You may choose to spend a portion of your capital gains as if it were income, and if you do, remember that whilst you are getting a tax advantage by using your CGT-free allowance and thus converting some or all capital gain into income, you must include the amount so expended in your records when you are monitoring the performance of your portfolio from the point of view of return on capital employed.

An investor

The philosophy of an investor is the complete antithesis of that of a trader.

The first thing to remember is that you are going to take a much longer view of the expected return on your capital.

This does not mean that you expect to make a great deal less than a trader might for two reasons:

- you will incur far fewer dealing costs because you will not expect to change your investments very often, and

- because if a trader gets three winners out of five he is considered to be successful, and so the winners have to cover both the dealing costs of all the trades as well as the capital losses incurred.

> ...The market rate of fall tends to be faster than its rate of rise. ....

It does mean that it is absolutely essential that you do your homework in depth before you buy a particular share, and plot your expected annual increase in the price at the outset in accordance with your strategy, and watch it like a hawk.

Where a trader is interested in the price movement of an individual investment only over a short term (possibly days, or even hours if it is a traded option), an investor is much more concerned with all the news items relating to the company concerned, to see whether they either confirm or negate his original expectations of the likely progress of the share price.

An investor will expect to see the price of a share fluctuate within acceptable limits based on historical patterns but such variation should not be the cause for alarm provided that:

- there has not been any disturbing news which might lead you to alter your belief that the company can continue to increase its earnings in line with your projections, and

- the trend in the share price over a period of, say, 90 days is upwards and at a rate which confirms your projected rate of annual increase.

The main objective of an investor should be to choose a portfolio which is designed to produce the income and capital growth desired after he has allocated his resources in the way described above and then leave it alone.

SUMMARY

In this chapter we have demonstrated the way to approach the formulation of your strategy, and emphasized the need to arrange all the facts at your disposal concerning your assets and liabilities. Without going through this essential exercise, you will never be able to keep control over your capital and income needs, nor will you be able to ensure that the return you are getting on your assets is as high as possible, bearing in mind the aspect of safety. As a stockbroker responsible for advising other people of the best arrangements available, I can assure you that this basic groundwork is absolutely vital if you are going to succeed in doing your own portfolio management.

We have examined in particular the importance of establishing the overall trend of the market first in order to make sure that you are not attempting to achieve something which is patently impossible at that time, e.g., trying to get good capital growth in a falling market. We have also demonstrated how to apportion your capital into different categories of investment instrument to achieve your objectives, and we have listed the type of function which each instrument is designed to do best.

Finally we have explained the need to make your capital work to produce a reasonable and achievable return each year, and consequently the need to monitor the progression of your portfolio constantly and keep records of all transactions in order to keep control of your wealth and to maximise your income.

What we are aiming to demonstrate is that by using the techniques described in this book, you will be better placed to limit any damage on the downside, as well as to be more able to pick successful investments which will achieve your targets as long as they are realistic.

10

Sharpening your investment tactics

Some basics

A portfolio for income and growth

A portfolio for growth alone

Creating a portfolio for growth

A portfolio for income

A portfolio for trading

A portfolio for inheritance tax planning

Summary

We have described the different types of instrument which you can invest in and the uses for which they have been designed.

We have looked at the different types of research which you should carry out in order to satisfy yourself that you are aware of all the potential risks and rewards which exist in specific markets, sectors and individual shares.

We have shown how to monitor the performance of markets and individual shares and calculate the optimum price levels at which to buy and sell shares within your portfolio.

In this chapter we pull together all the elements and show how to construct portfolios to achieve:

- income and growth;
- capital growth only;
- income only;
- successful trading;
- maximum protection against inheritance tax.

SOME BASICS

The individual shares which have been used to illustrate the ways to achieve given objectives are not meant to be recommendations to buy those stocks or shares, and should be regarded as being for demonstration purposes only. The prices and yields shown were correct at the time when this book was being constructed, and will bear no relation to their price levels or forecast earnings by publication date. As we have demonstrated only too clearly, share prices are not static and they can rise as well as fall, sometimes with great rapidity.

What we are aiming to demonstrate is that by using the techniques described in this book, you will be better placed to limit any damage on the downside, as well as be more able to pick successful investments which will achieve your targets as long as they are realistic.

Two important points should be borne in mind when you are starting from a cash base, whether you are faced with the selection for investment of a small sum, or the creation of an entire portfolio.

- Prevailing market conditions will dictate whether your objectives can be met at the outset. The factors which will determine your ability to achieve your strategic targets include current rates and yields of instruments commensurate with safety.

- The bullish or bearish phase of the market.

You may be starting to implement your tactical plan at a time when the market trend is against you, and thus find it impossible to get either the yields you require from fixed-interest stocks, or the growth you need from equities.

Do not be dismayed and above all do not jump into shares which are much more risky than you would have chosen otherwise. Do not alter your strategy simply because you cannot find a safe home for some of your money at that particular time. If necessary leave it on deposit and wait for conditions to change in your favour. Alternatively, put more of your cash than you would have done into a government stock, where you will get a better return than from a building society or bank deposit, pending the opportunity to buy the shares you have selected at the right price.

> **It is foolish to expect to buy shares for growth in a falling market.**

It is foolish to expect to buy shares for growth in a falling market. On the other hand, since the stock market always over-reacts to economic conditions, whether it be for an individual share or a whole sector, those who wait for the sentiment to improve can find rich pickings. So it might take time for your strategic plan to be implemented tactically into the final shape that you want.

The most common requirement for investors is a balanced portfolio, but before it can be constructed in detail, you have to evaluate how much income and how much growth is required and over what period of time the portfolio is to be made to perform.

A PORTFOLIO FOR INCOME AND GROWTH

This is by far the most common request which I get from new clients. Let me say that it is impossible to give any sort of advice, let alone good advice, if there is no more information than that to go on. I need to have all the details of income and expenditure (particularly if there are any regular major payouts such as school fees or nursing home charges), quite apart from where and how the capital is situated at present. So you will save yourself time if you do all your homework on drawing up a domestic statement of affairs before you do anything else. Apart from producing a clear picture of what is required in terms of cash flow, it will help you enormously in defining how much risk you are prepared to take. It will also demonstrate later on, as you do your market research, whether that which you would like to achieve is possible.

✳ EXAMPLE We shall assume that you have listed your assets and liabilities and that you have a capital sum of £75,000 available for investment. We shall take the current inflation rate (RPI) as being 2.6 per cent.

Since it is probably unlikely that such a low rate of RPI inflation can be sustained it will be more realistic to look for protection against an inflation rate of 5 per cent.

Thus on a capital sum of £75,000, the minimum growth to be achieved is £78,750 (£75,000 x 5% = £3,750 net of tax + £75,000) within 12 months.

The requirement is:

(a) to obtain enough capital growth for protection against inflation, and

(b) to produce an income of £4,000 per annum net of tax.

The first step is to decide what amount of capital you wish to put aside for a contingency fund to which you have immediate access.

We shall assume that you are happy to assign £5,000 for this purpose, and that the chosen depository is a building society.

Thus the residual capital available is reduced to £70,000.

The picture which starts to emerge is shown in Table 10.1.

Table 10.1

Investment instrument	Amount £	Growth %	Potential £	Net income at % yield	25% tax £
Building Society	5,000	nil	nil	5.25	262.00
Balance	70,000				
Fixed-interest securities	35,000	2	700	7.6	2,660.00
Balance	35,000				
Total income so far:					2,922.00

Reserve £6,000 to invest in a PEP to provide maximum capital growth in this type of investment but without any income attached.

This will leave a balance of £29,000 to be invested in equities.

Types of fixed-interest securities

Before we deal with the equity investment, let us look at the types of fixed- interest shares which might be considered in this portfolio.

Gilts are an obvious choice because, apart from the safety element which we have described earlier, any capital gain which is achieved is completely free from CGT.

Another group of shares which is well worth considering here are permanent interest bearing shares (PIBS), which are issued by several building societies. They too are free of any liability to CGT, but the inherent risk in these shares is considerable. In the event of the building society collapsing, there would be no return whatsoever to the holders of these shares. However, their yields have been quite high and in times of high interest rates, if you had been able to buy them at the time of issue, the growth in the prices has been more than just pleasing.

Another group to consider is **convertible preference shares.** As we have explained they will not participate in the growth of the company's earnings to the same extent as the ordinary shares to which they are attached, but some will increase in value at a faster rate than others, particularly as the yield of the ordinary shares gets closer to that of the convertible. However, you must be aware of the predetermined conversion terms attached to each one that you are considering, because you might find that the price of the convertible reduces as you get nearer to exercise of the conversion option.

If you choose to buy such a share, you should buy one where the accrued interest is included in the price of the share rather than one where the interest is separated from the share price. The reason is because when you come to sell the share, the interest accrued comes to you as a capital gain within your annual CGT free allowance, thus converting an element of income into capital, rather than attracting income tax on the interest element.

Debentures and other loan stock would also be considered in this category.

In all the above types of instrument, you must always bear in mind the factors which are likely to affect the underlying stock prices. Apart from any adverse market sentiments concerning the underlying companies to which they are attached, the main threat comes from fears of a rise in interest rates. Any Press comment about changes to the Bank base rates which you think is more than idle speculation should make you start to review these holdings in your portfolio, and if there are any significant profits in any of the stocks you should consider taking them. You can always use some or all of the gain in place of the lost income until you have found a suitable alternative home for the capital.

The other instrument to consider is the income section within **split-level income investment trusts.** If you do so, make sure that such shares do not end up being worthless at the time that the investment trust is liquidated. Ideally you should choose an investment trust which, at the time when you buy the shares, has at least 14 years to run before liquidation.

Now we have two targets to try to achieve for this portfolio. The first is to make up the shortfall on the income front, and the second is to deal with the requirement for growth over the whole amount of the initial capital.

✳ EXAMPLE | **Income shortfall**

Thus far we have raised an income of £2,922 and this leaves a balance of £1,078 net of tax to be found from investing the remaining capital sum of £29,000.

The *net* yield needed is £ $\dfrac{1,078 \times 100}{29,000} = 3.71\%$

The calculation required to establish what gross yield you must find to arrive at a given net yield is very simple.

(a) In order to obtain a net return of x % if you are a 25 per cent tax payer, you require a gross yield of $x + \frac{1}{3}x$.

: Thus to get a net return of 5%, you need to find a stock which is yielding 5% + ($\frac{1}{3}$ x 5%) = 6.667% gross.

(b) In order to obtain a net return of x % if you are a 40 per cent tax payer, you require a gross yield of $x + \frac{2}{3}x$ %.

Thus to get a net return of 5%, you need to find a stock which is yielding 5% + ($\frac{2}{3}$ x 5%) = 8.333% gross.

Beware of the danger of moving into a higher tax band

It is vital that you make sure that any additional income that you generate from investments does not take you from a lower tax band into a higher one, because if you fall into this trap and it does, all your calculations will be wrong. If there is any danger of this situation arising then you should buy the stock in the name of your spouse and register it in his or her name so that you maximise the tax allowances of each other before getting into a higher tax band.

For the purpose of this example we shall assume that you are paying tax at the rate of 25 per cent and that you have plenty of room to accommodate the extra income within that tax band.

We shall address the question of the amount of capital growth required further on in this chapter, but in the meantime, continue to examine the way to obtain the extra income. Two more questions must now be asked:

- Is the yield required achievable?
- How much risk am I running by investing in equities with the minimum level of yield required to achieve my target?

Is the yield achievable?

We have assumed a gross yield requirement of 5.00 per cent per annum based on a tax rate of 25 per cent which will produce a net yield of 3.71 per cent being necessary to achieve the target income. The first place to look is the sector analysis shown in the City section of the leading newspapers. The information is provided by the Stock Exchange even though it is published under the title of FT-SE Actuaries Share Indices.

The figures which are given show those for the current date, the percentage change on the previous day, those for each of the last three business days, and the figure for the same day one year ago. In addition, figures are given showing the percent dividend yield, the percent earnings yield and the P/E ratio.

All this information is shown for the FT-SE 100 shares, the FT-SE 250 shares, the FT-SE 350 shares and the FT-SE-A All-Share list. There are other sub-divisions such as the FT-SE Smallcap, etc.

The same data is displayed by sector. For example, there is a sector headed CONSUMER GOODS, and one of the sub-divisions of this sector is labelled Breweries.

You will see that there is a number shown in brackets after both Consumer Goods (99) and Breweries (17). These refer to the numbers of companies whose shares are listed within that category. Under the general category of Consumer Goods, in addition to Breweries there are sub-divisions labelled:

- Spirits, Wines and Ciders (10)
- Food Manufacturers (24)
- Household Goods (13)
- Health Care (21)
- Pharmaceuticals (12)
- Tobacco (2).

The total number of listed companies shown against the category is the sum of those contained in the sub-divisions.

The categories analysed in addition to Consumer Goods include Mineral Extraction, General Manufacturers, Services, and Utilities. Together these categories account for 640 listings and they make up the NON-FINANCIAL index. The category Financials (108) together with Investment Trusts (124) added to the Non-Financials make up the FT-SE-A All Share index. Unit trusts are not included because they are neither traded on the Stock Exchange nor settled through it.

On 19th December 1994 the FT-SE 100 index showed a Dividend Yield of 4.24 per cent gross.

Although the average yields available from the other groups of shares were lower, it does not mean that you cannot find individual shares outside the FT-SE 100 which will yield considerably in excess of 5 per cent gross, but the risks may well be greater.

You should always look at the indices for the FT-SE 100 first because these will set benchmarks for the 'quality' shares, and any other share which is offering substantially different or better yields should make you very alert. Next, you should look at the groupings shown lower down the table. You would see that there are plenty of sectors to choose from which are yielding from 5 to over 10 per cent. The next step will be to draw up a list of individual shares to examine in depth.

You should:

- select only those which are included in the top 100;
- remember that the requirement for capital growth still remains to be resolved.

In this example, the shares of Lloyds Bank, Bass, Scottish Hydro, BT and Severn Trent Water to name but a few, could be yielding over 5 per cent gross.

How much risk am I running?

It is relatively easy to plan for income provided that the yield required is not excessive. The difficulty is to find safe ordinary shares which will compensate for the lack of capital growth inherent in low-risk fixed- interest shares. The more capital you invest into fixed-interest high-yielding securities, the greater the burden for growth production you are loading on to the reducing balance of capital available for investment in ordinary shares. In times of low inflation it will be easy to compensate for the erosion of the value of your capital. If you believe that inflation has been conquered and will remain below 2.5 per cent per annum for the next five years, then you can afford to accept a lower target growth figure.

I have a more cynical view, and do not believe that the way in which this country is run makes it possible for any government to hold down public expenditure to levels which ensure that inflation can be restricted to present levels for more than a few months.

There is a widely held belief that inflation is good for share prices. This is an over-simplified generalisation. An increase in inflation will cause higher prices for goods and services from food to transport, and on through the spectrum. Higher prices may produce increases in earnings initially for the companies which provide the goods and services, but it is not long before they generate increased wage demands. Higher wage costs will reduce profits and consequently companies' earnings. If the companies wish to maintain their cost/profit differentials, they have two options open to them. Either they replace people with machines, or they increase their product prices, or do both.

Replacing people with machines requires extra capital investment which they will have to raise from shareholders by issuing more shares. This is long-term capital. Issuing more ordinary shares dilutes existing holdings. Issuing preference shares or loan stock means that the extra interest rates payable may deplete the EPS (earnings per share) for the ordinary shareholder. The alternative is to increase bank borrowing (short term gearing) which will probably deplete the EPS also.

> If you believe that inflation has been conquered and will remain below 2.5 per cent per annum for the next five years, then you can afford to accept a lower target growth figure.

There is a limit to which manpower can be replaced by machines, and the initial costs of both redundancy and extra capital investment can be high. It may be some time before the benefits filter through the earnings line, and unless the market for the goods or services can be expanded the EPS will not grow.

Increasing product prices will make the company less competitive and therefore will almost certainly be detrimental to the company's earnings in the longer term.

Thus price increases caused by inflation will have an initial effect of increasing earnings, perhaps for the next year of trading. It will become apparent that the ability to maintain such levels of earnings is in jeopardy only when wages are increased above the rate of inflation.

Finally, there are two more elements which can cause inflationary pressures on companies and which represent a potential threat to their ability to maintain or increase their level of earnings.

The first is the cost of raw materials. As the world is generally considered to be emerging from recession in the second half of the 1990s, the demand for minerals and other raw materials is increasing, and in accordance with the natural laws of supply and demand, the prices are set to rise for such items as zinc, copper, silver, gold, etc. Since these materials are widely used in the manufacture of such things as microchips and electronic equipment, for example, there will be increasing pressures on profit margins.

Historically, many of these raw materials have been produced by countries where labour rates are extremely low compared with the developed countries in the western hemisphere. However that situation is changing fairly rapidly, and costs of production are increasing considerably. When you couple that with an increasing world demand for the material, you have all the ingredients of a substantial inflationary element.

The second is taxation. An increase in the levy on oil products such as petrol and diesel will have an immediate effect on the cost of transport and distribution. Obviously there will be an extra cost for any company which is using oil or oil derivatives for heating or within its manufacturing processes. Either the company has to try to absorb these extra costs or pass them on the customer. The result is a danger of reduced profit margins or lower turnover as a result of uncompetitive product prices.

I have spelled out the dangers of inflation deliberately, yet again, for two reasons.

The first is because when you want to invest your capital, and are looking at a list of shares from which to choose, you should always be aware of all the potential dangers which lurk around the corner in each individual case. I prefer to adopt the attitude of a bookmaker. When he accepts a bet on a horse, he calculates how much money he will **lose** if the horse wins, not how much money he will make on the race. In the same way, I prefer to examine all the dangers inherent in a particular investment, rather than what profit I might make. When you buy a ticket in the lottery, you know that the most you can lose is £1. What you might win is irrelevant. The only question is, ' Can I afford to lose £1?'

I realise that the question of inflation does not arise when you are having a punt on the lottery, but it certainly does when you are investing your capital long term, and you are not being very clever if you ignore the potential risks which exist. In the end it boils down to judgement, and you are foolish if you do not carry out as exhaustive research as possible to discover all the dangers, actual and potential, before you make your final decision.

The second is to emphasize the need to keep a constant watch on this insidious cancer which can eat away at your capital. The corollary is, of course, that when the possibility of such dangers become obvious, market sentiment towards the share price may well change from positive to negative, and you may have to be quick on your feet to take steps to limit the damage to the value of your investment.

So now let us go back to assess the general direction of the market. If the overall trend of the market is downwards, then you have three choices in essence.

- You have to find a market which is growing somewhere else in the world.
- You have to find a share which is UK-based, but which really is going to buck the trend and grow when most of the rest are declining.
- You play safe and buy more fixed-interest stocks, and forgo the growth requirement for the time being, until you find a suitable investment which will give you the income and growth needed.

Types of equity

What types of share should I consider?

My advice at this stage of the construction of the portfolio is to stick to safe, well-capitalised shares, and to look first at those sectors which are generally expected to benefit from any strengthening of the economy. Look for companies which have any of the following benefits:

- Strong overseas markets particularly in developed countries such as Europe, the USA or Japan.
- Products which have to be consumed whatever the state of the economy such as gas, oil, water, electricity or communications including telephones. Beware of companies where there is likely to be strong competition for their goods or services which could lead to a

price war such as food retailing, motor cars, clothes (both manufacturing and retail), and companies which are likely to be affected by adverse tax impositions on their products such as breweries and tobacco manufacturers. A product price war hits profit margins, and therefore earnings and the ordinary shareholders will suffer more than any else.

The essential points to check for every share you consider buying

How do the professional fund managers select their shares to buy?

They carry out market and sector analysis.

At this point I should like to introduce you to a system of analysis which is used by the better fund managers every time they are considering buying a share or investment trust. You will be able to do your own checking by following the format shown here.

The first checklist is shown in Table 10.2.

Table 10.2   Market and sector checklist

Movement		Yesterday	3 months	1 year	5 years
Currency (against £) (If applicable)	US$	+0.1	+0.3	−0.1	−0.5
Market	London	+2.2	+1.8	−11.9	+18.6
Sector	Oil	+1.8	+3.6	+5.0	+2.8
Share	Shell	+0.3	+4.5	+7.2	+3.9

The fund manager is establishing the overall movement in a given market in which he is interested, and measuring the performance of a particular share in which he is interested. He is looking to see whether it is out-performing or under-performing both the market as a whole (the All-Share Index), and its own sector. He will include currency data in his analysis although the average UK investor may not need to do so unless he is analysing a possible investment in an investment trust, for example, which specialises in a foreign country. Don't forget that all oil is dealt in US$, so the direction in which that currency is moving against the £ is important. The movement and all the values shown are invented, but the examples which I have chosen will suffice for most purposes. The figures will be the percentage changes against the current or today's prices.

What does this tell you ?

Currency

You will see from Table 10.2 that the US$ has strengthened against sterling over the period, even though it has fluctuated in the process as you would expect. However the most important thing here is that the risk of currency loss is not that great, as you can see, probably not more than 2 per cent. It would be a very different picture if you were analysing the yen.

Market movement

The volatility here has been substantial over the last 12 months, but the market has risen over the longer term. Thus, unless you think that there is reason to believe that there will be a significant rise in the market in the short term, you would expect the general level to show slow growth over one to two years.

Sector performance

The sector has performed well against the market as a whole, and so you have no reason to worry about this element.

Share price

The share price has maintained its stability and shown a reasonable growth under the prevailing conditions. Since the share yields about $4^{1}/_{2}$ per cent per annum at current prices, you can see that it produced an overall return of more than 10 per cent over the last 12 months.

Followed by a more detailed analysis

Assume that the share you have shortlisted has passed the first inspection. When you have drawn up your shortlist then you should then carry out the following nine steps of analysis for each one:

1. Measure the share price and PER relative to the other shares in its own sector.
2. Note the 'High' and 'Low' of the price over the last 12 months and calculate how far off its high it is standing today. Express the difference in percentage terms.
3. Note the latest movement in the price (actual and percentage) since yesterday.
4. Ask your broker what is the normal market size in which the prices are quoted. If the prices are being made in 1,000 shares only, and you are

considering buying 10,000, it might be as well to look for another share.

5. Check the market capitalisation for the company. These numbers are published in the quality newspapers each week, or you can ask your broker to send you a copy of the Extel card. My advice is to avoid a company with a market capitalisation of less than £150 million unless there are very good reasons to buy the stock.

6. Ask your stockbroker for the Reuters graph of the share price over the last three years, including the 30-day and 200-day moving average, and the Extel report showing the accounts for the last five years.

7. Check the dividend cover multiple for the last five years and see whether it has been falling, remaining constant or increasing. If you are happy with the finds, then:

8. Re-calculate the dividends for the last five years adjusting each one for inflation using indexation tables. If the result is showing an upward trend, then:

9. Check the net cash flow record and satisfy yourself that any anomalies can be demonstrably acceptable.

When you have carried out the analyses, and assuming that you now have a shortlist which consists of acceptable shares, you turn to the graphs of those shares and look at the current share price in relation to its trading range.

- If the share price is on an upward trend but near to the bottom of its trading range, you should mark it a buy.

- If the share price has broken through the upper level of its trading range, you should mark it as a definite buy and the sooner you get in the better.

- If the share price is on a downward trend within its trading range you should not buy it until it has turned upwards. Do not write it off necessarily but try to get as much current information about the company to explain the reasons for the lack of support.

- If you decide to include an investment trust in your shortlist, and this is recommended particularly if you are considering investing in overseas markets, choose one whose gross yield is 5 per cent or more, and whose share price is standing at a discount to the net asset value (NAV) shown in the *Financial Times*.

How much money should I invest in each stock or share ?

It is a common mistake to buy lots of little holdings in a great number of different shares. By doing so, you are increasing the dealing costs considerably, which is extravagant and unnecessary. Also this practice produces a portfolio which is unwieldy and inefficient. Suppose you have invested £10,000 in ten stocks in equal amounts. Further, suppose that one of them increases in value by 50 per cent and the rest stay just about where they are, your portfolio has increased overall by £500 or 5 per cent. Not very clever.

As a general rule, it is sensible to invest in parcels of £5,000 to £10,000 in each share, and not less than £10,000 in a gilt.

Thus, in this portfolio, it would be sensible to invest as follows:

- *£10,000 in each of two gilts at a price below 100 and with an interest yield of over 8 per cent.*

✳ EXAMPLE

At the time of writing, there were plenty of gilts which could be bought for less than 100 yielding well in excess of 8 per cent. For example, Treasury 8% 2003 was yielding 8.35 per cent and standing at $95^{27}/_{32}$; Treasury $8^{1}/_{2}$% 2007 was yielding 8.59 per cent and was standing at $98^{15}/_{16}$; and Treasury $7^{3}/_{4}$% 2006 was yielding 8.29 per cent and was standing at $98^{15}/_{16}$.

- *£7,500 in each of the two fixed-interest shares yielding not less than 8 per cent gross.* An example is shown below.

✳ EXAMPLE

Hambros $7^{1}/_{2}$% Convertible Pref.	Price 102.5
	Yield 9.1% gross
	High 191
	Low 99.5
British Aerospace 7.75p *net* Convertible Pref.	Price 109
	Yield 9.0% gross
	High 111
	Low 105.5
Hanson $9^{1}/_{2}$% Bond 2006	Price 104
	Yield 9.1%
	High 108.25
	Low 103

- *£7,000+ in each of four ordinary shares with a gross yield of not less than 5 per cent selected after carrying out the market sector analyses described above.*

Achieving the required growth

So far we have dealt with the income requirement demanded by the mandate for capital available for investment in this portfolio. This element is relatively simple, in that the yields which are available are known in advance and, provided you have chosen companies which are safe and well established with substantial market capital, you should be able to sleep at nights without too much worry about the ability to maintain your income.

The unknown element, of course, is whether the growth required is achievable within the timescale which has been set.

In this case we are looking for a growth overall of £3,750. We have assumed that it is reasonable to expect a growth of not less than 2 per cent from the fixed-interest element of the portfolio. This will produce an increase in value of £700 which leaves a further £3,050 to be found 12 months hence.

Now we come to the sum of £6,000 reserved for a personal equity plan.

From the start of the financial year 6 April 1996, the rules concerning what is allowed to be included in a PEP have been changed. From that date it is permissable to include fixed-interest stock which hitherto has been excluded. Although the scope of shares which are eligible has been extended, unfortunately gilts are not included within the range. However, the opportunity to convert income into capital and receive the proceeds of sale completely free of tax is a great bonus. When you realise that all income arising from such investments is also free from any tax which would normally have been deducted at source, you will see that a whole new tactic is opened to you.

The way to get the maximum benefit from such an investment is to regard such a PEP plan as a 'savings' fund rather than an 'income producing' one. If you buy a preference share, loan stock or debenture which is yielding 10 per cent gross (and under PEP rules gross is the same as net), and if you reinvest the income each year then you will have doubled your capital within ten years. Also, when you come to realise your investment, there will not be any liability to CGT. To get the best possible growth out of this arrangement you should make provision to pay the dealing costs of reinvestment of income and the annual management charges with money outside the PEP fund.

So in the portfolio, the sum of £6,000 should be invested in such a preference share and you should leave it there unless some fearful news occurs concerning the company. This portion of the capital will not be considered as a revenue producer within the overall plan, but it will certainly assist in part of the growth provision.

The value of this growth element in the portfolio will amount to £600 and thus the sum of £2,450 remains to be obtained from growth derived from the capital invested in the equities.

The capital to be invested in equities is £29,000, as we have demonstrated above. Therefore, the minimum growth required is:

$$\frac{£2,450 \times 100}{29,000} = 8.45 \text{ per cent}$$

In order to cover dealing costs when and if you decide to change any of the shares in this part of the portfolio, you should set a minimum target for growth of 10 per cent in this case.

Thus when you are making your selections from the shares mentioned above, you will see that they have to conform to two criteria.

The first is that they are yielding the minimum percentage required under the income demands at current price levels.

The second is that there is sufficient upside potential at the current price within the share price trading range. So, in this case, you must select those shares which, when you add 10 per cent to their present price, will not reach a figure that is above the 'high' shown on the graph.

Now, unless some disaster occurs, you will have constructed a portfolio which meets the demands set at the outset.

The picture which emerges is shown in Table 10.3.

Table 10.3

Investment instrument	Amount £	Growth %	Potential £	Net Income % yield	25% tax £
Building Society	5,000	nil	nil	5.25	262.00
Fixed-interest securities	35,000	2	700	7.6	2,660
PEP	6,000	10	600	nil	nil
Equities	29,000	10	2,900	3.75	1,087
TOTAL	75,000		4,200		4,009

So much for the construction of the portfolio. You will realise that if yields in general are much lower it may not be possible to build a portfolio which will satisfy the requirements of both income and capital growth, without being driven to shares which have a much greater degree of risk.

Whatever shares you decide to include, remember that timing is everything, as it is in so much of life. There is an old adage in the market 'where there is a tip, there is a tap'. So when a 'friend' whispers to you that you should be buying shares in the Square Cannon Ball company, ask yourself whether he bought a bundle of them at a much lower price, and is anxious to ensure he gets a good profit by getting a buyer to mop up the shares he is anxious to unload. Make sure the mug is not you!

Monitoring performance

You have set targets for your capital to achieve, both in terms of income provision and capital growth. These targets have got to be reached within a specific period and, as with gardening, you must

> Make sure the mug is not you!

watch the progress of each plant to see that it is growing and remains healthy. You must not be afraid to be quite ruthless and prepared to abandon any that fail to perform. Show no mercy in stripping out any which get sick and replace them with better ones.

However, a couple of points to remember.

First, you may well be faced with a difficult dilemma. Suppose you have bought a share at a price which is yielding a really attractive return, but which has risen in value subsequently, to a point where you are looking at a substantial capital profit if you sold the investment. Do you sell and take the profit, or do you stick with the share because it will be difficult, if not impossible, to replace the level of income elsewhere?

There is no hard and fast rule to cling to, and each person's circumstances will vary. However it never hurts to take a profit, and this is particularly so if, for example, an instrument such as a PIB or a gilt is free of any liability to CGT. A profit is only a profit when you have converted it into cash; that way you do not run the risk of seeing it evaporate because the market turns sour. Also, you will be able to afford to use some of the profit to replace lost income until you find a suitable replacement home for the capital.

Second, when you set your targets for each share price to achieve in order to secure the requisite growth, you examined the 'highs' and 'lows' and so you know what is reasonable to expect from the performance. Now unless the share price breaks through the upper level, you would expect the next movement to be downwards. If this level is reached more quickly than you thought it would be, **and** if it does not look like continuing upwards, take the profit. For example, if such an event occurs with one of the equities in the above portfolio, say three months after you invested the capital, then not only would you have secured the growth required for that particular share, but you would have a further nine months to make some more profit with the same capital.

Your money has to work for you and produce a minimum return each and every year, otherwise you are failing to manage it properly. But do not be reckless and let greed get the better of you, or your judgement will become warped and your capital will disappear. Remember your targets must be reasonable and achievable.

The targets which we set in the portfolio may well not be achievable if you were to start when the market was in a different shape. If, for example, the average gross yield of the fixed-income interest stocks was 5 or 6 per cent, then you would have to commit a much greater proportion of your available capital to this section of the market and you would have to compromise on your requirement for growth. Alternatively you might have to settle for a lower income from your investments at the outset and wait to re-arrange your portfolio until the market had changed more to your advantage.

- Do not make the mistake of buying stocks or shares with a much greater risk simply to achieve a target which is unreasonable at the time when you start.

- It will reward you handsomely if you keep a record of both the reasons for choosing a particular stock or share at the time when you make your investment, and the bid price which you expect to achieve in each case. Thus subsequent actual performance can be measured in terms of price, elapsed time from the date of purchase and whether your assessment of the reasons for selecting that particular instrument were valid and vindicated your judgement. It is so easy, at a later date, to forget what were the prevailing economic conditions and the separate items which you took into consideration when you made each selection.

A PORTFOLIO FOR GROWTH ALONE

The objective in this case is to produce the maximum amount of growth commensurate with safety of the capital each year.

It is almost impossible to look ahead further than the next 12 months at any given moment, and so any target which is set must be limited in its life to one year at a time. It goes without saying that the degree of growth for which you will be planning will vary according to prevailing market conditions. However, we shall make recommendations in the climate which exists in the market at the end of 1996.

The mandate is to invest £75,000 to achieve maximum growth with safety.

Risks

There are more risks inherent in investments in equities alone, and they are increased if you use traded options, so the need to monitor your investments is much greater.

We start in the same way by looking at the overall picture of the market and examine the published data.

The equity market has been rising for the last 12 months, largely because of fears of the possibility of increases in interest rates have been allayed. In addition rolling settlement was introduced during this period, and its immediate effect was to reduce the number of bargains executed because of the abolition of account trading. This last item reduced the liquidity in the market, and you can see evidence of this from the daily reports of the number of trades completed.

The questions are, where is the market going from here, and what information do we have available to help in coming to a conclusion?

As to the first one, the answer is that it is anyone's guess. If you ask six different 'experts' you will probably get six different answers. The fund managers compete annually to produce a forecast which subsequently proves to be the most accurate. It may be worth noting that it is usually a different one each year who gets closest to the actual results.

Historically, the stock market has roughly followed a pattern each year, and it is this. The market has tended to rise at its fastest rate from September until the end of December. It has continued to rise but at a slower rate from January until around the time of the budget in March/April, and then it has drifted downward during the summer, until the cycle begins again in the autumn when the main Budget announcements are made, thus increasing the factors of uncertainty.

However, not only is that pattern unreliable, but also there is no factual basis upon which to base your conclusions. So many extraneous events could upset the market, such as a sudden political upheaval, or an extension of existing hostilities, or a significant increase in interest rates in

America or Germany, or a collapse of a major bank somewhere in the world. Unfortunately the list of potential disasters is endless.

...If you ask six different 'experts' you will probably get six different answers. ......

So let us look at what factual evidence there is to direct our thinking.

Company results

There has been a tremendous shakeout in British industry as a result of the recession. Many companies, including some large ones, have gone to the wall. Nevertheless, many of those which have survived have slimmed down their labour force, and the reduction of inflation has placed some of those which remain in good shape in a position to increase their earnings. Increases in profits have been reported by many leading manufacturers.

The money markets

The pound is relatively strong against the US dollar which makes British exports to America more difficult to expand. When corporate earnings are generated overseas and subsequently converted into sterling, they will enhance the profits – if the currency of that market for their products strengthens against the pound. The converse is valid also, and when the pound strengthens against that currency, profits will suffer.

Countries with expanding economies

The Far East and parts of the Pacific Rim are generally forecast to continue their considerable rate of expansion, which has been well established over the last two years. These markets have had one tremendous benefit above all else for manufacturers situated in these areas. The cost of labour has been minuscule when compared with that of Europe, America and Australia.

... The Far East and parts of the Pacific Rim are generally forecast to continue their considerable rate of expansion, which has been well established over the last two years. ....

Share selection

That is global picture – it is now time to select those shares which are likely to prosper the most under current market conditions.

First, you should draw up a list of companies which have established strong export markets in America and the Far East. You should look at their accounts over the last five years and select those whose sales to these areas have been expanding each year because the management will have built up experience of trading conditions alien to those within the UK. The fact that they have been expanding such trade means that they have learned the lessons and got it right.

Second, you should look at the types of product which they are exporting. For example, the Chinese have a virtual endless supply of cheap labour at present, but they lack technological expertise, and so they are hungry for such things as precision-engineered and computer-controlled equipment, manufacturing processes and so on.

However, do not forget that they are very quick to learn, and once their technical education systems are established and experienced, their dependence on foreign knowledge will diminish. They are at the same stage of industrial development as Japan was in the late 1930s. Political restraints may well restrict the growth of imports of western articles which the government might consider to be subversive or a potential threat to a controlled modernisation of the country, so it may not be sensible to expect a large increase in the sales of a company trying to export luxury goods to China at present. That is for the future.

You would be best advised to select investment trusts which specialise in such markets and which have a good track record of growth of their net asset value (NAV). For reasons which have been described earlier in this book, it is much less risky than buying individual shares direct from Britain. However, because the funds in the investment trust are spread over a number of individual companies, you will not expect to see the percentage growth that you might obtain from direct investment.

In Chapter 9, we showed a list of British companies which derive a substantial amount of turnover from trade in the USA and such companies as these would certainly be included for examination. Within the UK, the clearing banks would also be potential candidates, as would advertising and communications and data disseminating organisations, because these will all be well-placed to benefit from an upturn in the domestic economy. With the exception of the construction and house building industry, it is always sensible to look closely at a sector which has been out of favour in the last 12 months.

So now that you have drawn up your list of shares, and you have carried out your analysis of the earnings history for each one and thus arrived at a short list, what do you do next?

Set targets and stop-loss limits

Assume that the FT-SE 100 index is standing about 15 per cent below its high achieved during 1996. If the recession both in Britain and in Europe is over, and given that the economy in America is growing fast (perhaps too fast), then it is reasonable to set a minimum target for growth of 15 per cent. You would aim to beat this figure comfortably, so perhaps you would choose 20 per cent as a target for growth over the next 12 months.

In just the same way as described above, the individual target which you set for every share must be achievable and realistic under current market conditions. If the share price is standing at a level within its trading range, and there is a potential upside movement of, say, 20 per cent, then you should record this price level as your target. You might possibly select a level just below its previous high, because there is a danger that a lot of other people will be waiting to unload their holdings when the share price reaches the top of its previous range. When the share price gets near to your target, you do not necessarily have to sell it. Rather you should re-assess the whole background to the share when that situation occurs. You may decide to hold on and set a new target for the share.

Beware the speed with which the share has risen, particularly towards the final stages of its approach to your target price. There may well be some reason other than a re-rating of the PER which is driving the price upwards, such as the possibility of a bid arriving. Frequently a rapid rise in a share price which is based on speculative reasons that do not materialise is the precursor of a fall which can be just as quick and often by a greater amount than the recent rise. A sharp increase in a share price puts the spotlight on the company and causes intensive research into its current and future earnings potential. This can result in a reappraisal of the desirability of retaining holdings of the share, so that the market could find itself overloaded with selling orders – the price could come down quickly.

How do I set a stop-loss limit?

Let us take the share price of British Steel as an example (see Figure 10.1). During 1994 the price movement was as follows:

High	Low	% movement
172p	121p	42

Assume that you had bought the share at its low and you have decided to limit your potential loss on the investment to 10 per cent.

If, having bought the share, the price starts to go down, you would sell immediately the price dropped to 109p. However, if the price starts to rise and some time after you bought the share, the price starts to stabilise at around, say, 150p, you would reset your stop-loss to 10 per cent of 150 and thus you would sell immediately if the price dropped to 135p (150–[15% x 150]p). Under these circumstances, although you would not have got out at the top of the price level achieved, you would have made a profit of 14p per share.

However, let us assume that the price fluctuates but does not trigger a sale by falling to your limit, but it recovers and continues upwards. You are happy with your reappraisal of the company and the share price rise stops at 172p. You re-set your stop-loss at a level 10 per cent lower, and round it up to 155p, the price at which you would sell (172 – [10% x 172]p). If such a situation occurred, you would have made a profit of 28 per cent. If the share continues on upwards you simply reset your stop-loss limit until a sale is triggered.

> ...Beware the speed with which the share has risen, particularly towards the final stages of its approach to your target price. ......

In the examples given above, no account has been taken of dealing costs or stamp duty.

CREATING A PORTFOLIO FOR GROWTH

You can invest the whole of the capital available into those shares which you have selected, provided that each one is at a relatively low price within its trading range, in parcels of about £10,000 each.

Or you can make investments, but keep a sum aside to use to augment the performance of your portfolio by buying traded options as and when the market conditions present opportunities which have a reasonable chance of success. Bearing in mind the risks attached to this type of invest-

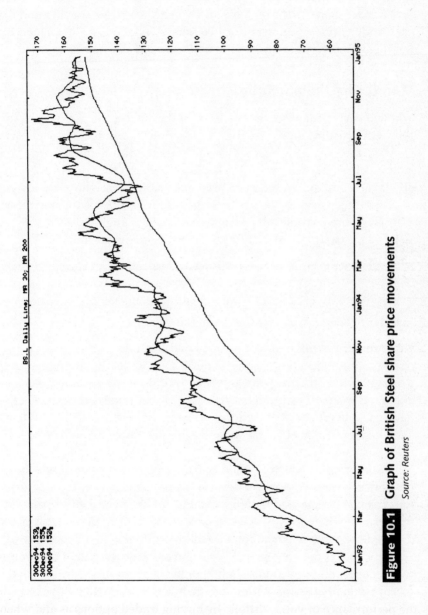

Figure 10.1 **Graph of British Steel share price movements**
Source: Reuters

ment, it would be prudent to limit the sum allocated for such use to, say, £5,000.

If you decide to 'write' any 'put' options you would be well-advised to limit your selection to those shares which you hold in your portfolio, and for no more shares than you have purchased already, bearing in mind that each traded option contract is for 1,000 shares, no more, no less. Thus your holding in the portfolio must be in multiples of 1,000 shares.

Monitoring the portfolio

You will need to monitor the share prices daily at the very minimum, and you will probably find that the construction of a graph for each share showing the price movement is useful. You can draw a line showing your stop-loss limit in each case. You should read everything that is published about the companies and their principal markets in whose shares you have invested, so that you are both well-informed about them and fore-warned of any possible adverse influences which might arise.

There are two main objectives in constructing this portfolio:

- to achieve the targets for growth set at the begining of each investment year;
- to make as few changes as possible during each investment year in order to keep dealing costs to a minimum.

However, preservation of your capital and consolidation of your profit is of paramount importance, and so you should not let the fear of incurring dealing costs influence your judgement at all, if, by so doing, you put either your capital or profits at risk. One of the Rothschilds said that he had made his fortune by selling too soon, so beware of the tendency exhibited by so many to hang on for the last few pence of profit before selling a particular share.

The other point which I would make concerns the price at which you buy any given share. A recent 'low' in the price range may have occurred for reasons unconnected with the earnings potential of the company. The market as a whole may have been going through a fit of depression and dragged the price down along with all other prices. So it is possible that you will not see the 'low' price level again in the near future if the company is inherently sound, and a slightly higher price is still one at which it is worth buying the share. Within reason, it is true to say that if the share is worth buying, it does not matter if you pay slightly more than you would prefer.

Capital Gains Tax management

The successful result of managing your portfolio for growth as described above will be a profit of £15,000 on your capital of £75,000, if you achieve a growth rate of 20 per cent by the end of 1995. Along the way you will almost certainly have taken some profits, and circumstances could arise when you decide to liquidate all your holdings. It is essential that you keep an eye on your potential liability to CGT. You should use your tax-free allowance to its full and that of your spouse if you have one. Remember when using your spouse's unused tax-free allowance to transfer any shares at least three months before you anticipate selling them, so that you avoid problems arising subsequently with the Inland Revenue. It is better still if you buy shares and register a proportion of the portfolio in the name of your spouse at the outset. Also you should make the greatest possible use of Bed and Breakfast techniques because the cost of carrying out such dealing far outweighs the potential cost of CGT. Any unused losses, whether actual or established as a result of B&B transactions can be carried forward indefinitely to be offset against future profits.

> **Within reason, it is true to say that if the share is worth buying, it does not matter if you pay slightly more than you would prefer.**

It might help if you operate your own trading or investment year so that it runs concurrently with the tax year. In that way sometimes you can decide to realise profits, so that the sales can be made to straddle the year-end, thereby utilising two separate annual tax-free allowances for both you and your spouse.

Remember also that the **real** value of your profits, whether realised or on paper, will be eroded by inflation. You will need to index your actual gains when you do your CGT computations but do not forget to make similar provisions for your paper gains when you are reviewing your existing investments.

A PORTFOLIO FOR INCOME

This portfolio is much easier to establish than one for growth only. The fundamental approach to constructing such a portfolio was described in detail in the first section of this chapter. The total capital of £75,000 would be invested in fixed-interest stocks, chosen from the following list of instruments:

- gilts;
- Tessas;
- permanent interest bearing shares;
- preference shares;
- loan stock.

The exact apportionment of capital into any or all of such investments would depend upon the amount of income required per annum. To ensure safety of the capital, it would be reasonable at the time of writing to look for a gross yield of 7 per cent per annum, which could be achieved by buying a gilt at below 100. Thus if it was held to maturity there would be a very small element of capital growth, but almost certainly not enough to give protection against erosion from inflation. Depending upon the reasons for wanting such a portfolio, and the length of time over which the income is required, you would consider changing an individual stock only if there was a change in interest rates.

Any other stock described above, other than a Tessa, will carry an element of risk to the underlying capital through fluctuation in the prices of the stocks, and it is impossible to lay down any rules as to what is best, because so much depends on the circumstances of the person to whom the capital belongs. If the requirement is for a finite period of, say, five years or so and the objective is to meet the cost of school fees, for example, then you would have to take a risk that at the end of the period the market was buoyant and interest rates low, so that the prices of the instrument were standing at or above the original costs. If they are not when the time comes, then you have to decide whether to wait for the market in each individual stock to recover sufficiently to sell and re-invest into a different mix of investment, at which point a whole new plan has to be drawn up within the constraints of the market conditions which are prevailing.

The disadvantage of a Tessa is that you have to leave the money locked away for a minimum of five years in order to get the maximum tax benefit. If, for reasons beyond your control, you are forced to liquidate the Tessa before it has matured you lose all the tax advantage. There is no protection for the capital from inflation in a Tessa.

The most important point to be made above all else is this.

Do not be persuaded by yourself or anyone else to put money into an investment which is yielding a rate of return which is well above the top rates available from a safe government stock.

You can get a gross return from a gilt as high as 13.8 per cent per annum, but you would be paying a premium over the redemption price of about eight points, and so you know that if you hold the stock to redemption your capital invested in that particular instrument will be depleted. Nevertheless, you can take this yield from a gilt as a bench-mark, and if any other investment of whatever sort promises to produce a yield in excess of that level you should not touch it with a barge pole.

...**There is no protection for the capital from inflation in a Tessa.** .....

The net yield which you will receive will depend upon your rate of tax and you should ensure that as much of the income as possible is payable to you or your spouse, whichever is on the lower rate.

A PORTFOLIO FOR TRADING

Essentially a trader is a speculator because he is taking a very short-term point of view and is prepared to put much larger amounts of money into very few shares thereby increasing the risk of loss considerably.

A portfolio for trading carries the most risk because you are trying to maximise your capital growth by using short-term investments to make a relatively small amount of profit each time. If, for example, you could generate 5 per cent net of all dealing costs on the capital sum of £75,000 every month of the year, you would make pretax profits of £45,000. **Naturally, whilst this result is very desirable, it is very difficult to achieve.**

Not only have you got to find shares which will perform for you each and every month, but if you can only find two, for example, then you have to commit half your capital into each and the risk of the market turning against you is huge. Also it is very difficult to find shares which are going to rise and fall in price to the degree required, with any certainty beforehand.

The benefit of hindsight is that you have 20/20 vision of the performance after the events have occurred.

You would probably have to divide your tactics between buying and selling ordinary shares and using traded options both to enhance your returns or protect your capital.

If you reserved £25,000 to invest in traded options, then you would try to find five ordinary shares which are moving up and down in price and invest £5,000 in each. An example of such a share is Dalgety.

✳ EXAMPLE **Dalgety**

You will see from Figure 10.2 that if you had bought the share in November 1991 at about 352p and sold in May 1992 at 420p, you could have bought again in August 1992 at about 365p and sold at any time during the period November 1992 to March 1993 at around 480p. You could have repeated the process again in June 1993 to August 1993, and yet again in September 1993, with a sale in January 1994. Such trading would have shown very handsome profits even after dealing costs and you could have safeguarded your capital and profits by buying put and call options at the same time.

If you are going to trade in this way, you will need access to share prices and traded option prices on an hourly basis or you could miss the boat. Even so, the risks are very much greater. You should limit the amount of money which you are going to put into such trading activities to that which you are prepared to lose at the outset. You should never get involved in such dealing if you are depending upon regular income or growth from your capital upon which to live.

A PORTFOLIO FOR INHERITANCE TAX PLANNING

There are many misconceptions about the hazards of inheritance tax and the need to make provision for any liabilities which might arise after the death of the owner of the capital.

First, let us establish what the rules are as applied to those who do not have very large amounts of capital in one form or another, under current legislation.

- There is no liability to inheritance tax between husband and wife. During the lifetime of both, gifts can be made between spouses which are valued at the original price of purchase without any liability to tax arising until such gifts are sold or otherwise disposed of. Such concessions do not include any living generation whether previous or subsequent to the husband or wife, nor does it extend to any other relations of the husband or wife. Annual gifts to other generations are allowed, provided they do not exceed £3,000 in total in any one

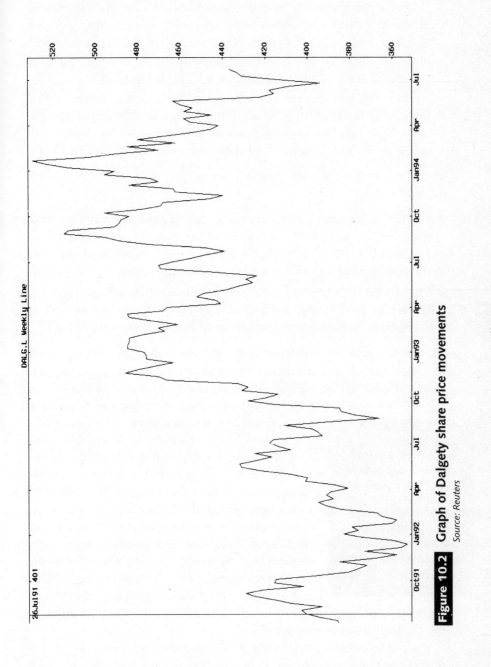

26Jul91 401

DALG.L Weekly Line

Figure 10.2 **Graph of Dalgety share price movements**
Source: Reuters

financial year, and the same rules apply for valuation at the time of the gift and its subsequent disposal by the recipient.

- Upon the death of one spouse, the ownership of any assets including all capital invested is transferred to the remaining spouse, other than any bequests made to other nominations in the will of the deceased. If both husband and wife die together, for example in an accident, then the husband is deemed to predecease the wife for tax purposes.

- At present (and subject to any changes in the Budget in 1996), the first £150,000 of the value of an estate at the date of death is allowed free of inheritance tax. The value of all assets in the estate of the deceased in excess of £150,000 is liable to inheritance tax at the rate of 40 per cent.

There are two important points arising out of these general rules described above.

- The first is that any provision which you may feel necessary to make need only be limited to such value of your whole estate which is in excess of £150,000, and that such provision need only be made to cover the potential liability which is 40 per cent of that value.

- The second is that the tax is levied on such assets as are considered to be part of your estate: this includes property of any sort as well as marketable investments and shares in unlisted companies.

The whole subject of tax avoidance is a minefield and you should get professional advice from a solicitor or a chartered accountant, or in some cases both, but in general terms there are two avenues to consider.

> **Depending on the income tax laws governing the country which you choose to act as domicile for your trust, you can manage your portfolio in just the same way as if it were under your control within the UK.**

The first is to make a gift during your lifetime of such capital as you would intend to bequeath to a third party on your death, and hope that you would survive for the minimum period of seven years from the date of making the gift. Under this concession, if death were to occur within the seven year period, the liability to inheritance tax from your estate would remain at 100 per cent for the first two years, and then diminish in each subsequent year by a percentage until the end of the seven year period, by which time the liability would be nil. You must not have any control over the capital or benefit from any income arising from the moment you make the gift or at any time thereafter.

You can, of course, protect your estate from any such potential liability during the seven-year period by buying diminishing term life assurance to cover the amount of the liability, and this is probably the most cost-effective way of covering the risk. However, you will lose the income arising from such capital which you give away. There is no reason why the recipient of the gift should not use some or all of the income arising to pay the premiums for the life assurance cover, but such payments must be made by that person directly to the insurance company, not via your bank account. Any such arrangements would have to be informal and you would have no recourse to enforce them.

The second is to set up a trust which is resident outside the European Union, and control the investments yourself. This is an expensive exercise, and you will not find it worthwhile to do unless you are able to put at least £100,000 into such an arrangement. During the lifetime of such a trust, you can be a trustee with all the powers that are included in that position, but you cannot be a beneficiary as far as any income or the proceeds of sale of any investments are concerned. However, depending on the income tax laws governing the country which you choose to act as domicile for your trust, you can manage your portfolio in just the same way as if it were under your control within the UK.

Since the objective of a portfolio for inheritance tax planning would probably be to achieve maximum growth, you would aim to make as few changes to individual investments as possible, because the costs of dealing and the annual management charges levied by the trust administrators can be quite high. Nevertheless, the assets within the trust will remain outside your estate for inheritance tax purposes until and if you chose to terminate the trust and repatriate its assets.

SUMMARY

In this chapter we have demonstrated the way to approach the creation of: a portfolio to provide income and growth, and how to design the shape of the portfolio to produce a balanced distribution of your capital to ensure that you have access to cash when you need it, the right amount of capital invested in fixed-interest securities to provide the net income you require to meet your living and leisure expenses, and the right amount of capital invested to provide growth which at the very least will protect your wealth against erosion by inflation.

In addition we have described how to analyse markets and sectors and the nine essential points to check for each share before you buy, so that you reduce the risk of loss to the absolute minimum.

We have examined the ways to create portfolios for growth only and income alone. We have discussed the risks involved in a trading portfolio, and shown how to watch for the right opportunities to buy shares whose price is extremely volatile, how to monitor the price movement, set stop-loss limits, as well as when to take your profits.

We have looked at ways to reduce your liabilities to inheritance tax payable on your estate by your heirs, including the use of trusts and offshore funds, whilst keeping control of the investment management of your portfolio in your own hands.

In particular we have shown the need for:

- buying shares at the right price and, if necessary, waiting for the right moment;
- research and access to share price information at all times;
- constant monitoring and reappraisal of your investments without which your capital is at risk unnecessarily;
- setting targets which are reasonable and achievable;
- making your capital work for you, both as to production of yield and growth, as well as achieving these returns within a specified time.

Finally, we have noted the fact that most of the money paid to the Inland Revenue by way of Capital Gains Tax is a voluntary donation and, we have shown how to cut down on such luxuries to your advantage unless you enjoy making such gifts.

The more data you can record, the more easily and quickly you can make machinery do the analysis work for you.

11

The role of information technology (IT)

Data required

Charts

What are the signals?

How do we interpret the signals?

Further interpretation of charts

Summary

At the beginning of this book, I emphasised the vital need for research. I have described the sort of data which you need to accumulate about a company, its management, its products, its markets, its competitors and so on. By now you should be much better equipped to satisfy yourself that you can isolate the potential investments whose ordinary shares are most likely to go up in value, and by using charts you can select the optimum time to buy (or sell), or re-set stop-loss limits.

You will understand that the need for collating information is just as important as the necessity for monitoring the progress of your investments. Both are time-consuming, particularly if you are to do the job properly.

In this chapter we show you how to use your time to the maximum advantage whilst keeping the tedious but essential data processing to the minimum. We demonstrate how IT can:

- save you hours of research into share price history;
- let you see, at a glance, the share price performance over two years or more as often as you like;
- enable you to monitor the share price history of all 2,300 plus shares traded on the London Stock Exchange whether you have invested in any of them or not;
- read and interpret the 'Buy', 'Sell' and 'Hold' signals which charts give;
- set targets for growth using charts and stop-loss limits.

DATA REQUIRED

The more data you can record, the more easily you can make machinery do the analysis work for you. However there is a limit to what is useful data which can be analysed advantageously, and what is perhaps interesting information but which is unimportant for comparison purposes. In the latter category, if we take Glaxo Welcome as an example, whilst it is most useful to know when the patent rights of Zantac will run out, it is of no consequence when comparing the company's current share performance with that of a competitor, the sector, or the market as a whole. Likewise, whilst you ignore at your peril any particular and specific information published about a company's changes in directors, products, markets or market share, it would not serve any useful purpose to include such items in your data controls.

Basic information required

The basic information which you need to record in any IT system is that which will give you the ability to carry out the following exercises *at least once a week*:

- see the *actual* profit/loss which you are making on your portfolio at any time;
- see the *indexed* profit you are making at all times, whether you sell or not, thereby being aware of your potential liability to Capital Gains Tax (CGT);
- plot the trading range of each share or unit trust, whether you hold them in your portfolio or not;
- see at a glance whether or not each investment is out-performing the sector or the Index;
- keep your CGT to a minimum;
- record all purchases, sales, dividends received, interest received and current cash balances.

The way to maximise profit and protect your capital against possible loss depends upon two main factors:

- *up-to-date share price information with an ability to read future trends from the graphs;*
- *the control of the vital decisions – which shares to choose, when to buy and when to sell.*

You should choose a software program which enables you to record the following data:

- name of security;
- Sedol number – this is the identifying code given to all listed stocks and shares by the Stock Exchange;
- date purchased/date sold;
- purchase price/selling price;
- costs including commissions, Stamp Duty, etc;

- number purchased/number sold;
- type of security, for example bank, brewery, oil;
- sector value (as shown in the *Financial Times*);
- FT All Share Index;
- RPI factor – this value is published around the 15th of each month and is *not* the same as the Retail Price Index.

Share price data

It is clear that the time taken to collate and enter the essential data can become considerable if you posses a portfolio with a large number of holdings. Also, and this is very important, you will need to be keeping a record of the share price movement of other shares in which you are interested and which you may want to buy when some of your existing investments have achieved their targets or started to go the wrong way. In addition, although you may have got a list of shares to watch and be keeping a record of their price movements, you may read or hear about an interesting share whose prices you have *not* been logging. So you have to make a decision as to what is the most economical way of obtaining your data on a regular basis.

Methods of recording data

There are essentially four ways in which you can enter your data:

- **Manually**   This is the most time-consuming but the cheapest. It suits a small portfolio (say up to 10 holdings) mostly comprising investment or unit trusts where there is going to be infrequent change in individual investment.

- **Via the television**   The charge for this facility is made at the outset and from then onwards there are no further costs. The charge will be approximately £200 and you can download the prices of all 2,300 shares exhibited on Teletext as often as you like. The PC program will accept all the new prices for all 2,300 shares in about 15 minutes, and automatically re-calculates the current values of all your holdings. It will enable you to record the share price history of all 2,300 shares so that you can build charts for future reference. For the average home-based investor this is probably the most economic and efficient system of data supply. At present, the Teletext system does not include unit trust prices, nor those of fixed-interest securities, such as gilts or preference shares, or loan stocks.

- **Via subscription** Some program suppliers will supply a disc on a regular basis for a fee; this you install into your PC. The advantage of this system is that if you are away on holiday, for example, you can subsequently bring your database up-to-date. The disadvantage is that you are locked in to a financial commitment which may not be what you want.

- **Via the Internet** Provided you have a telephone modem attached to your PC, you can gain access to the Internet and down load your data whenever you want. However, before you choose this option, you will be well advised to look before you leap. The data available on the Internet is voluminous and a great deal of it is superfluous to the needs of the average investor. Unfortunately, you can not be selective when downloading and so you will be recording a vast amount of unnecessary information and using up memory on your hard disk to no purpose.

There are PC software programs available which include a whole host of additional items of data including currencies and exchange rates, and their relationships, but for the ordinary investor such extra 'bells and whistles' are not necessary. A program which will give you most of what you require, and which can be updated manually or linked to Teletext via a Microtext Card is called *Portfolio Control*. It is available either as DOS-based or in Windows, and can be obtained from CPV Associates Ltd, 93 Eastern Road, Romford, Essex. RM1 3PB. The price of the DOS version is £47.50, and the Windows version is £65.50, both prices are inclusive of VAT, postage and packing.

CHARTS

Charts are a very useful tool for decision making. Properly used they will save you a great deal of time and alert you to ask the right questions about the shares in which you are interested.

The movement of share prices will tell you a great deal if you know how to interpret the signals and the purpose of this chapter is to explain the lessons which can be learned from them. The patterns which emerge from recording such share price movements graphically will enable you to predict future movements with more accuracy, as well as helping you to make 'buy' or 'sell' decisions which are based on fact rather than guess-work or hunch.

The use of charts to assist you in the planning and control of your investments will reduce the risks of missing opportunities either to sell at around the top end of the trading range, or to buy at around the bottom.

Chart construction

Why use a chart?

To some people, a row of figures is all that is required to be able to see trends in the historical record of a share price. By using mental arithmetic they can measure the rise or fall in the value of a share over a period of time and calculate the percentage change accurately, without the need to see history recorded in a pictorial form. I have to say that I envy such people because I have never been able to do this, and I am sure that there are many like me for whom graphic representation of the past history of a share price is much easier to read and understand.

> The use of charts to assist you in the planning and control of your investments will reduce the risks of missing opportunities.

Also I find it easier to measure changes in values, or to set targets for growth for each individual investment, if I can see lines rather than a mass of figures. Anything which gives me a clear picture of what is happening, and which saves time is, as far as I am concerned, worth having.

Since it is very rare that the price of a share remains unaltered, or static, it is essential for successful portfolio management that you are able to measure the amount of price fluctuation quickly and accurately.

What is a chart?

A chart is a symbolic representation. Essentially, it is a line joining up dots on a piece of paper. Each dot represents a figure and for our purposes, each dot represents a share price. In order to locate the right spot to place the dot on the chart, you have to establish two sets of measurements – one vertically, the other horizontally.

These lines on which measurements are recorded are called the *axes*. In order to demonstrate the movement of a share price by using a chart, you would record a range of share prices on the vertical axis and time along the horizontal axis. The horizontal axis is usually referred to as the *x-axis*, and the vertical axis as the *y-axis*.

The time record (x-axis) could be anything from every minute during market hours, daily, weekly, monthly, or some specific period of your own selection. The share price record (y-axis) would cover a range of prices with enough room to accommodate a considerable variation from the current price. The range does not have to start at 1, for example, but it should be sufficiently wide to allow for a movement of 100 per cent in either direction from the current level.

If you make the time scale (x-axis) using very short periods (eg hourly), you will get a picture which is fairly meaningless. It will show you the price movements over a period of one or two days which, in the context of the normal private investment, is of no real value. There are two main reasons for this:

- You would not expect a share price to fluctuate much during such a short period, if at all, other than by a penny or two. The exception to this would be a traded option or bid target perhaps, but for that sort of investment you would find a graphical record useless because the whole process would be too slow.

- The picture which would emerge would be over such a short relative time-scale that you would have to paper the walls of your house with the charts to get any real history of the share movement. Obviously this would be a waste of time.

The most useful time-scale to adopt is to record the prices of your shares once a week. Thus the horizontal axis should be able to demonstrate the record over a period of at least two years and so it requires not less than 104 divisions.

> *It is most important that you do not alter your chosen frequency and that you do not miss recording the prices in accordance with your chosen frequency.*

Any gaps which occur in your data recording will give you a picture which is possibly difficult to read and perhaps inaccurate. This will become obvious later on when we consider the signals which charts can give you.

The vertical axis should be designed to give you as much room as possible so that a gain or loss of a few pennies in the price is reflected by an obvious change of direction in the chart.

> **The most useful time-scale to adopt is to record the prices of your shares once a week.**

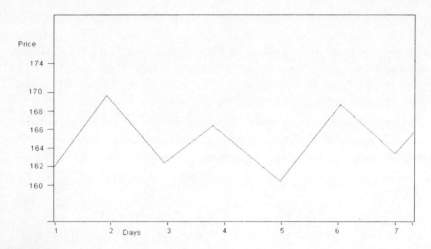

Figure 11.1 Too short a time-scale

Figure 11.1 shows a chart measured over a time-scale which is far too short to have any significant meaning. The price has fluctuated between about 164p and 170p over seven working days. The variation in price was about 6p on 164p, or 3.6 per cent. As an isolated picture in the life of that particular share it is meaningless.

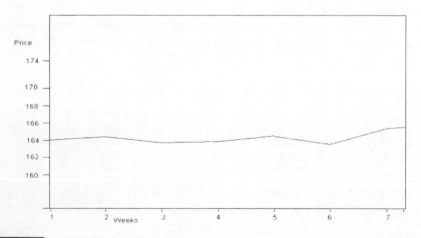

Figure 11.2 Still too short a time-scale

Figure 11.2 shows a chart that is also measured over too short a time-scale, although it gives a fraction more information than is available from Figure 11.1. A trend is begining to emerge but since there is no historical pattern to compare with, you would not be able to see whether this trend was always to be expected at the same time each year, or whether the trend shown is conforming to a longer term overall pattern or not.

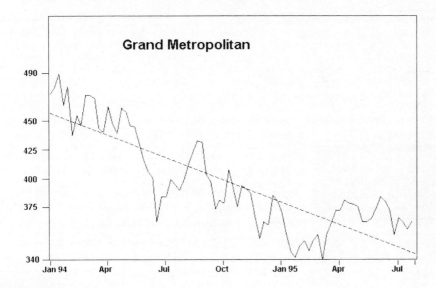

Figure 11.3 **A more meaningul chart on a realistic time-scale**

Now let us look at a chart which is much more meaningful. Figure 11.3 shows the movement of a share price which has been plotted over 27 months on a weekly basis. You will see that the divisions are shown at intervals of three months on the *x-axis*, but in order to get an accurate picture of the movement, the prices had to be fed into the database once a week.

Now that we have demonstrated how to construct a chart which contains sufficient information for analysis, the next questions must be:

• What are the signals that are being given?

• How do we interpret them?

WHAT ARE THE SIGNALS?

Benchmarks

It is necessary to establish *benchmarks* for each aspect that you are going to use as a 'control' when setting your targets for individual share achievement. Whilst the *values* will be different for each share, the *measurement devices* will not. In order to set realistic and achievable values, the more historic data you have the better able you are to make realistic forecasts.

Trends

Usually a graph of the historic movement of a share price will show an uneven line. If you plot the movement over the last two years (or better still over the last five years), you will be able to see the overall trend whether it be annually or over the whole period. This will give you a far better picture of its history than you will get by looking at a row of figures, or by relying on your memory. **Memory is notoriously fallible**. Thus you will see

> There is no point in buying a share for growth if the overall trend is downward.

at a glance whether the overall trend is rising or falling. There is no point in buying a share for growth if the overall trend is downward. The same thing is true for the market as a whole and it is generally difficult for a share to buck the trend unless there are very good reasons as to why it should.

What does a trend reflect?

As we have explained earlier in this book, the market prices reflect the overall direction of demand for a share, or lack of it. There are two elements that cause share prices to alter:

- **Market opinion**. This dictates the popularity or otherwise of a share. Such opinion is generated by Press and analytical comment, particularly with regard to the future earnings of the company. Good or bad Press comment will generate interest in a share, and the more frequently such comment is published, the more the share price is in the limelight.

- **Investor demand**. Investors will want to buy a popular share and so this chases the share price upwards. Likewise, they will want to dump a share which is receiving bad Press comment and this will help to depress the share price even more.

Anything which prompts you to investigate the reasons for abnormal or dramatic change in the historical pattern of progression of a share price is useful. A chart will enable you to see when such changes have occurred and so you can concentrate your research on the information which was published around the appropriate dates. It may be that substantial changes occurred for reasons which had nothing to do with the perceived earnings potential of the company, such as the crash of 1987 or the outbreak of war in the Middle East, but at least you will have satisfied yourself as to whether the reason was pertinent to the market as a whole or that share in particular.

Thus the overall trend, if measured over a sufficiently long period, will show you what is the general market consensus. In the case of a demonstrable falling trend, you need to have very good reasons for believing that the market has got it wrong for one particular share over such a long time, if you think that the trend is going to be reversed, and the reversal sustained.

> **Anything which prompts you to investigate the reasons for abnormal or dramatic change in the historical pattern of progression of a share price is useful.**

EXAMPLE ✳

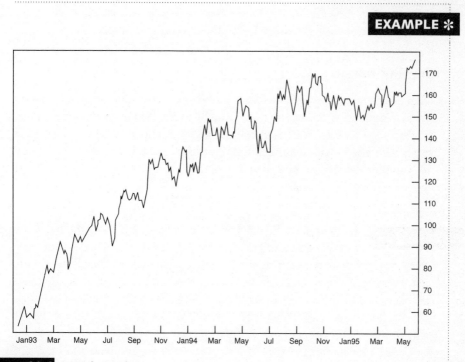

gure 11.4 **British Steel**

The price history of British Steel is shown above for the period January 1993 to May 1995. During that time, the price has risen from around 52p to 174p, an increase of 122p over 28 months. This represents a growth rate of 4.3 per cent per month.

Since prices do not move in a straight line for a sustained period, the increase is an average rate and serves as a factor to be built into your calculations for future projected performance.

Thus, a simple conclusion might be to expect a continuous growth rate of around 50 per cent per annum, but such a view would probably be over simplistic.

You will see that the *angle* of the upward trend has reduced from around August 1994 to May 1995. The trend was still upwards during that period, but the angle of climb was considerably less steep when compared with the period from January 1993 to August 1994. For this reason, to be realistic, you would expect to extrapolate future percentage growth at a much lower amount.

HOW DO WE INTERPRET THE SIGNALS?

So now let's look in detail at the signals which you can expect to see emerging from your charts and how these should be interpreted.

Trading range

This device enables you to see and measure the amount by which a share price is oscillating about the trend line. It fulfils two important functions. It allows you to measure the expected 'high' and 'low' of the share price in the future after you have projected the trend line, and it shows you when will be the best time to buy or sell the share.

✳ EXAMPLE If a share price (middle) is standing at say 220p and the trend line for the last year has been increasing at the rate of 10 per cent, then if you extrapolate that for a further 12 months, you could reasonably expect the middle price to rise to 242p by that time. Then, if you measure the amount between the top and bottom of the trading range, you might find that the share price fluctuates by, say, 20 per cent. This would give you a variation of 10 per cent above and 10 per cent below the trend line. So you might set your target for selling the share at 266p in a year's time. (Mid-price to have risen to 242p plus 10 per cent of 242 = 24.2p if you sell at the top of the trading range.)

Of course, neither life or the markets are so predictable, nor do they conform so neatly to such precise anticipated behaviour. However, now that you have set a realistic and achievable target in this example, you can defer making a decision to sell, either until the share price reaches the level required in the time allotted, or if the price changes direction suddenly and dramatically.

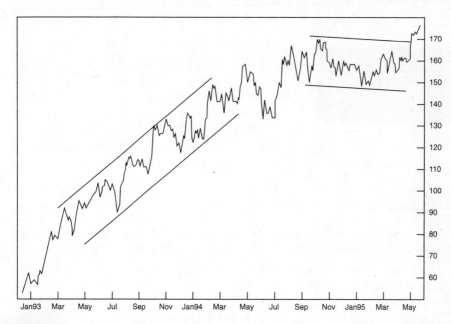

Figure 11.5 Graph showing trading range

Figure 11.5 shows the same graph as that in Figure 11.4 but with two sets of parallel lines superimposed on it. By drawing such lines, **which must be parallel** and which join the high and low points over a period, you establish the *trading range* of the share. This enables you to:

- measure the amount of the upward and downward movement of the price in pence;
- measure the average time which elapses between the 'highs' and the 'lows'.

There are two lessons to be learned from this information:

- If you are thinking of buying the share, you can see when will be the most advantageous time to make your purchase. This will occur when the share price has reached the bottom of its trading range **and has turned upwards again**. You do *not* buy before it has turned upwards in case it continues to fall below the projection of the lower limits of the trading range.

- If you are considering selling the share, you wait until the share price has reached the top of its trading range **and has turned downwards**. You do *not* sell before it has turned downwards in case it continues to rise beyond the upper limits of the trading range.

> ...You ignore the signals which moving averages give at your peril. ....

You will be lucky to buy at the bottom or sell at the top because these points can only be established after they have occurred but you will maximise your profits and minimise your losses if you follow these two rules. It goes without saying that it is as foolish to buy when the share price is falling as it is to sell when the price is rising, but it is much easier to see what is happening if you show the progress graphically.

Indices

There are many indices which you can use as further aids to decision making, but you should beware of ending up with a picture which is more likely to confuse than be helpful. The more you include, the more difficult it becomes to read the signals with any reasonable clarity. We will deal with other signals later on in this chapter, but at this stage we confine ourselves to those which are useful to the average investor.

Moving averages

A moving average is a useful control which should be regarded as a device to alert you to the likelihood of possible future movement in the share price. It is not something which should initiate action by itself. However, you ignore the signals which moving averages give at your peril.

30 day index

This is a line consisting of the average price of the share over the last 30 days. It is also called a *moving average* because each time that a new daily price is added to the total (making 31 days), the price for day one of the total is subtracted (bringing the total back to 30 days), and a new average price is calculated.

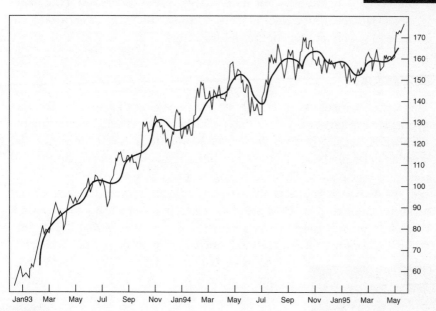

Figure 11.6 30 day moving average

Figure 11.6 shows the 30-day moving average superimposed on to the share price record.

The effect is to smooth out the volatility of the price movement: this is interesting but not much else by itself. Remember that because the index consists of an average of the prices over the last 30 days, it will be slower to react to the latest price movement, whether that is up or down, and particularly if such a movement has been dramatic. This is a short-term index.

There are two points to remember when you read the signals which emerge from such factual evidence.

- If the share price line **cuts through** the 30-day moving average line in a downward direction, you can expect the price to continue to fall. Such a situation should immediately alert you to watch the price line closely to see if it continues downwards to a point where it cuts through the lower limit of the trading range. If the drop in price is fast and sustained then you should sell the share to protect your capital from further loss.

- If the share price cuts through the 30-day moving average line in an upward direction, you can expect the price to continue to rise and you might consider buying some more shares to take advantage of the rising trend. However, you should only do this if the lines cross at a point close to the lower level of the trading range.

90-day index

This index is identical to the 30-day index, except that it is the moving average of the share price over the last 90 days. The effect of increasing the number of days to be included in the total is to iron out the peaks and troughs in the line so that you are looking at an even more obvious trend over a longer period. This index will be even slower to respond to any sudden change in direction of the share price, but it provides a useful and more stable picture of the share price performance over a longer period. One of its main benefits, from a visual point of view, is that it puts into perspective any abnormal and dramatic variation in share price which has not been sustained. It may be, for example, that the share price jumped for no other reason than the emergence of a bid for another company in the same sector and the market thought that this company could be a possible bid target also. In the absence of any such interest being shown, the share price would be expected to return to its proper level which is dictated by the actual and anticipated earnings and market sentiment.

> **The 90-day index puts into perspective any abnormal and dramatic variation in share price which has not been sustained.**

Any indices which are based on shorter or longer periods than 30 or 90 days will simply accentuate the fluctuations in share price, or flatten them out even more. They will not add to your tool kit for reading the signals and so they are unnecessary. They just clutter up the chart.

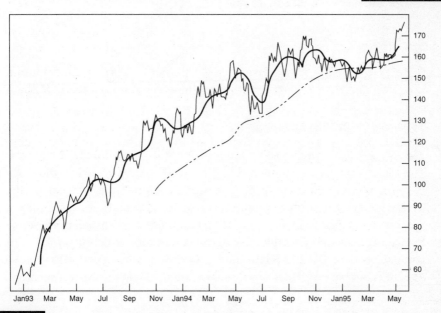

Figure 11.7 30-day and 90-day moving averages

In Figure 11.7 both the 30-day and 90-day moving averages are combined. The 90-day line gives a more simplified picture of the overall trend of the share price, and it moves in a much more leisurely way.

There are two important points to remember when you read these signals, if they occur:

- If the 30-day moving average line cuts through the 90-day line in a downward direction **and they are both moving in a downward direction**, then you can expect the share price to fall and probably by a long way. If the 30-day line cuts downwards through the 90-day line while the 90-day line is moving horizontally, or better still in an upward direction, the reduction in the share price will probably be small.

- If the 30-day moving average line cuts upwards through the 90-day line **while it is also rising**, the share price will rise considerably and you should buy the share if you do not hold it in your portfolio already, or perhaps you should add to your holding. If the 30-day line cuts upwards through the 90-day line while the 90-day line is moving horizontally or in a downward direction, you cannot necessarily expect a sustained rise in the share price.

Sectors

In order to measure the performance of a particular share in a meaningful way, you need to compare it with something. The choices are as follows.

The FT-SE 100 Share Index

This is the most widely used comparison but it has some disadvantages. The 100 Share Index is composed of the top 100 shares traded on the Stock Exchange measured by their market capitalisation. Thus, to measure the performance of a company with a much smaller market capitalisation against the giants, seems to be fairly meaningless. It is much more sensible to measure like with like. Also, the companies which form the constituent parts of the 100 Share Index are only a small proportion of the total number of companies whose shares are listed on the Stock Exchange.

The FT-SE 250 and 350 Share Index

The component companies of these two indices are, as you would expect, the top 250 and 350 companies measured by their market capitalisation. Since there are over 3000 shares listed on the Stock Exchange, the same comments apply as described above.

The FT-SE Allshare Index

The component parts of this index consist of the top 800 companies measured by their market capitalisation. Whilst this list is not exhaustive, it does cover a much wider selection of the market than do the other indices. You get a much broader picture of what the market as a whole is doing – both in terms of its overall trend as well as the average percentage movement in share price, dividend yield and price earnings ratios (PER) – than you do from the rather more narrow picture which the other indices produce.

Company Sectors

This index, combined with the FT-SE Allshare will give you the most meaningful comparison. Every company which is listed is categorised and placed for record purposes in the *Financial Times* with other companies carrying on a similar type of business. The market capitalisation is ignored so that you will find small companies' prices shown alongside those of market leaders. Thus if you measure the performance of a company against that of its own sector, you are better able to judge its degree of success or otherwise in its ability to earn profits as well as its standing in the market opinion ratings.

It is usual to measure the price earnings ratio (PER) against that of its sector. The reason is that you will get a distorted view if you try to compare prices between a company and those of the component parts of the sector because of the wide variations in values.

EXAMPLE ✳

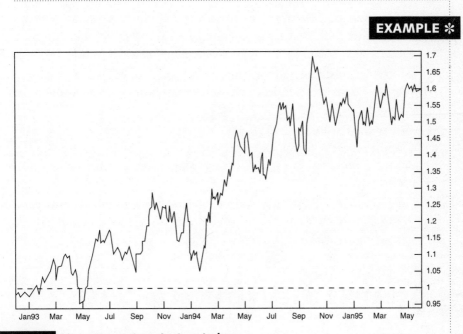

Figure 11.8 **Measurement against an index**

In the chart shown in Figure 11.8 the PER is measured against the Allshare Index. The Allshare Index has been reduced to the value of 1 and the individual share PER is shown relative to it. When the relative PER has a value in excess of 1, then the share is performing better than the market. If the value is less than 1 then the share is under-performing the market.

From the picture that emerges you can see that the share has out-performed the market average considerably in this case. Measurement against an index is a very useful tool for use in your control systems, and helps in your decision making.

Key points

The key points to be remembered when reading the signals which emerge from plotting the price movement of a share together with 30-day and 90-day moving averages are as follows:

- You can see the overall trend of the share price at a glance.
- You can measure the annual rise or fall of the share price and thus establish a realistic expectation of future performance.
- You can measure the performance of an individual share against the performance of its own sector. Thus you can see at a glance whether an individual share is doing better or worse than other shares in the same industry.
- You can measure the performance of an individual share against the performance of the market as a whole to see whether the share is doing better or worse than the average investment.
- You can establish the trading range of each share price so that you know when to buy and when to sell to maximise your profit and minimise any potential loss.
- You can use the 30-day and 90-day moving averages to alert you to even closer monitoring of your investments in order to make more profits or remove a potential danger to your capital by selling before any loss increases.
- You can analyse the performances of shares which you hold in your portfolio as well as those in which you are interested and which represent potential investments.

■ FURTHER INTERPRETATION OF CHARTS

We now examine some further signals which charts can give and explain how to interpret them. It is important to remember that they are only signals, not instructions to do anything. View signals as being rather like the amber traffic lights, a warning that something is about to change, and if you can interpret them properly they will enhance your control over your investments and give you the ability to concentrate your time and energy in research which may be required urgently.

The points which we discuss here are not by any means exhaustive. The science of interpreting charts is well researched and there have been many books written on the subject. They go into much greater depth and detail than we are covering in this book, but since the average investor will not want to get involved in lengthy and abstruse discussion on the subject we confine the data here to the bare essentials which will give you sufficient knowledge to become competent in chart interpretation.

There are two configurations which often occur in the charts of share price movements and more often than not they precede a firm and sustained change in direction.

Head and shoulders

The term 'head and shoulders' is given to a configuration which is symmetrical and looks like an apex with either two lower ones on either side or a horizontal line on either side.

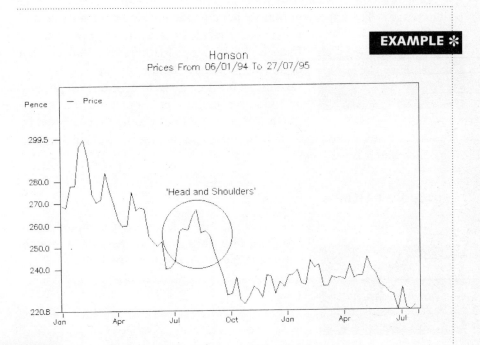

EXAMPLE ✳

Hanson
Prices From 06/01/94 To 27/07/95

Figure 11.9 Head and shoulders

In Figure 11.9 you will see the chart of Hanson and if you look at the price movement between August and September 1994 you will see a good example of a 'head and shoulders'. Note that the price rose from a level of around 230p to form a small apex between 248p and 255p and then fell back to about 248p. Then it rose to form a new apex at about 260p and then fell back to form another smaller one, similar to the first. When such a configuration occurs, it is usual for the share price to drop substantially and over a short time span. It does not always happen but it is generally accepted that the likelihood is that it will and the professionals tend to get out of the share because there is no telling where the bottom is likely to be. In fact, in this instance, the share price was following an established downward trend as you can see from the earlier part of the chart and it did not change direction until the end of October that year. This is a company which is often the subject of Press comment and opinions are divided as to whether to hold the share or not. You can look at the history now with more enlightened eyes and make your own decisions.

Sometimes the 'head and shoulders' configuration is spread over a longer time span. The important thing is to be on the look out for the shape and to remember its likely implications when you are finalising your targets for any given share, or, if it occurs after you have bought the stock, you might seriously consider abandoning the investment and look for another as a replacement. Alternatively, if you are trading, you might be alerted by such a configuration to consider buying a put option and buying the share in at a much lower level.

> The important thing is to be on the look out for the shape.

Double bottoms

In the same way that a 'head and shoulders' is generally accepted as the precursor of a drop in the share price, a 'double bottom' is taken to indicate the reverse.

> There is more excitement generated by a double bottom configuration in charts.

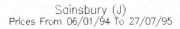

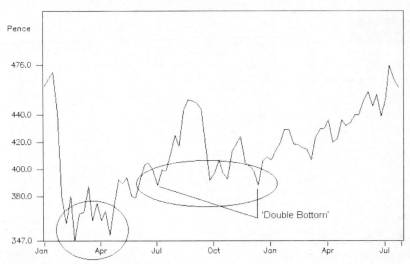

Figure 11.10   'Double bottom'

Figure 11.10 shows the chart of Sainsbury and here are two interesting examples of 'double bottoms'. The first one occurred in March/May 1994 and it was evident over a very short time span. After the second low of the double bottom in May, the price climbed erratically to a high of 405p before establishing the first leg of a second double bottom in July when it dropped to 395p. The second leg of this double bottom occurred towards the end of December when the price reached a similar low level. In both cases there was a substantial rise in the share price following the double bottoms and this pattern remained until a new trading range became established from January 1995 onwards.

There is more excitement generated by a double bottom configuration in charts because many people believe that it is the forerunner of a worthwhile rise in the price and consequently they jump in to the market to buy the share. This, of course, adds to the demand for the share which itself helps to boost the price.

You can see an example of both double bottoms and head and shoulders in Figure 11.11.

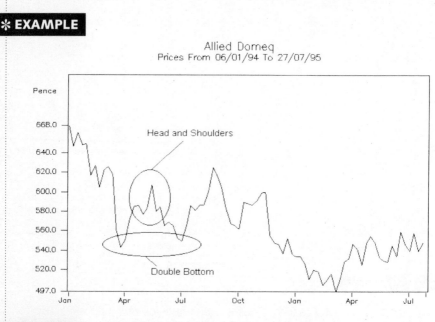

Allied Domeq
Prices From 06/01/94 To 27/07/95

Figure 11.11 'Double bottom' with 'head and shoulders'

Figure 11.11 is the chart of Allied Domeq. The head and shoulders occurred between May and June 1994, and the double bottom between March and July 1994.

Find the reason for price changes

In all cases you should be prompted to find out what has been the reason for market sentiment to force the price down so far. There is always a reason, even though sometimes it can be trivial, particularly with hindsight. Very often an unexpected note of caution may appear in the Chairman's statement when the figures are announced. Because it is unexpected, particularly if the company is one of the leaders, it is frequently the case that the market over-reacts and the market makers push the price down much further than may be justified. When this occurs, and it is really only common sense and a feel for where the right level should be, you can often find buying opportunities. The market has a tendency to behave rather like a pendulum and swing too far in either direction. Charts will help you to identify such events but it is essential that when such a situation

> **The market has a tendency to behave rather like a pendulum and swing too far in either direction.**

occurs you check carefully using all available means to ensure that there really is no fundamental bad news which could not only keep the price down, but might depress it even further.

SUMMARY

In this chapter we have described how IT and charts can save a vast amount of time and enable you to reap the following benefits:

- By recording historic facts you will be in a much better position to ask the right questions about the future movement of an individual share price, and therefore you will be able to concentrate your research on those aspects which directly affect the company and thus its share price.

- You will be using the same methods as the professional fund managers do when they are monitoring the progress of an existing investment, or watching the progress of a share in which they are interested and waiting for the right time to buy.

- You will avoid falling in to the trap of hanging on to a share for too long and thus miss getting out just before the price starts to fall away.

- You will save yourself a great deal of time and uncertainty over what shares to buy and when to buy them.

- You will be able to spend more time on profitable research into other shares to choose as potential candidates to include in your portfolio in the future.

- You will be in **control** of your investment decisions and they will be **based on fact**.

Unless you feel convinced that your financial adviser completely understands you and your particular needs, you will not be likely to respect the advice you get.

12

Getting the most from financial advisers

General advice on do's and don'ts

Questions you should ask your financial adviser

Execution-only service versus full advisory service

Summary

At the beginning of this book I explained that you have to use the services of a stockbroker or firm which is authorised to deal on the market, whether you choose to construct and manage your own portfolio or not. Whether you choose to employ an execution-only service, or opt to have a full advisory service, there are some golden rules to follow.

These are divided into two sections.

The first section applies to whichever service you choose, and I strongly recommend that you follow the advice here in order to ensure that, not only do you safeguard your money, but you get the right relationship at the start. Unless you feel convinced that your financial adviser completely understands you and your particular needs, you will not be likely to respect the advice you get.

◼ GENERAL ADVICE ON DO'S AND DON'TS

- **Never pay a cheque to an individual.** If you are settling an account, or applying for new shares or any form of investment, always make your cheque payable to a firm.

- **Which regulatory authority does the firm answer to?** Your safeguard is the regulatory authority which governs and controls the business and behaviour of all firms engaged in handling money belonging to the public. It is to the relevant authority that you should send any complaints which you might have concerning dealing ethics or business practices, and so you should find out which one is responsible for your adviser at the start.

- **Financial protection.** All regulatory authorities have compensation funds to cover loss which occurs as a result of malpractice such as fraud or bankruptcy on the part of their members. This does not cover losses arising through bad advice, because at the end of the day, you are the one who decides to accept or reject the advice which is given to you as far as any investment is concerned.

- **Commission rates or fees.** Always ask for all scales of charges, commission rates or fees and any other costs involved in dealing which an adviser demands for his services. You must get them in writing and keep them on file.

- **Check the independence of the adviser.** If an adviser is independent, he is able to suggest all the products available on the market which are pertinent to your particular requirement and discuss them. A bank manager, for example, is allowed to recommend only the unit trusts managed by his own bank, even if there are better ones available elsewhere. The same applies to insurance-linked financial advisers.
- **Length of existence.** Ask how long the adviser and his firm have been in existence. It will probably pay you to use those who have some substantial experience.

QUESTIONS YOU SHOULD ASK YOUR FINANCIAL ADVISER

It is, in my view, absolutely essential to go and see your financial adviser at his office. You will be able to get a view of the substance, or lack of it, from the state of the building, whether you feel that the office seems chaotic or well organised and so on. When you do so, arm yourself with all the relevant information about yourself and your financial assets and sources of income, both current and expected, as we have described in this book. You should interview several firms of advisers, and in order to be able to make your decision as to which one to choose, list all your questions and ask them all the same ones. That way you can compare their answers and recommendations, like with like.

Don't forget they all want to earn commission from your money and so you should feel important. Too many people start by feeling overawed by financial gurus. It is your money, and however small your capital may be, it is all you have got and it is just as important to you as a large fortune is to a millionaire. So it is vital that you make the right choice in whom you place your trust.

I suggest that you include the following questions in your list.

Information services

Ask whether the firm subscribes to Reuters and Extel. Avoid those that do not. Ask whether you can have information on demand from these sources, and whether such data will be provided free of charge. What research does the firm provide, either by newsletter or company or sector or country? Is such information free? You should avoid firms which require payment for such research.

Dealing information

Ask whether the firm executes orders immediately on receipt of instructions, or whether they only deal once or twice a day like the banks. Avoid any firm that does not carry out your instructions immediately. Ask whether the firm negotiates prices with the market makers or only deals on screen prices. Any firm worth its salt will pride itself on getting a better price for you than is shown on the screen. It is not always possible, of course, but you ought to feel that at least they will try.

EXECUTION-ONLY SERVICE VERSUS FULL ADVISORY SERVICE

The purpose of this book is to show you how to create and manage your own tailor-made portfolio, and to equip you with all the technical knowledge required to do just that. It may be that you would like to have an advisory service in addition to keeping full control of your investments and being, as a result of what you have learned from this book, well-equipped to manage your own money.

Table 12.1 gives the differences costs involved between the two services.

Table 12.1

	Dealing costs
Execution-only	From £9 minimum per bargain. Average 1.0 per cent, reducing for bargains over £10,000
Full advice	From £ 25 minimum per bargain Average 1.85 per cent, reducing for bargains over £10,000

Extra costs such as handling or administration charges will vary from firm to firm.

Some firms charge for portfolio valuations, some do not.

Charges for registering shares in nominee companies will vary, sometimes by quite a lot.

Depot charges for safe custody will vary also. These are levied for each shareholding and are normally made on an annual basis irrespective of how long the share is kept.

There is not that much difference between the costs, but there is a world of difference between the services on offer, and this becomes apparent when something goes wrong, as it does inevitably. A good firm of stockbrokers will give all sorts of help free of charge when it is needed, and as a stockbroker myself, I know just how often clients need assistance. Also, and the most important of all, my clients are my friends and this makes the whole business much more satisfactory.

 SUMMARY

In this chapter we have looked at the questions you should ask a financial adviser to satisfy yourself that you are making the right choice. We have also described the items of information which you must get regarding costs of dealing and charges for services provided, so that you know exactly what you can expect from the firm, and at what price. We have stressed the need to get several 'quotations' before you decide which one to choose, and emphasised that the most important point of all is that you should feel a rapport exists between yourself and your adviser.

It is generally considered in the stockbroking fraternity that if you can get three right out of five, you are doing fairly well. I hope that you will improve on that ratio.

Conclusion

In this book, I have described two main aspects which you need to understand in some depth if you are going to manage your financial affairs in the way in which a good stockbroker would do.

- What the various financial instruments are and what you can expect them to do for you.
- What the external factors are which influence their performance.

Since I spend a great deal of time with a new client at the first meeting trying to find out all I need to know about his or her affairs, I know that I cannot do a good job in creating a portfolio for anyone without the essential information at the outset. You have all the facts which I would have to have, and so now there is no reason why you cannot do your own research, make your own selections, create your own portfolio and keep your own records.

The first part of the book is devoted to explaining what the various 'tools' are designed to do, and you must be fully *au fait* with both the uses for which they are designed and their limitations, before you build any of them into your portfolio. You must know how they work, what you can and cannot expect from each one and, above all, what degree of risk is attached to each instrument.

There is no mystique attached to this, it is simply a question of reading and learning. Anyone can do it.

But even if you become a walking encyclopaedia on every type of stock and share you will not be able to create or manage a portfolio successfully until you are aware of the external factors which elevate or depress share prices. You cannot create a portfolio in isolation from the economy, the political climate, or market sentiment and have any hope of success. It helps to think laterally. As a very simple example, if you read about the possibility of a takeover bid arriving for the ABC company, your immediate concern should be to inspect the share prices of the other companies in the same sector to see whether any of them might be considered as a potential victim, and thus whether its share price too may go up if it looks as though the market has overlooked it. With a little practice you will be able to get a 'nose' for a bargain and you will find that it can be very exhilarating as well as profitable. You will get a great deal of satisfaction from beating the market. The opportunity does not occur every day, but if you persevere and commit yourself only when you are satisfied that you have done all your checks and analyses and you are happy with the share, you should be able to congratulate yourself.

The second part is dedicated to showing how important it is to set your strategic targets, so that they are reasonable and achievable within the current market conditions. There is no point in trying to make the car maintain an average speed of 50 miles an hour across country when what you have got to drive is an ancient vehicle.

People often wring their hands, metaphorically, when they have picked their investments in much the same was as many amateurs have a bet on the Derby – 'liked the name' or 'the jockey looks nice'!

Investing is a business, and to be successful you have to work at it. The need for revision is constant. It is rather like gardening. When you see a really well laid out garden, you know that there has been a great deal of planning before a single plant is sown. Not only that, but every plant is looked at daily, pruned where necessary, fed with all sorts of nutrients including tender loving care. Even when all this is being done, there is no control over the weather, and a sudden and totally unexpected frost in the middle of the summer can damage or kill the prize blooms. People spend more time and effort on their gardens than they do on making their capital grow or taking steps to protect it against disasters. When all is said and done, you can't use flowers to pay the bills.

> .... **With a little practice you will be able to get a 'nose' for a bargain.** ...

The best way to regard the undertaking is to put yourself in the frame of mind where you have to advise someone else on investing their money. What questions would you ask them in order to establish targets for income or growth, or both?

Remember that if you are actually doing this for a living, you run the risk of being sued if your advice proves to be bad because you had not done your research properly. As you can imagine, such a risk concentrates the mind wonderfully.

Successful planning and execution of investment requires a knowledge of the tools, obviously, and **common sense.**

This book teaches you about the tools. It also shows you where to get most of the information you need to make as best an evaluation as you can including risk assessment. The rest is up to you to keep yourself fully informed about the progress, whether good or bad, of each share in your portfolio. Do not be squeamish about cutting out those which do not perform, cut them out ruthlessly. There is a saying in the market when a share goes wrong – 'the first cut is the cheapest cut'.

There are three things which make a share go up in price, and they are 'earnings, earnings and earnings'. Earnings grow because of good management. Companies are run by people, and the only way to judge whether the management is successful in their market is their track record. No market is static whether it be a stock market or a street market. Good management is only going to continue to be successful if it is able to anticipate the subtle changes which are constantly taking place and adapt its products and practices to gain the most advantage at all times.

If you stick to the large international and well-capitalised companies and do your analyses of ROCE and EPS, allowing for inflation, you will be able to sleep at night. Such shares may be considered boring and pedestrian, but generally they will look after you and, in the longer term, they will out perform the more risky ones.

It is generally considered in the stockbroking fraternity that if you can get three right out of five, you are doing fairly well. I hope that you will improve on that ratio. So now you are on your own. You should be able to create an interesting portfolio which you can manage happily without feeling dominated by your investment or the market. You should feel completely in control of your 'garden' and I wish you the best of luck.

Appendix 1
Registrars

AXA Equity & Law International Fund Managers Ltd
Victory House, Prospect Hill, Douglas, Isle of Man
Telephone: 01624 677877 Fax: 01624 672700

Abacus Asset Management Ltd
La Motte Chambers, St Helier, Jersey JE1 1BJ Channel Islands

Allied Dunbar International Fund Managers Ltd
Allied Dunbar International Centre, Lord Street, Douglas, Isle of Man
Telephone: 01624 661551 Fax: 01624 662183

Bank Leumi (UK) plc
Balfour House, 390-398 High Road, Ilford, Essex IG1 1NQ England
Telephone: 0181 478 8241 Fax: 0181 478 2876

Bank of England
Chief Registrar, Southgate House, Southgate Street, Gloucester GL1 1UW
England
Telephone: 01452 398080/398054

Bank of Ireland
Registration Department, Donegal House, 7 Donegal Square North, Belfast BT1
5LU Northern Ireland
Telephone: 01232 321092 Fax: 01232 313134

Bank of Scotland
Registrar Department. Apex House, 9 Haddington Place, Edinburgh EH7 4AL
Scotland
Telephone: 0131 243 5317 Fax: 0131 243 5327

Bermuda International Securities (UK) Ltd
3rd Floor, Austin Friars House, 2–6 Austin Friars, London EC2N 2HE England
Telephone: 0171 296 4000 Fax: 0171 867 0037

Birmingham Registrars Ltd
Charterhouse, 165 Newhall Street, Birmingham B3 1SW England
Telephone: 0121 200 3077 Fax: 0121 200 2454

C.1. Registrars Ltd
PO Box 30, Victoria Street, Luton, Bedfordshire LU1 2PZ England
Telephone: 01582 405333 Fax: 01582 458908

CMG Computer Management Group (UK) Ltd
CMG Share Registration Division, Astra Centre, Edinburgh Way, Harlow, Essex
CM20 2BE England
Telephone: 01279 444488 Fax: 01279 419616/412387

Canadian Pacific Ltd
62–65 Trafalgar Square, London WC2N 5DY, England
Tel: 0171 798 9898 Fax: 0171 925 2796

Capital House Administrators (C.I.) Ltd
PO Box 348, Capital House Building, Bath Street St Helier, Jersey JE4 8XL
Channel Islands
Telephone: 01534 285700 Fax: 01534 285754

Capital House Fund Managers (C.I.) Ltd
Capital House Building, Bath Street, St Helier, Jersey JE2 4ST Channel Islands
Telephone: 01534 285700

Carey Langlois & Co
PO Box 98, 7 New Street, St Peter Port, Guernsey GY1 4BZ Channel Islands
Telephone: 01481 727272 Fax: 01481 711052

Central Registration Ltd
1 Redcliffe Street, Bristol BS1 6NT England
Telephone: 0117 929 3296 Fax: 0117 925 2187

Chase Bank & Trust Company (C.I.) Ltd
PO Box 289, Chase House, Grenville Street, St Helier, Jersey JE4 8TH Channel
Islands
Telephone: 01534 626262

Citibank (Channel Islands) Ltd
PO Box 104, 38 Esplanade, St Helier, Jersey JE4 8QB Channel Islands
Telephone: 01534 608000 Fax: 01534 608296

Clydesdale Bank plc
Corporate Investment Services, PO Box 124, 150 Buchanan Street, Glasgow G1
2JS, Scotland
Telephone: 0141 223 4093/4094 Fax: 0141 223 2062

Cocke, Vellacott & Hill
29 Weymouth Street, London W1N 3FJ, England
Telephone: 0171 629 2936 Fax: 0171 629 9273

Connaught St Michaels Ltd
PO Box 30, Victoria Street, Luton, Bedfordshire LU1 2PZ England
Telephone: 01582 405333 Fax: 01582 458908

EBC Fund Managers (Jersey) Ltd
PO Box 556, EBC House, 1–3 Seale Street, St Helier, Jersey JE4 8XL Channel
Islands
Telephone: 01534 36331 Fax: 01534 39495

Ernst & Young Fund Administrators Ltd
PO Box 621, Le Gallais Chambers, 54 Bath Street, St Helier, Jersey JE4 8YD
Channel Islands
Telephone: 01534 501000

Exchange Registrars Ltd
18 Park Place, Cardiff CF1 3PD Wales
Telephone: 01222 371210 Fax: 01222 388455

Fidelity International (C.l.) Ltd
40 Esplanade, St Helier, Jersey, Channel Islands
Telephone: 01534 71696

Gartmore Fund Managers International Ltd
45 La Motte Street, St Helier, Jersey, Channel Islands
Telephone: 01534 27301 Fax: 01534 32848

Geoghegan Co CA
6 St Colme Street, Edinburgh EH3 6AD Scotland
Telephone: 0131 225 4681 Fax: 0131 220 1132

Grant Thornton
1 Stanley Street, Liverpool L1 6AD England
Telephone: 0151 227 4211 Fax: 0151 236 3429

Grooved Secretaries Ltd
34 Southborough Road, Bickley, Bromley, Kent BR1 2EB England
Telephone: 0181 857 9335 Fax: 0181 851 7897

Guernsey International Fund Managers Ltd
PO Box 255, Barfield House, St Julian's Avenue, St Peter Port, Guernsey GY1 3QL
Channel Islands
Telephone: 01481 710651 Fax: 01481 710285

Guinness Flight Fund Managers (Guernsey) Ltd
Guinness Flight House, PO Box 250, La Plaiderie, St Peter Port. Guernsey GY1
3QH Channel Islands
Telephone: 01481 710404 Fax: 01481 712065

Hambros Fund Managers (Channel Islands) Ltd
PO Box 255, Barfield House, St Julian's Avenue, St Peter Port, Guernsey GU1 3QL
Channel Islands
Telephone: 01481 715454 Fax: 01481 715299

Harford Registrars
Harford House, 101-103 Great Portland Street, London W1N 6BH England
Telephone: 0171 637 9523/4/5 Fax: 0171 580 7689

Hereward Philips
Prospect House, 2 Athenaeum Road, Whetstone, London N20 9AE England
Telephone: 0181 446 4371 Fax: 0181 446 7606

Hill Samuel Fund Managers (Jersey) Ltd
PO Box 63, 7 Bond Street, St Helier, Jersey JE4 8PH Channel Islands
Telephone: 01534 604814 Fax: 01534 75139

I.A.H. McPake SSC
66 Queen Street, Edinburgh EH2 4NE Scotland
Telephone: 0131 226 4771 Fax: 0131 225 3676

IBI Managers (l.O.M.) Ltd
Christian Road, Douglas, Isle of Man
Telephone: 01624 622676 Telex: 628270

INVESCO International Ltd
INVESCO House, PO Box 271, Grenville Street, St Helier, Jersey JE4 8TD Channel
Islands
Telephone: 01534 73114 Fax: 01534 73174

Ian Brockie FCIS
33 Pinkhill, Edinburgh EH12 7BA Scotland
Telephone: 0131 337 7373 Fax: 0131 316 4420

Independent Registrars Group Ltd
Balfour House, 390-398 High Road, llford, Essex IG1 1NQ
England
Telephone: 0181 478 8241 Fax: 0181 478 7717

Independent Registrars Group Ltd
Broseley House, Newlands Drive, Witham, Essex CM8 2UL England
Telephone: 01376 515755 Fax: 01376 510609

John Lewis plc
171 Victoria Street, London SWIE 5NN England
Telephone: 0171 828 1000 Fax: 0171 828 6679

Johnson Fry Secretaries Ltd
20 Regent Street, London SWIY 4PZ England
Telephone: 0171 321 0220 Fax: 0171 437 4844

Jupiter Tyndall (Jersey) Ltd
PO Box 679, 7-11 Britannia Place, Bath Street, St Helier, Jersey JE4 8US Channel
Islands
Telephone: 01534 37331 Fax: 01534 504575

KPMG Peat Marwick
Festival Way, Hanley, Stoke-on-Trent, Staffordshire STI 5TA England
Telephone: 01782 216000 Fax: 01782 216050

Kidsons Impey
Breckenridge House, 274 Sauchiehall Street, Glasgow G2 3EH Scotland
Telephone: 0141 307 5000 Fax: 0141 307 5005

Kleinwort Benson (Guernsey) Fund Services Ltd
PO Box 44, The Grange, St Peter Port, Guernsey GY1 3BG Channel Islands
Telephone: 01481 727111 Fax: 01481 728317

Kleinwort Benson (Jersey) Ltd
PO Box 76, Wests Centre, St Helier, Jersey JE4 8PQ Channel Islands
Telephone: 01534 613000

Lambert Storey
John Dalton House, 121 Deansgate, Manchester M3 2AB England
Telephone: 0161 832 5696 Fax: 0161 834 5689

Lazard Fund Managers (Channel Islands) Ltd
Lazard House, 1 St Julian's Avenue, St Peter Port, Guernsey, Channel Islands
Telephone: 01481 710461 Fax: 01481 711438

Ledingham Chalmers
I Golden Square, Aberdeen AB9 1HA Scotland
Telephone: 01224 647344

Lloyds Bank Fund Managers (Guernsey) Ltd
Sarnia House, Le Truchot, St Peter Port, Guernsey, Channel Islands
Telephone: 01481 724983 Fax: 01481 727344

Lloyds Bank International (Jersey) Ltd
Commercial House, Commercial Street, St Helier, Jersey JE4 8WZ Channel
Islands
Telephone: 01534 22271 Fax: 01534 22280

Lloyds Bank Registrars
54 Pershore Road South, Kings Norton, Birmingham B30 3ER England
Telephone: 0121 433 8000 Fax: 0121 433 8030

Lloyds Bank Registrars
Antholin House, 71 Queen Street, London EC4N 1SL England
Telephone: 0171 248 9822

Lloyds Bank Registrars
The Causeway, Worthing, West Sussex BN99 6DA England
Telephone: 01903 502541 Fax: 01903 702481

London Pacific Secretaries Ltd
Minden House, 6 Minden Place, St Helier, Jersey, Channel Islands
Telephone: 01534 38578

M & G Financial Services Ltd
M & G House, Victoria Road, Chelmsford CM1 1FB England
Telephone: 01245 390390 Fax: 01245 267789

M.P. Evans (UK) Ltd
3 Clanricarde Gardens, Tunbridge Wells, Kent TN1 1HQ England
Telephone: 01892 516333 Fax: 01892 518639

MSP Secretaries Ltd
112 West Street, Farnham, Surrey GU9 7HH England
Telephone: 01252 733683 Fax: 01252 717233

MacIntyre & Co
28 Ely Place, London EC1N 6RL England
Telephone: 0171 242 0242 Fax: 0171 405 4786

Matrix-Data Ltd
Gossard House, 7-8 Savile Row, London W1X 1AF England
Telephone: 0171 734 8334

Merrill Lynch International Capital Management (Guernsey) Ltd
Barfield House, St Julian's Avenue, St Peter Port, Guernsey GY1 3QL Channel
Islands
Telephone: 01481 710651 Fax: 01481 710285

Midland Bank Fund Managers (Jersey) Ltd
28/34 Hill Street, St Helier, Jersey JE4 8NR Channel Islands
Telephone: 01534 606335 Fax: 01534 606356

Mr I.C. Parkinson
ICI Registrar's Department, PO Box 251, Wexham Road, Slough SL2 5DP
England
Telephone: 01753 877008 Fax: 01753 512226

Neville Registrars Ltd
Neville House, 18 Laurel Lane, Halesowen, West Midlands, B63 3DA England
Telephone: 0121 585 1131 Fax: 0121 585 1132

Northern Registrars Ltd
Northern House, Penistone Road, Fenay Bridge, Huddersfield, West Yorkshire
HD8 0LA England
Telephone: 01484 606664 Fax: 01484 608764

Pannell Kerr Forster
52 Mount Pleasant, Liverpool L3 5UN England
Telephone: 0151 708 8232 Fax: 0151 708 8169

Price Waterhouse
Royston House, 34 Upper Queen Street, Belfast BT1 6HG Northern Ireland
Telephone: 01232 244001 Fax: 01232 246597

Prudential Registrars Ltd
142 Holborn Bars, London EC1N 2NH England
Telephone: 0171 405 9222

R & H Fund Services (Isle of Man) Ltd
19/21 Circular Road, Douglas IM1 1AF Isle of Man
Telephone: 01624 629420 Fax: 01624 627515

R & H Fund Services (Jersey) Ltd
Ordnance House, 31 Pier Road, St Helier, Jersey, Channel Islands
Telephone: 01534 75141

R & H Registrars (Jersey) Ltd
Ordnance House, 31 Pier Road, St Helier, Jersey JE4 8PZ Channel Islands
Telephone: 01534 75141 Fax: 01534 32876

Richards & Co
11 Marsh Street, Bristol BS1 4AL England
Telephone: 0117 9294142 Fax: 0117 9211278

Rothschild Asset Management (C.l.) Ltd
PO Box 242, St Peter Port House, Sausmarez Street, St Peter Port, Guernsey GY1
3PH Channel Islands
Telephone: 01481 713713 Fax: 01481 723965

Royal Bank of Canada Offshore Fund Managers Ltd
PO Box 246, Canada Court, Upland Road, St Peter Port, Guernsey, Channel
Islands
Telephone: 01481 723021 Fax: 01481 723524

Royal Trust Asset Management (C.I.) Ltd
PO Box 194, 19-21 Broad Street, St Helier, Jersey JE4 8RR Channel Islands
Telephone: 01534 27441 Fax: 01534 24760

Save & Prosper Registrars Ltd
Administration Centre, Sovereign House, 16-22 Western Road, Romford, Essex
RM1 3LB England
Telephone: 01708 766966

Schroder Management Services (Jersey) Ltd
PO Box 195, Waterloo House, Don Street, St Helier, Jersey JE4 8RS Channel Islands
Telephone: 01534 284200

Security Exchange Ltd
James Yard, 480 Larkshall Road, London E4 9UA England
Telephone: 0181 504 3630 Fax: 0181 559 1086

St Helier Trust Co Ltd
PO Box 393, 7–11 Britannia Place, Bath Street, St Helier, Jersey, Channel Islands
Telephone: 01534 504504 Fax: 01534 504575/76/77

Standard Bank Fund Management (Jersey) Ltd
PO Box 583, One Waverley Place, St Helier, Jersey JE4 8XR Channel Islands
Telephone: 01534 67557 Fax: 01534 89642

Stanley Wilkinson & Co
288 Church Street, Blackpool FY1 3QA England
Telephone: 01253 22324

TSB Fund Managers (Channel Islands) Ltd
PO Box 538, 25 New Street, St Helier, Jersey JE4 8XE Channel Islands
Telephone: 01534 503002 Fax: 01534 617082

Taylor, Lauder & Gemmill
4th Floor, Savoy House, 140 Sauchiehall Street, Glasgow G2 3DH Scotland
Telephone: 0141 333 0034 Fax: 0141 353 2158

The Bank of Bermuda (Guernsey) Ltd
PO Box 208, Bermuda House, St Julian's Avenue, St Peter Port, Guernsey GY1 3NF Channel Islands
Telephone: 01481 726268 Fax: 01481 726275

The Chase Manhattan Bank NA
Woolgate House, Coleman Street, London EC2P 2HD England
Telephone: 0171 962 5000 Fax: 0171 962 5480

The R-M Trust Co
Balfour House, 390 High Street, Ilford, Essex IG1 1NQ England
Telephone: 0181 478 1888 Fax: 0181 478 7717

The Royal Bank of Canada Trust (Jersey) Ltd
PO Box 194,19–21 Broad Street, St Helier, Jersey, Channel Islands
Telephone: 01534 27441

The Royal Bank of Scotland (I.O.M.) Ltd
Victory House. Prospect Hill. Douglas IM99 1NJ Isle of Man
Telephone: 01624 629111 Fax: 01624 612769

The Royal Bank of Scotland plc
Registrar's Department. 15 Featherstone Street, London EC1Y 8QS England
Telephone: 0171 714 2000

The Royal Bank of Scotland plc
Registrars Department, PO Box 435, Owen House, 8 Bankhead Crossway North,
Edinburgh EH11 4BR Scotland
Telephone: 0131 556 8555 Fax: 0131 442 4924

The Royal Bank of Scotland plc
Registrars Department, PO Box 82, Caxton House, Redcliffe Way, Bristol BS99
7NH England
Telephone: 0117 930 6600 Fax: 0117 930 6509

Unibank Fund Managers (I.O.M.) Ltd
19-21 Circular Road, Douglas IM1 1AF Isle of Man
Telephone: 01624 629420 Fax: 01624 627515

Warburg Asset Management Jersey Ltd
PO Box 190, Forum House, Grenville Street, St Helier, Jersey JE4 8RL Channel
Islands
Telephone: 01534 600600 Fax: 01534 600687/88/89

White Rose Registrars Ltd
Portland House, 11-13 Station Road, Kettering, Northamptonshire NN15 7HH
England
Telephone: 01536 517548 Fax: 01536 411013

Yamaichi Capital Management (Guernsey) Ltd
22 Smith Street, St Peter Port, Guernsey, Channel Islands
Telephone: 01481 717717 Fax: 01481 717860

Appendix 2

Firms of stockbrokers offering execution-only service

ALLIED PROVINCIAL
155, St Vincent Street, Glasgow G2 5NN
Telephone: 0141 204 1886

Aberdeen
25 Albyn Place, Aberdeen AB1 1YL
Telephone: 01224 589345

Birmingham
Beaufort House, 94–96 Newhall Street, Birmingham B3 1PE
Telephone: 0121 609 4000

Bristol
40 Queen Square, Bristol BS1 4DU
Telephone: 01272 293901

Cardiff
Westgate House, Womanby Street, Cardiff CF1 2UD
Telephone: 01222 397672

Carlisle
1 Cecil Street, Carlisle CA1 1NL
Telephone: 01228 21200

Colwyn Bay
15 Wynnstay Bay, Colwyn Bay LL29 8NN
Telephone: 01492 530354

Dundee
41 North Lindsey Street, Dundee DD1 1PW
Telephone: 01382 21081

Edinburgh
12 Melville Crescent, Edinburgh EH3 7LU
Telephone: 0131 226 4466

Exeter
Broadwalk House, Southernhay West, Exeter EX1 1TS
Telephone: 01392 410277

Hereford
35 Bridge Street, Hereford HR4 9DG
Telephone: 01432 264646

Hull
7 Marina Court, Castle Street, Hull HU1 1TJ
Telephone: 01482 226293

London
51/55 Gresham Street, London EC2V 7EH
Telephone: 0171 606 1777

Lymington
98 High Street, Lymington S041 9AP
Telephone: 01590 674288

Manchester
PO Box 419
St. James's Court, 30 Brown Street, Manchester M60 2JE
Telephone: 061 832 4812

Middlesbrough
City House, 206–208 Marton Road, Middlesbrough TS4 2JE
Telephone: 01642 249211

Newcastle
Central Exchange Buildings
128 Grainger Street, Newcastle NE1 5AF
Telephone: 0191 232 6695

Nottingham
Norwich Union House, South Parade, Nottingham NG1 2LN
Telephone: 0115 9476772

Peterborough
Trinity Court, Trinity Street, Peterborough PE1 1DA
Telephone: 01733 555131

Plymouth
St Catherine's House, Notte Street, Plymouth PL1 2TW
Telephone: 01752 220971

Ramsey (IOM)
PO Chambers
2 Court Row, Isle of Man IM99 4BD
Telephone: 01624 812925

Redruth
27a Fore Street, Redruth TR15 2BQ
Telephone: 01209 214488

Torquay
Provincial House, 1 Strand, Torquay TQ1 2RH
Telephone: 01803 297337

ARNOLD, STANSBY & Co.
Dennis House, Marsden Street, Manchester M2 3JJ
Telephone: 0161 832 8554 Fax: 0161 834 7710

ASTAIRE & PARTNERS
40 Queen Street, London EC4R 1DD
Telephone: 0171 332 2600 Fax: 0171 332 2626

Cheltenham
115 Promenade, Cheltenham, Glos GL50 1NW
Telephone: 01242 251000 Fax: 0242 251551

M.D.BARNARD & Co. LIMITED
61 Broadway, Stratford, London El5 4BQ
Telephone: 0181 534 9090

BARCLAYS STOCKBROKERS LIMITED
2nd Floor, 21 St Thomas Street, London SE1 9RY

Glasgow
The Guild Hall
57 Queen Street, Glasgow G1 3DT

BARRATT & COOKE
5 Opie Street, Norwich, Norfolk NR1 3DW
Telephone: 01603 624236

Mansfield
The First Floor, 8 Queen Street, Mansfield, Nottingham NG18 1JN
Telephone: 0115 923596

BLANKSTONE SINGTON LIMITED
91 Duke Street, Liverpool L1 5AA
Telephone: 0151 707 1707 Fax: 051 707 1247

JAMES BREARLEY& SONS
56–60 Caunce Street, Blackpool FY1 3DQ
Telephone: 01253 21474

Burnley
5 Grimshaw Street, Burnley,
Lancashire, BB11 2AX
Telephone: 01282 422042

Carlisle
9 Devonshire Street, Carlisle, Cumbria CA3 8LG
Telephone: 01228 20299

Kendal
1 Beacon Buildings, Stramongate, Kendal, Cumbria LA9 4BH
Telephone: 01539 733979

Southport
47 Hoghton Street, Southport, Merseyside PR9 0PG
Telephone: 01704 501511
152A Lord Street, Southport, Merseyside PR9 0QH
Telephone: 01704 532282

Stockport
467 Buxton Road, Great Moor, Stockport SK2 7HE
Telephone: 0161 487 4191

BREWIN DOLPHIN BELL LAWRIE LIMITED

Brewin Dolphin & Co.
5 Giltspur Street, London EC1A 9BD
Telephone: 0171 248 4400 Fax: 0171 236 2034

Jersey
Burrard House, Don Street, St Helier, Jersey JE2 4WS
Telephone: 01534 27391 Fax: 01534 31910

Redhill
Seloduct House, 30 Station Road, Redhill, Surrey RH1 1NH
Telephone: 01737 778810 Fax: 01737 778862

Manchester
Central Buildings,11 Peter Street, Manchester M2 4QR
Telephone: 0161 833 0961 Fax: 0161 839 1651

Eastbourne
49 Gildredge Road, Eastbourne, East Sussex BN21 4RY
Telephone: 01323 411585 Fax: 01323 411525

Swindon
17 Wood Street, Old Town, Swindon, Wiltshire SN1 4AN
Telephone: 01793 616001 Fax: 0793 481900

Nottingham
Ellington, Tattershall Drive, The Park, Nottingham NG7 1AD
Telephone: 0115 9414344

BELL LAWRIE WHITE & CO
7 Drumsheugh Gardens, Edinburgh EH3 7QH
Telephone: 0131 225 2566 Fax: 0131 225 3134

Cardiff
Sutherland House, Castlebridge, Cowbridge Road East, Cardiff CF1 9AB
Telephone: 01222 340100 Fax: 01222 344999

Cheltenham
Imperial House, Lypiatt Road, Cheltenham GL50 2QJ
Telephone: 01242 577677 Fax: 0242 520030

Dumfries
52 Buccleuch Street, Dumfries DG1 2AH
Telephone: 01387 52361 Fax: 01387 57288

SUBSIDIARY OFFICES:
Aberdeen
20 Rubislaw Terrace, Aberdeen AB1 1XE
Telephone: 01224 633700 Fax: 01224 646659

Stocktrade
Norloch House, Kings Stables Road, Edinburgh EH1 2EU
Telephone: 0131 529 0101 Fax: 0131 220 6047

BROADBRIDGE
Wellington Plaza, 31 Wellington Street, Leeds LS1 4DL
Telephone: 0113 2422211 Fax: 0113 2420134

Halifax
12–14 Fountain Street, Halifax HX1 1LX
Telephone: 01422 367707/8 Fax: 01422 348362

Wakefield
Rishworth House, 8a Rishworth Street, Wakefield WF1 3BY
Telephone: 01924 372601
0924 371594 Fax: 0924 361367

BROWN SHIPLEY STOCKBROKING LIMITED
Reading
30–31 Friar Street, Reading RG1 1AH
Telephone: 01734 595511

London
10 Foster Lane, London EC2V 6HH
Telephone: 0171 726 4059

Bexhill-on-Sea
65 Devonshire Road, Bexhill-on-Sea, East Sussex TN40 1AJ
Telephone: 01424 219111

Bristol
Stock Exchange Building, 34 St Nicholas Street, Bristol BS1 1TW
Telephone: 0117 9276521

Chichester
60a North Street, Chichester PO19 1NB
Telephone: 01243 786472

Cirencester
Ewbank House, Dyer Street, Cirencester GL7 2PP
Telephone: 01285 659671

Exeter
Norwich Union House, 12 Bedford Street, Exeter EX1 1LG
Telephone: 01392 423423

Gloucester
2 Beaufort Building, Spa Road, Gloucester GL1 1XB
Telephone: 01452 525444

Oxford
4 King Edward Street, Oxford, Oxon OX1 4HJ
Telephone: 01865 243581

BWD RENSBURG
Woodsome House, Woodsome Park, Fenay Bridge, Huddersfield HD8 OJG
Telephone: 01484 608066 Fax: 01484 604099

Belfast
St Georges' House, 99–101 High Street, Belfast BT1 2AH
Telephone: 01232 321002 Fax: 01232 244852

Birmingham
City Plaza, Temple Row, Birmingham B2 5AB
Telephone: 0121 643 0330 Fax: 0121 643 4999

Bradford
Broadway House, 9 Bank Street, Bradford BD1 1HJ
Telephone: 01274 729406 Fax: 01274 729406 (extension 42)

Glasgow
De Quincey House, 48 West Regent Street, Glasgow G2 2RB
Telephone: 0141 333 9323 Fax: 0141 332 9920

Leeds
3 Park Court, Park Cross Street, Leeds LS1 2QH
Telephone: 0113 2434631 Fax: 0113 2468500

Liverpool
100 Old Hall Street, Liverpool L3 9AB
Telephone: 0151 227 2030 Fax: 0151 227 2444

Manchester
18 Ralli Courts, Manchester M3 5FT
Telephone: 0161 832 6868 Fax: 0161 832 1233

Sheffield
Wharncliffe House, Bank Street, Sheffield S1 2DS
Telephone: 01742 722292 Fax: 01742 701503

CAMPBELL O'CONNOR & CO.
8 Cope Street, Dublin 2
Telephone: 010 353 1 6771773 Fax: 010 353 1 6791969

CAVE & SONS LIMITED
PO Box 32, 9–11 Hazelwood Road, Northampton NN1 1LQ
Telephone: 01604 21421 Fax: 0604 234335

Ferndown
3 Princes Court, Princes Road, Ferndown, Dorset BH22 9JG
Telephone: 01202 861534

Banbury
PO Box 167, Banbury, Oxon OX15 5BN
Telephone: 01608 85688

CAWOOD, SMITHIE & CO
22 East Parade, Harrogate, North Yorkshire HG1 5LT
Telephone: 01423 530035

Hartlepool
90 York Road, Hartlepool, Cleveland TS26 9DQ
Telephone: 01429 272231

Middlesbrough
48a High Street, Stokesly, Middlesbrough, Cleveland TS9 5AX
Telephone: 01642 712771

CENTRAL STOCKBROKERS LIMITED
Lloyds House, Albert Square, Manchester M60 2EN
Telephone: 0161 832 2924 Fax: 0161 832 0296

Leigh-on-Sea
120 Rectory Gove, Leigh-on-Sea, Essex SS9 2HL
Telephone: 01702 470870 Fax: 01702 470817

CHAMBERS & REMINGTON LIMITED
Canterbury House, 85 Newhall Street, Birmingham B3 1LS
Telephone: 0121 236 2577

CHARLES STANLEY & CO LIMITED
25 Luke Street, London EC2A 4AR
Telephone: 0171 739 8200 Fax: 0171 739 7798

Bournemouth
2 Westover Road, Bournemouth, Dorset BH1 2BY
Telephone: 01202 317788 Fax: 01202 317754

Cambridge
25 City Road, Cambridge CB1 1DP
Telephone: 01223 316726 Fax: 0223 321215

Ipswich
16 Northgate Street, Ipswich, Suffolk IP1 3DB
Telephone: 01473 210264 Fax: 01473 225735

Newbury
58a Northbrook Street, Newbury, Berkshire RG13 1AN
Telephone: 01635 551331 Fax: 0635 44720

Norwich
24 Castle Meadow, Norwich NR1 3DH
Telephone: 01603 665990 Fax: 01603 610560

CHRISTOWS LIMITED
The Lodge, 10a Southernhay West, Exeter EX1 IJG
Telephone: 01392 210510 Fax: 01392 426176

Dorchester
4 Trinity Street, Dorchester, Dorset DT1 1TT
Telephone: 01305 268979 Fax: 01305 251086

Bournemouth
Clifton, St Peter's Road, Bournemouth BH1 2LT
Telephone: 01202 299344 Fax: 01202 293178

CITY & INTERNATIONAL SECURITIES LIMITED
11 Hill Street, Douglas, Isle of Man
Telephone: 01624 627134 Fax: 01624 624903

CLIFTON STOCKBROKERS LIMITED
Clifton House, 5–7 Park Hill Road, Torquay TQ1 2AN
Telephone: 01803 292441 Fax: 01803 292615

Bristol
Wessex House, 25 Oakfield Road, Bristol BS8 2AT
Telephone: 0117 9467557 Fax: 0117 9466348

London
150 Minories, London EC3N 1LS
Telephone: 0171 816 0606 Fax: 0171 264 2123

DAVY STOCKBROKERS
Davy House, 49 Dawson Street, Dublin 2
Telephone: 010 353 1 679 7788 Fax: 010 353 1 679 6340

DEALWISE
Sturge Court, 120 Wellington Street, Leeds LS1 4LT
Telephone: 0113 234 5555

DENNIS MURPHY CAMPBELL
6 Broad Street Place, London EC2M 7DA
Telephone: 0171 638 0033 Fax: 0171 638 1318

DERIVATIVE SECURITIES LIMITED
43 Eagle Street, London WC1R 4AP
Telephone: 0171 404 2888 Fax: 0171 404 2920

DUNBAR BOYLE & KINGSLEY LIMITED
Gun House, 1/4 Artillery Passage, London E1 7LJ
Telephone: 071 247 8898 Fax: 071 377 8886

DURLACHER & CO plc
First floor, 10 Throgmorton Avenue, London EC2N 2DL
Telephone: 0171 628 4306 Fax: 0171 638 8848

Hove
32 Church Road, Hove, East Sussx BN3 2FF
Telephone: 01273 205217 Fax: 01273 726782

Rotherham
16 Percy Street, Rotherham, South Yorkshire S65 1ED
Telephone: 01709 368490 Fax: 01709 370037

ELECTRONIC SHARE INFORMATION LIMITED (ESI)
Mount Pleasant House, 2 Mount Pleasant, Huntingdon Road, Cambridge CB3 0RN
Telephone: 01223 566926 Fax: 01223 506288

ELLIS & PARTNERS LIMITED
Talisman House, 16 The Courtyard, East Park, Crawley RH10 6AS
Telephone: 01293 517744 Fax: 01293 521093

FAIRMOUNT STOCKBROKERS LIMITED
Huntingdon House, Princess Street, Bolton, Greater Manchester BL1 1EJ
Telephone: 01204 362233 Fax: 01204 362525

FARLEY & THOMPSON
Pine Grange, Bath Road, Bournemouth BH1 2NU
Telephone: 01202 556277

FIDELITY BROKERAGE SERVICES LIMITED
Kingswood Place, Tadworth, Surrey KT20 6RB
Telephone: 01800 222 190

J.M.FINN & CO
Salisbury House, London Wall, London EC2M 5TA
Telephone: 0171 628 9688 Fax: 071 628 7314

GALL & EKE LIMITED
Charlotte House, 10 Charlotte Street, Manchester MI 4FL
Telephone: 0161 228 2511 Fax: 0161 228 2237

GERRARD VIVIAN GRAY LIMITED
Burne House, 88 High Holborn, London WC1V 6LS
Telephone: 0171 831 8883

Ipswich
25 Lower Brook Street, Ipswich, Suffolk IP4 1AQ
Telephone: 01473 225055

Colchester
73 East Hill, Colchester, Essex CO1 2QW
Telephone: 01206 869992

SOUTHARD GILBY, MCNISH & CO
65 London Wall, London EC2M 5TU
Telephone: 0171 638 6761 Fax: 0171 628 3064

Canterbury
62 Burgate, Canterbury, Kent CT1 2HJ
Telephone: 01227 456085/6

GOODBODY STOCKBROKERS
122 Pembroke Road, Dublin 4
Telephone: 010 353 1 667 0400 Fax: 010 353 1 667 0230

GREIG, MIDDLETON & CO LIMITED
66 Wilson Street, London EC2A 2BL
Telephone: 0171 247 0007

Bristol
The Stock Exchange, St Nicholas Street, Bristol BS1 1TH
Telephone: 0117 9264013

Cambridge
Francis House, 112 Hills Road, Cambridge CB2 1PH
Telephone: 01223 327657

Glasgow
Pacific House, 70 Wellington Street, Glasgow G2 6UD
Telephone: 0141 221 8103

Guildford
York House, 38/42 Chertsey Street, Guildford GU1 4HD
Telephone: 04183 300585

Norwich
De Vere House, 90 St Faith's Lane, Norwich NR1 1NE
Telephone: 01603 760226

Truro
Eagle Star House, Lemon Street, Truro TR1 2PX
Telephone: 01872 222485

York
23 High Petergate, York YO1 2HS
Telephone: 01904 647911

GREIG, MIDDLETON & CO (CI) LIMITED
Guernsey
2nd Floor, TSB Weighbridge Premises, Le Truchot, St Peter Port, Guernsey
Telephone: 01481 726511 Fax: 01481 711483

Jersey
19 Seaton Place, St Helier, Jersey JE2 3QL
Telephone: 01534 280068 Fax: 01534 280070

HARGREAVE (MARSDEN W.) HALE & CO
PO Box No 7, 8–10 Springfield Road, Blackpool FY1 1 QN
Telephone: 01253 21575 Fax: 01253 293511

Bangor
204 High Street, Bangor, Gwynedd LL57 1NY
Telephone: 01248 353242

Carlisle
24 Spencer Street, Carlisle CA1 1BG
Telephone: 01228 818110

London
Brookfield House, 44 Davies Street, London W1Y 1LD
Telephone: 0171 409 0840

St Anne's-on-Sea
Royal Bank of Scotland Chambers, St Anne's-on-Sea, FY8 1RW
Telephone: 01253 722166

Isle of Man
The Elms, Westmead, Glen Vine, Isle of Man
Telephone: 01624 852330

HARGREAVES LANSDOWN STOCKBROKERS LIMITED
Embassy House, Queens Avenue, Clifton, Bristol BS8 1SB
Telephone: 0117 9741309 Fax: 0117 9739902

HEDLEY & CO
Springwell House, 2 Shear Bank Road, Blackpool BB1 8AP
Telephone: 01254 699333 Fax: 01254 692847

HITCHENS, HARRISON & CO plc
Bell Court House, 11 Blomfield Street, London EC2M 1LB
Telephone: 0171 588 5171

HILL OSBORNE & CO
Royal Insurance Building, Silver Street, Lincoln LN2 1DU
Telephone: 01522 513838 Fax: 01522 513965

Bradford
Auburn House, 8 Upper Piccadilly, Bradford BD1 3PA
Telephone: 01274 728866

Leicester
Permanent House, Horsefair Street, Leicester LE1 5BU
Telephone: 0116 2629185

Scarborough
17 York Place, Scarborough YO11 2NP
Telephone: 01723 372478/9

INFOTRADE
3600 Parkside, Birmingham Business Park, Birmingham B37 7YG
Telephone: 0121 717 3764 Fax: 0121 717 3650

JEFFERSON SEAL LIMITED
PO Box 534, 38 Esplanade, St Helier, Jersey JE4 8XZ Channel Islands
Telephone: 01534 25225/74725 Fax: 0534 32786

KEITH BAYLEY ROGERS & CO
Ebbark House, 93/95 Borough High Street, London SE1 1NL
Telephone: 0171 378 0657 Fax: 0171 378 1795

KILLIK & CO
45 Cadogan Street, London SW3 2QJ
Telephone: 0171 589 1577
24/25 Manchester Square, London W1M 5AP
Telephone: 0171 224 2050
2A Devonshire Hill, London NW3 1NR
Telephone: 0171 431 6314
24 Royal Exchange, Threadneedle Street, London EC3

LE MESURIER JAMES & CO LIMITED
PO Box 16, 29 Broad Street, St Helier, Jersey JE4 8NL Channel Islands
Telephone: 01534 58367 Fax: 01534 27821

LLEWELLYN GREENHALGH & CO
20 Mawdsley Street, Bolton, Lancashire BL1 1LF
Telephone: 01204 21697 Fax: 01204 380354

LLOYDS BANK STOCKBROKERS LIMITED
48 Chiswell Street, London EC1Y 4XX

MATHESON SECURITIES LIMITED
63 St Mary Axe, London EC3A 8AA
Telephone: 0171 369 4800 Fax: 0171 369 4888

MATHESON SECURITIES (CHANNEL ISLANDS) LTD
PO Box 177, 12 Esplanade, St Helier, Jersey
Telephone: 01534 76222 Fax: 01534 30185

Guernsey
PO Box 286, First Floor, Frances House, St William Place, St Peter Port Guernsey
Telephone: 01481 728950 Fax: 01481 726008

MIDLAND STOCKBROKERS
Mariner House, Pepys Street, London EC3N 4DA

NATWEST STOCKBROKERS LIMITED
55 Mansell Street, London E1 8AN
Telephone: 0171 895 5144 Fax: 0171 895 5639

NEILSON COBBOLD
Martins Building, 4 Water Street, Liverpool L2 3UF
Telephone: 0151 236 6666 Fax: 0151 236 4996

Offices at:	**Bristol**
	Telephone: 0117 291919
Bowness-on-Windermere	**Chichester**
Telephone: 01539 442141	Telephone: 0243 775373
Edinburgh	**Taunton**
Telephone: 0131 225 6630	Telephone: 01823 259711
Newport, IoW	**Tunbridge Wells**
Telephone: 01983 520922	Telephone: 01892 515156
Southampton	**Winchester**
Telephone: 01703 330130	Telephone: 01962 852362

NICHOLSON BARBER & CO
New Oxford House, Barkers Pool, Sheffield S1 1LE
Telephone: 0114 2755100 Fax: 0114 2701109

Chesterfield
91A New Square, Chesterfield, Derbyshire S40 1AH
Telephone 01246 550380 Fax: 01246 550346

Doncaster
Cameron House, 9 Thorne Road, Doncaster DN1 2HP
Telephone: 01302 320322 Fax: 01302 340300

O'BRIEN STOKES STOCKBROKERS
36 Dame Street, Dublin 2, Telephone: 010 353 1 679 8066 Fax: 010 353 1 679 1292

PILLING & CO
12 St Ann's Square, Manchester M2 7HT
Telephone: 0161 832 6581 Fax: 0161 832 0815

London
2 Bath Place, Rivington Street, London EC2A 3DR
Telephone: 0171 613 3000 Fax: 0171 613 4066

POINTON YORK SECURITIES LIMITED
The Crescent, King Street, Leicester LE1 6RX
Telephone: 0116 2547545 Fax: 01533 548529

P.H. POPE & SON
6 Pall Mall, Hanley, Stoke on Trent ST1 1EU
Telephone: 0782 202154 Fax: 0782 202018

I.A. PRITCHARD STOCKBROKERS LIMITED
1 Richmond Hill, The Square, Bournemouth BH2 6HW
Telephone: 01202 297035 Fax: 01202 555177

Bath
38 Gay Street, Bath BA1 2NT
Telephone: 0225 335616 Fax: 0225 311375

Bristol
Equity and Law House, 28 Baldwin Street, Bristol BS1 1NG
Telephone: 0117 9257337 Fax: 0117 9257671

Glasgow
20 Strathview Park, Netherlee, Glasgow G44 3LA
Telephone: 0141 637 0000 Fax: 041 637 1111

Weston-super-Mare
The Turret Rooms, Lloyds Bank Chambers, 115 High Street, BS23 1HQ
Telephone: 01934 413355 Fax: 01934 417332

PRIVATE FUND MANAGERS LIMITED
17 Sun Street, London EC2M 2PU
Telephone: 0171 247 8080 Fax: 0171 247 0774

QUILTER GOODISON CO LIMITED
Exchange House, Primrose Street, London EC2A 2NR
Telephone: 0171 600 4177

Birmingham
39 Bennetts Hill, Birmingham B2 5SZ
Telephone: 0121 212 2120

Coventry
30 Warwick Road, Coventry CV1 1EY
Telephone: 01203 632323

Guernsey
Quilter Goodison Channel Islands
PO Box 339, 10 Lefebre Street, St Peter Port
Guernsey GY1 3UL
Telephone: 01481 710541

Jersey
Quilter Goodison Channel Islands, 5 Britannia Place, Bath Street, St Helier, Jersey
JE4 8TE
Telephone: 01534 506070

Liverpool
Ashton Tod McLaren, 35 Dale Street, Liverpool L2 2HF
Telephone: 0151 236 8281

Manchester
3rd Floor, Brazenose House, Brazenose Street, Manchester M2 5BP
Telephone: 0161 832 9979

Warrington
Ashton Tod McLaren
Stanley House, 29 Stanley Street, Warrington WA1 1EZ
Telephone: 01925 572671

RAMSEY CROOKHALL & CO LIMITED
25 Athol Street, Douglas, Isle of Man
Telephone: 01624 673171/2/3/4 01624 623884/5 (dealers) Fax: 01624 6777258

RAPHAEL ZORN HEMSLEY LIMITED
10 Throgmorton Avenue, London EC2N 2DP
Telephone: 0171 628 4000 Fax: 0171 628 5986

REDMAYNE-BENTLEY
Merton House, 84 Albion Street, Leeds LS1 6AG
Telephone: 01532 436941 Fax: 01532 445516

Beverley
St Mary's Court, North Bar Within, Beverley, North Humberside HU17 8DG
Telephone: 01482 864090 Fax: 01482 871807

Bury St Edmunds
27 Churchgate Street, Bury St Edmunds, Suffolk IP33 1RG
Telephone: 01284 723761 Fax: 01284 723760

Chislehurst
68 High Street, Chislehurst, Kent BR7 5AQ
Telephone: 0181 295 515 Fax: 0181 467 6352

Glasgow
104 West Campbell Street, Glasgow G2 4TY
Telephone: 0141 248 6941
0141 248 1183
Fax: 0141 248 6844

Harrogate
Victoria House, Albert Street, Harrogate, North Yorks HG1 1JU
Telephone: 01423 526886 Fax: 04123 530738

Henley-on-Thames
Rotherfield House, 7 Fairmile, Henley-on-Thames, Oxon RG9 2JR
Telephone: 01491 411022 Fax: 01491 410613

London
12 Well Court, London EC4M 9DN
Telephone: 0171 489 9955 Fax: 0171 489 8531

Manchester
113/115 Chorley Road, Swinton, Manchester M27 2AA
Telephone: 0161 794 8018 Fax: 0161 727 7042

Perth
19 Marshall Place, Perth PH2 8AG
Telephone: 01738 441144 Fax: 01738 30933

Stroud
23 High Street, Stroud, Glos GL5 1AJ
Telephone: 01453 758100 Fax: 01453 753111

THE SHARE CENTRE
St Peter's House, Market Place, Tring, Hertfordshire
Telephone: 01800 800008/01442 890800

Postal address:
Post: PO Box 1000, Tring, Herts HP23 4JR

SHARELINK LIMITED
ShareLink Limited, Cannon House, 24 The Priory Queensway
Birmingham B4 6BS
Telephone: 0121 200 2242 Fax: 0121 200 7745

ALBERT E SHARP & CO
Edmund House, 12 Newhall Street, Birmingham B3 3ER
Telephone: 0121 200 2244

London
Moor House, 199 London Wall, London EC2Y 5ER
Telephone: 0171 638 7275

Bristol
2 Trinity Street, College Green, Bristol BS1 5TE
Telephone: 0117 9260051

Manchester
1 St James Square, Manchester M2 6DN
Telephone: 061 834 2040

SPIERS & JEFFREY LIMITED
36 Renfield Street, Glasgow G2 1NA
Telephone: 0141 248 4311 Fax: 0141 221 4764

STANDARD BANK STOCKBROKERS (C.I.) LIMITED
PO Box 583, One Waverley Place, St Helier, Jersey JE4 8XR
Telephone 01534 67557 Fax: 01534 59969

STIRLING HENDRY & CO
Royal Exchange House, 100 Queen Street, Glasgow G1 3DL
Telephone: 0141 248 6033 Fax: 0141 204 2155

Dundee
10 Panmure Street, Dundee DD1 9BA
Telephone: 01382 26282 Fax: 01382 23573

Inverness
Ballantyne House, 84 Academy Street, Inverness IV1 1LU
Telephone: 01463 220113 Fax: 01463 232678

R.L. STOTT & CO
Exchange House, 54/58 Athol Street, Douglas
Isle of Man
Telephone: 01624 662400 Fax: 01624 672444

TEATHER & GREENWOOD
Salisbury House, Circus Place Entrance, London Wall, London EC2M 5TH
Telephone: 0171 256 6131 Fax: 0171 628 6931

Leigh-on-Sea
Broadway House, 74–76 Broadway, Leigh-on-Sea, Essex SS9 1AE
Telephone: 01702 471143 Fax: 01702 471640

TILNEY & CO
Royal Liver Buildings, Pier Head, Liverpool L3 1NY
Telephone: 0151 236 6000

Aberdeen
7 Rubislaw Terrace, Aberdeen AB1 1XE
Telephone: 01224 624066

Birmingham
35/37 Great Charles Street, Birmingham B3 3JP
Telephone: 0121 627 6267

Edinburgh
10 Hill Street, Edinburgh EH2 3JZ
Telephone: 0131 225 7846

Glasgow
130 St Vincent Street, Glasgow G2 5SE
Telephone: 0141 248 6271

London
85 Watling Street, London EC4M 9BJ
Telephone: 0171 248 4000

Manchester
Clarence House, Clarence Street, Manchester M2 4DW
Telephone: 0161 832 1300

Peterborough
84 Lincoln Road, Peterborough PE1 2SN
Telephone: 01733 311611

Shrewsbury
Central Chambers, 15 Pride Hill, Shrewsbury SY1 1DQ
Telephone: 01734 351374

TORRIE & CO
132 Rose Street, Edinburgh EH2 3JD
Telephone: 0131 225 1766 Fax: 031 220 2363

VARTAN & SON
The Singing Men's Chambers, 19 Minster Precincts, Peterborough PE1 1XX
Telephone: 01733 315155 Fax: 01733 346619

WALKER, CRIPS, WEDDLE, BECK & CO
Sophia House, 76–80 City Road, London EC1Y 2BJ
Telephone: 0171 253 7502 Fax: 0171 253 7500

Colchester
9 West Stockwell Street, Colchester C01 1HN
Telephone: 01206 769001 Fax: 01206 769156

Newton Abbot
1 St. Paul's Road, Newton Abbot TQ12 2HP
Telephone: 01626 335533 Fax: 01626 334366

Stowmarket
Capital House, 18 Bury Street, Stowmarket IP14 1HH
Telephone: 01449 771882 Fax: 01449 771415

WATERS LUNNISS & CO LIMITED
2 Redwell Street, Norwich, Norfolk NR2 4SN
Telephone: 01603 622265 Fax: 01603 630127

Cambridge
27 St Andrew's Street, Cambridge, CB2 3AX
Telephone: 01223 303101 Fax: 01223 302964

London
114 High Holborn, London WC1V 6JJ
Telephone: 0171 405 4865 Fax: 0171 831 2474

Northampton
71B Abington Street, Northampton NN1 2BH
Telephone: 01604 602998 Fax: 01604 39698

Nottingham
10 Wheeler Gate, Nottingham NG1 2NB
Telephone: 0115 9503666 Fax: 0115 9508823

Peterborough
5 Cathedral Square, Peterborough PE1 1XB
Telephone: 01733 896949 Fax: 01733 558178

WESTONS SECURITIES LIMITED
8–9 Botolph Alley, London EC3R 8DR
Telephone: 0171 283 8466 Fax: 0171 623 9167

WILKINFORM STOCKBROKERS
Victoria House, The Moor, Hawkhurst, Kent TN18 4NR
Telephone: 01580 754488

WILSHERE, BALDWIN & CO
19 The Crescent, King Street, Leicester LE1 6RX
Telephone: 01533 541344 Fax: 01533 550969

D.M. WRIGHT & PARTNERS
15 The Diamond, Londonderry BT48 6HW
Telephone: 01504 263344

Appendix 3

Client agreement forms

When you approach a firm of stockbrokers for the first time you will be asked to complete a 'New Client Agreement' form. The Finance Act demands that you supply certain information about yourself.

You may feel that it is an impertinence that you should be asked to list all your assets and names and addresses of your professional advisers, including your bank, as well as details of your income. There are many folk who do feel that way, and it is very easy to understand.

However, it is worth making the point that the intention behind the request is to protect the investor, rather than to collect data just for its own sake.

Some of the questions have to be answered, and some can be ignored, but, if you decide to leave out those which are not mandatory, you are reducing your ability to make successful claim for recompense in the event that you may have a claim for unprofessional advice.

There are two separate forms to be signed. The layout may vary between firms but essentially the information should be the same, and here are two examples.

The first is a description of the terms and conditions of business under which the broking firm is prepared to deal with you. It spells out the different services which the firm offers and the instruments in which it is prepared to transact dealings.

It explains the firm's position with regard to any responsibility for giving investment advice, types of business which it will and will not entertain, conflict of interest, aggregation of orders, illiquid investments, and a list of the firm's charges.

When you sign this form, you are acknowledging both your understanding and acceptance of the terms and conditions of business applicable to this firm.

Therefore it is essential if you do not understand or accept any part of these conditions you must challenge them before you sign.

The SFA demands that a member firm must be in posession of a signed client agreement form before it executes any instructions to deal in securities for a client.

The second form is a questionnaire and is an integral part of the client agreement. It is an extension of the item concerning your investment objectives. It is this element which arouses the feeling of invasion of privacy.

1. **THE SERVICES WE WILL PROVIDE**
The services we will provide are:–
General investment advisory and dealing services in the following investments, together with related research, valuation and safe custody facilities:–

(a)   shares in British or foreign companies;
(b)   debenture stock, loan stock, bonds, notes, certificates of deposit, commercial paper or other debt instruments, including government, public agency, municipal and corporate issues;
(c)   warrants to subscribe for investments falling within (a) or (b) above;
(d)   depositary receipts or other types of instrument relating to investments falling within (a), (b) or (c) above;
(e)   unit trusts, mutual funds and similar schemes in the United Kingdom or elsewhere;
(f)   traditional options or traded options as detailed by The international Stock Exchange (a separate agreement is required for traded options);
(g)   life assurance, pensions, mortgage and related services;
(h)   investments which are similar or related to any of the foregoing.

Our understanding is that when you give us some orders it is possible that you will not expect us to be responsible for advising you about the investment merits of the transaction concerned. **If this understanding is not correct, please notify us as soon as possible.**
We may also provide other services if agreed between us.
We will not sell a security on your behalf where it will result in your having a short position. This situation arises when you contract to sell a security which you do not currently own.

2. **YOUR INVESTMENT OBJECTIVES**
The attached questionnaire forms an integral part of this agreement. Please complete question 3 for any specific or general objectives you have. Otherwise we will proceed on the basis that there are no specific or general investment objectives to which we must have regard when giving you advice or dealing for you.

3. **TRANSACTIONS NOT ON REGULATED MARKETS**
The Securities and Investments Board, the central regulatory authority for UK investment business, will recognise or designate certain stock exchanges or investment exchanges, both in the UK and elsewhere, which meet certain standards as regards safeguarding investors.
Unless we receive written notification to the contrary we will assume that we can deal for you on an exchange which has not been recognised or designated by the Securities and Investments Board.
However, your attention is drawn to the fact that we may deal with or for you in circumstances in which the relevant deal is not regulated by the rules of any stock exchange or investment exchange.

4. **UNSOLICITED CALLS**
We may 'cold' call you where we reasonably believe that the call is necessary for the purpose of this agreement and will be to your advantage in connection with the investment which is the subject of the call. We shall endeavour to ensure that the call will not be at an unsocial hour.
The ability to telephone you in this way is likely to increase the effectiveness of our services but you will forgo certain statutory rights that you might otherwise have entitling you to undo an investment transaction which you enter into as a result of the call.

5. **OUR CHARGES**
Our charges will be set out at the end of this agreement. Any alteration to these charges will be notified to you. You will also pay any applicable value added tax.
Any charges due to us (or to agents used by us) plus any applicable value added tax or stamp duty may be deductged from any funds held by us on your behalf or, at our discretion, shall be paid by you as stated in the relevant contract note or advice.
Any charges for services we provide for you under 1 above will be as agreed by us before or at the sme time we provide the services.

6. **CONFLICTS OF INTEREST**
Your attention is drawn to the fact that when we give you investment advice, we, or some other person connected with us may have an interest, relationship or arrangement that is material in relation to the transaction or investment concerned.
Under the rules of The Securities and Futures Authority, the employee who makes the recommendation has to disclose any such interest, relationship or arrangement of which he is aware unless (i) the recommendation is a reasonable one having regard to your interests, and (ii) we require (as we do) our employees to comply with an independence policy obliging them to

disregard the interest, relationship or arrangement concerned.

The following are some examples of the type of interest, relationship or arrangement that could be involved:

(a) being the financial adviser to the company whose securities you are buying or selling, or acting for that company in a takeover bid by or for it;

(b) sponsoring or underwriting the new issue involving the investment that you are buying or selling;

(c) having a holding or a dealing position in the investment concerned;

(d) receiving payments or other benefits for giving business to the firm with which your order is placed;

(e) being an associated company of the issuer of the investment.

Your attention is also drawn to the fact that when we recommend a transaction to you, we

(a) could be dealing as principal for our own account by selling the investment concerned to you or buying it form you; or

(b) could be matching your transaction with that of another customer by acting on his behalf as well as yours.

This will be shown on the relevant contract note or advice, but will not necessarily be disclosed to you at the time of the recommendation.

7. **AGGREGATION OF ORDERS**

We may combine your order with our own orders, orders of persons connected with us and orders of other customers. Combining your orders with those of other customers (not connected with us) may result in your obtaining on some occasions a more favourable price, and on others a less favourable price, than if your order had been executed separately.

8. **ILLIQUID INVESTMENTS**

Under The Securities and Futures Authority's rules, we have the following obligations to you as regards a transaction in an investment which is illiquid (ie difficult to sell), if at the time of the transaction there are not sufficient firms quoting a price for the investment for it to be possible to determine what is a proper market price:

(a) If we execute the transaction as principal, the price and the other terms of the transaction must be fair and reasonable to you.

(b) If we execute the transaction as agent, we must use reasonable care to execute the transaction at a price and on other terms which are fair and reasonable to you.

(c) We must explain the basis for arriving at the price in the transaction if you request; moreover, if you request, we have to include in that explanation an account of how the price relates to the prices in any previous arm's length bargain the other way which we have entered into.

9. **STABILISATION**

Please read carefully the following explanation about stabilisation which is likely to be an increasingly important factor in the UK markets.

Stabilisation is a price supporting process that very often takes place in the context of new issues, including rights issues.

The effect of stabilisation can be to make the market price of the new issue temporarily higher than it would otherwise be.

Stabilisation can also affect the market price of invesmtents of the same class which are already in issue and of other investments whose price affects the price of the new issue. For example, if a company has announced a rights issue, stabilisation may cause the market price of its shares which are already in issue to be temporarily higher that it would otherwise be; and the same may apply if the company has announced an issue of convertible loan stock or of eurobonds with warrants to subscribe for its shares.

The fact that there have been dealings in an investment in which stabilisation may be taking place does not necessarily mean that investors are interested in buying that investment or in buying it at the level at which those dealings have taken place. There are limits on the price at which shares, warrants or depositary receipts may be stablised but the limits do not apply where loan stock or bonds are being stablised.

Unless we receive written notification from you we shall assume that you wish us to recommend to you or execute your orders in, investments whose market price may be affected by stabilisation.

10. **YOUR MONEY**

We can only deal with your money in accordance with The Securities and Futures Authority's Financial Regulations which, among other things, require us to hold your money in a bank account at a bank approved by The Securities and Futures Authority.

Unless you notify us to the contrary, we shall assume that –

(a) all amounts of every kind which are payable by you to us and vice versa will be settled on a net basis;

(b) you will settle your accounts with us under The Stock Exchange Account System.

11. INTEREST

If you default in paying any amount when it is due, interest may at our discretion be payable by you at a rate not exceeding the base rate from time to time in force of Lloyds Bank Plc, plus 4%. We will pay interest on deposit accounts at rates not less favourable than those generally prevailing in the city in which the account is situated for money of its amount and currency and the time for which it is likely to be on deposit.

12. CUSTODY OF YOUR INVESTMENTS

Your investments will be registered in your own names or as instructed by you or at our discretion held in, or to the order of our Nominee Company. Without binding ourselves to do so we may, on your request, retain your certificate in our Safes or Strong Room, or where necessary in our Bank. Please note that some stocks (eg bearer) may be held, from time to time, by a third party including overseas agents and clearance systems for its or our account.

Whilst we accept responsibility for the safe custody of stock held by our Nominee Company, we do not accept responsibility for any default in the safe custody obligations of our Bank or any third party. You hereby agree to pay any charges incurred for safe custody services.

13. RIGHTS ISSUES, TAKEOVERS etc

Please note that as regards investments which we are holding on your behalf, we shall not be responsible for –

(a) taking up any rights;

(b) exercising any conversion or subscription rights;

(c) dealing with takeovers or other offers or capital re-organisations;

(d) exercising voting rights.

Although we shall make every reasonable endeavour to act in your best interests when we consider it appropriate.

14. RIGHT TO RETAIN YOUR FUNDS

Your attention is drawn to the fact that we reserve the following rights to retain, or make deductions from, amounts which we owe to you or are holding for you, where

(a) a late delivery of an investment results in our loss, for example, where stock is bought in results in our loss

(b) a late payment

(c) we have for any reason incurred a loss as a result of your default or of executing your instructions.

15. POWER OF SALE OVER YOUR INVESTMENTS

Your attention is drawn to the fact that we reserve the following right to sell or realise any investments which we are holding (or entitled to receive) on your behalf in order to meet any liabilities which you may have incurred to us.

We reserve the right to exercise our lien with power of sale (without prejudice to all rights and remedies exercisable at law):

(a) over your investments where you have failed to deliver investments or to pay on the due date and this had resulted in our loss; or

(b) over any investments which we are holding or are entitled to hold, for your account but for which you have not paid.

16. RESEARCH

Please bear in mind that, before publishing a research recommendation, we may have acted upon it or made use of information on which it is based.

17. CHANGES

We may amend these arrangements by sending you a written notice describing the relevant changes. Such changes will become effective on a date to be specified in the notice which must be at least one week after the notice is sent to you.

You can amend these arrangements in the following ways:

(a) by changing your investment objectives; or

(b) by imposing new restrictions under paragraph 2 or 4 above or changing or lifting any

(c) by notifying us that you do not agree to any of the matters set out in paragraph 3, 4, 9 or 10 above.

However, any such amendment which you wish to make will only become effective when the member of staff responsible for handling your account receives a letter from you setting out the amendment concerned.

No amendment will affect any outstanding order or transaction or any legal rights or obligations which may already have arisen.

18. **TERMINATION**

You are entitled to terminate these arrangements by giving us immediate written notice, as may we by giving you immediate written notice.

No penalty will become due from either you or us in respect of the termination of these arrangements; however, we may require you to pay the amount in respect of charges for transferring your investments to your new investment adviser.

If these arrangements are terminated, that will not affect any outstanding order or transaction or any legal rights or obligations which may already have arisen.

This letter is governed by the law of England.

Mr S. Broker
Partner

I/We agree to the above.

Signed: _____

Dated: _____

Name) Please Print _____

Address) _____

_____

_____

Please quote your Account Number: _____

Partner/Associate Contact Name: _____

We are obliged under the rules of The Securities and Futures Authority to take essential steps to obtain a client's investment objectives and those facts about your financial position which you believe we need to know. Whilst the full completion of this form would be helpful we understand that many clients may be unwilling to make a full disclosure of their affairs.

Questions 1, 2, 3 and 4 are essentially basic information and must be completed. The remaining questions must be stuck through if you are not prepared, or do not readily know the answers.

1. PERSONAL DETAILS

	Surname	Forenames	Title	Date of Birth
Self :				
Spouse :				
Children :				

Any other dependent relatives

	Home (for Tax Purposes)		Business
Addresss :			
	Postcode		Postcode

Telephone :   Self   Spouse   Telephone

Occupation :

2.. PROFESSIONAL ADVISERS

Solicitor :

Accountant :

Bankers :

Insurance
Bankers :

3. INVESTMENT OBJECTIVES

What are your aims?

Capital Growth ☐   Income ☐   Balance between Growth & Income ☐   Other Objectives (please specify)

_____

Degree of risk

Low Risk ☐   Medium risk ☐   High Risk ☐

_____

Period of Investment

Within 5 years ☐   Longer Term ☐

4. GENERAL INFORMATION

Please state where you wish us to send your certificates   Home ☐   Bank ☐

Portfolio valuations required   Yes ☐   No ☐

Name _____

Address _____

REGISTRATION

Securities to be registered in   Our Nominee Name ☐   Your Name at Your Address ☐

Sorting code _____

Account No. _____

DIVIDENDS

Income from your investments to be   (a) Sent to Your Address ☐   (b) Mandated to Your Bank Account ☐

INCOME BEFORE TAX (CURRENT YEAR)

5. PERSONAL DETAILS

Salary, Fees, Benefits in Kind etc.

	£5,000+	£10,000+	£20,000	£30,000+	£40,000+	£50,000+	£75,000+	£100,000+
Self	☐	☐	☐	☐	☐	☐	☐	☐
Spouse	☐	☐	☐	☐	☐	☐	☐	☐

6. INVESTMENT INCOME p.a.

(Dividends, Rents, Interest etc.)

	£5,000+	£10,000+	£20,000	£30,000+	£40,000+	£50,000+	£75,000+	£100,000+
Self	☐	☐	☐	☐	☐	☐	☐	☐
Spouse	☐	☐	☐	☐	☐	☐	☐	☐

7. TRUST INCOME

Amount

Self
Spouse
Children

8. RETIREMENT INCOME p.a.

(Pension, annuity etc.)

Amount

Self
Spouse

9. ASSETS

Amount

Home Value
Outstanding Mortgage

Owned by	Self ☐	Spouse ☐	Self/Spouse ☐

Other Properties

Value	£30,000+ ☐	£40,000+ ☐	£50,000+ ☐

Other Assets

	None	Less than £5,000	£5,000–£10,000
Equities Quoted			
Unquoted			
Gilt Edged			
Unit Trusts			
Overseas Investmentment			
Building society			
National Savings			
Investment Bonds			
Personal Equity Plans			
Other			

Please tick if you are enclosing a separate schedule of your assets ☐

Notes on the questionnaire

Question 1. The information required here is essential for obvious reasons. Quite apart from ensuring that the firm records the address correctly it is essential that your shares are registered accurately both as regards your full names and address for dividend remittance, share certificates, and company information of value to you, such as rights issues, company reports and accounts, etc.

Question 2. This information is useful, but not essential in my opinion. The name and address of your bank is helpful to have on record, particularly if you subsequently prefer to have dividends mandated directly to your account from the company paying the dividend. As for the rest, it is needed particularly if you die, because knowing who your other professional advisers are facilitates such things as probate valuations.

Question 3. This is probably the next most important data needed other than your name and address. The reason is because you are choosing the degree of risk that you are prepared to accept in your investments. Most people leave the assessment of risk to their stockbroker, and so by indicating how much or how little you are happy to entertain, you are putting the responsibility for some restraint on to your adviser. It is the answers to this section of the questionnaire that the inspectors from the SFA turn first when they are analysing the portfolio history of a client. If you indicate that your preference is for low risk, your broker will not be able to recommend such a wide range of opportunities, and if you instruct him to buy a stock which is considered to be outside this category, he may well refuse to execute your instruction unless he receives it in writing. If your investment objectives alter, you will have to complete another form, all of which takes time.

Question 4. All the data required here is sensible and important.

Questions 5–9. It is not mandatory to provide the answers to these questions. If a client of mine asks whether he should complete these, I explain that he or she may omit these answers if they so wish. A good stockbroker will have discussed these details in much greater depth than is demanded here, and it will be impossible to create a bespoke portfolio effectively without so doing anyway.

Appendix 4

Regulatory authorities

The Financial Services Act decreed that there should be accountability for good business practice by all firms and practitioners of those in the business of giving investment advice.

The main object is to protect the public from unscrupulous operators, as well as untrained individuals whether they are employed or working on a commission basis only.

The result is a number of Self-Regulating Organisations (SROs), all responsible ultimately to the Securities and Investments Board (SIB).

Apart from carrying out regular inspections of the member firms to monitor all aspects of their business and financial strength, they are the authorities to whom any complaints should be addressed by anyone who has reason to believe that he or she has been misled by a financial adviser.

In practice, if you have reason to feel that you have an objection which amounts to malpractice concerning advice which you have been given, you should take the matter up in the first instance with the Compliance Officer in the firm with whom you have had dealings. All firms must have a compliance officer. You will help yourself considerably if you keep copies of all correspondence, contract notes, statements and notes of all telephone conversations or meetings you may have had with any individuals representing the firm.

If you do not get satisfaction then you should write to the relevant SRO. Here are the addresses of those responsible for the sections of the investment industry.

The Securities and Futures Association (SFA)
The Cotton Centre, Cotton Lane, London SE1 2QB.
Telephone: 0171 378 9000

The Personal Investment Authority (PIA)
Hertsmere House, Hertsmere Road, London E14 4AB
Telephone: 0171 538 8860

The Investment Management Regulatory Organisation (IMRO)
Broadwalk House, 6 Appold Street, London EC2A 2AA
Telephone: 0171 628 6022.

Glossary of stock market terms

After hours dealing. Dealings done after the end of the Mandatory Quote Period which are treated as dealings done on the following business day. Shown on the Contract Note as EB and denoting that the bargain was not necessarily executed at the best price available.

Allotment Letter. See *Renounceable Documents*

APCIMS. Association of Private Client Investment Managers and Stockbrokers.

Arbitrage. Buying securities in one country, currency or market and selling in another to take advantage of price differentials.

Bargain. A deal made on or otherwise subject to the rules of the Exchange is an Exchange bargain. No 'special' price is implied.

Bear. An investor who has sold a security in the hope of buying it back at a lower price.

Bear Market. A market in which bears would prosper, that is a falling market.

Bearer Stocks/Shares. Securities for which no register of ownership is kept by the company. A bearer certificate has intrinsic value. Dividends are not received automatically from the company, but must be claimed by removing and returning the 'coupons' attached to the certificate.

Bed and Breakfast Deal. Selling shares one day and buying them back the next for tax purposes.

Beneficial Owner. The true owner of a security. The registered holder of the shares may act as a nominee to the true shareholder.

Bid. (1) The price at which the market maker will buy shares. (2) An approach made by one company wishing to purchase the entire share capital of another.

Big Bang. 27 October 1986, when the Exchange's new regulations took effect, and the new automated price quotation system was introduced.

Blue Chip. Term for the most highly-regarded shares. Originally an American term, derived from the colour of the highest value poker chip.

Bonus Issue. See *Capitalisation Issue*.

Broker/Dealer. A London Stock Exchange member firm, which provides advice and dealing services to the public and which can deal on its own account.

Bull. An investor who has bought a security in the hope of selling it at a higher price.

Bull Market. One in which bulls would prosper: a rising market.

Call. The amount due to be paid to the company by the purchaser of new or partly paid shares.

Call Option. The right to buy stock or shares at an agreed price on a future date.

Capitalisation Issue. The process whereby money from a company's reserves is converted into issued capital, which is then distributed to shareholders. Also known as a 'bonus' or 'scrip' issue.

Commission. The fee that a broker may charge clients for dealing on their behalf.

Consideration. The money value of a transaction (number of shares multiplied by the price) before adding commission, stamp duty, time of deal, and any other charges, etc.

Contract note. On the same day as a bargain takes place a member firm sends to the client a contract note detailing the transaction, including full title of the stock, price, stamp duty (if applicable), consideration, commission etc.

Coupon. (1) On bearer stocks, the detachable part of the certificate exchanged for dividends.

(2) Denotes the rate of interest on a fixed interest security – a 10 per cent coupon pays interest of 10 per cent a year on the nominal value of the stock.

Cover. The total net profit a company has available for distribution as dividend, divided by the amount actually paid gives the number of times that the dividend is covered.

Cum. Latin for 'with' used in the abbreviations *cum cap, cum div, cum rights*, etc to indicate that the buyer of a security is entitled to participate in the forthcoming capitalisation issue, dividend or rights issue. See *Ex*.

Daily Official List. The London Stock Exchange's *Daily Official List* is the register of listed securities and the prices of transactions published each day.

Debenture. A loan raised by a company, paying a fixed rate of interest and secured on the assets of the company.

Discount. When the market price of a newly issued security is lower than the issue price.

Dividend. That part of a company's post-tax profits distributed to shareholders, usually expressed in pence per share. See *Final Dividend* and *Interim Dividend* .

Equity. The risk-sharing part of a company's capital, usually referred to as ordinary shares.

Eurobond. A long-term loan issued in a currency other than that of the country or market in which it is issued. Interest is paid without the deduction of tax.

Ex. The opposite of cum, and used to indicate that the buyer is not entitled to participate in whatever forthcoming event is specified. *Ex cap, ex dividend, ex rights*, etc.

Final Dividend. The dividend paid by a company at the end of its financial year, recommended by the directors, but authorised by the shareholders at the company's Annual General Meeting.

FT-SE Actuaries 350. This index provides investors with a real-time measure of the largest 350 UK companies. It combines the FT-SE 100 and the FT-SE Mid 250 and is highly correlated to the FT-A All Share.

FT-SE Actuaries 350 Industry Baskets. Industry sectors within the FT-SE Actuaries 350.

FT Index. Refers to the Financial Times Industrial Ordinary Share Index, also known as the '30 Share Index'. This started in 1935 at 100, and is based on the prices of 30 leading industrial and commercial shares. They are chosen to be representative of British industry rather than that of the Exchange. Government stocks, banks and insurance companies are not included. The Index is calculated hourly during the day with a 'closing index' at 4.30pm.

FT-SE 100 Share Index. Popularly known as the 'Footsie': an index of 100 leading UK shares listed on the London Stock Exchange providing a minute-by-minute picture of how share prices are moving. It started on 3 January 1984 with a base number of 1,000. Also forms the basis of a contract on the London International Financial Futures and Options Exchange (LIFFE).

FT-SE Eurotrack 200 Index. Denominated in ECUs, this comprises the stocks of the FT-SE 100 Index plus constituents of the FT-SE Eurotrack 100 Index. The UK component is weighted to ensure that the 200 Index closely tracks the major bench-mark indices.

FT-SE Mid 250 Index. Index of medium-sized UK companies and calculated on a minute-by-minute basis; provides a measure of the next 250 companies outside the FT-SE 100.

FT-SE SmallCap Index. An end-of-day index, shows the movement of approximately 450 companies below those in the FT-SE Actuaries 350.

Fixed Interest. Loans issued by a company, the government (gilts or gilt-edged) or local authority, where the amount of interest to be paid each year is set on issue. Usually the date of repayment is also included in the title.

Flotation. The occasion on which a company's shares are offered on the market for the first time.

Futures. Securities or goods bought or sold for future delivery. There may be no intention to take them up but to rely on price changes in order to sell at a profit before delivery.

Gearing. A company's debts expressed as a percentage of its equity capital. High gearing means debts are high in relation to equity capital.

Gilts or Gilt-Edged Securities. Loans issued on behalf of the government to fund its spending. *'Longs'*: those with a redemption date greater than 15 years. *'Mediums'*: those with a redemption date of between 5-15 years. *'Shorts'*: those with a redemption date within five years.

Gross. Before deduction of tax.

Grossing-up. Calculating a gross or pre-tax rate of interest or dividend by adding a notional amount of tax to the net, or post-tax, amount received.

Index Linked Gilt. A gilt, the interest and capital of which change in line with the retail price index.

Insider Dealing. The purchase or sale of shares by someone who possesses 'inside' information about the company; that is, information on the company's performance and prospects which has not yet been made available to the market as a whole, and which, if available, might affect the share price. In the UK such deals are a criminal offence.

Interim Dividend. A dividend declared partway through a company's financial year, authorised solely by the directors.

Investment Trust. Company whose sole business consists of buying, selling and holding shares.

Issuing House. An organisation, usually a merchant bank, which arranges the details of an issue of stocks or shares,and the necessary compliance with Exchange regulations in connection with the listing of that issue.

Letter of Renunciation. This applies to a rights issue and is the form attached to an allotment letter which is completed, should the original holder wish to pass entitlement to someone else, or to renounce rights absolutely.

LIFFE London International Financial Futures and Options Exchange.

Listed Company. A company that has obtained permission for its shares to be admitted to the London Stock Exchange's *Daily Official List*.

Listing Particulars. The details a company must publish about itself and any securities it issues before these can be listed in the *Daily Official List*. Often called a prospectus.

Loan Stock. Stock bearing a fixed rate of interest. Unlike a debenture, loan stocks may be unsecured.

Mandatory Quote Period. The period of time Monday to Friday when all registered market makers in a security must display their prices. For *SEAQ* the period is from 8.30am–4.30pm, and for *SEAQ International*, 9.30am–4.00pm.

Market-Eye. Designed and developed for the London Stock Exchange to provide investors with real-time market information, via the BBC's Datacast service. Covers UK equities, international equities, gilts and fixed-interest securities, and traded options.

Market Maker. An Exchange member firm which is obliged to make a continuous two-way price, that is, to offer to buy and sell securities in which it is registered throughout the mandatory period.

Member Firm. A trading firm of the London Stock Exchange which may deal in shares on behalf of its clients or on behalf of the firm itself.

Mid Price. The price halfway between the two prices shown in the London Stock Exchange's *Daily Official List* under 'Quotation', or the average of both buying and selling prices offered by the market makers. The prices found in newspapers are normally the mid price.

Minimum Quote Size. (MQS) The minimum number of shares in which market makers are obliged to display prices on *SEAQ* for securities in which they are registered.

NPV or **No Par Value.** See *Par*.

Net Asset Value. The value of a company after all debts have been paid, expressed in pence per share.

New Issue. A company coming to the market for the first time or issuing additional shares.

Nil Shares. Shares newly issued by a company. These shares can usually be transferred on renounceable documents.

Nil Paid. A new issue of shares, usually as the result of a rights issue, on which no payment has yet been made.

Nominal Value. See *Par*.

Nominee name. Name in which a security is registered and held in trust for the beneficial owner.

Normal Market Size (NMS) The *SEAQ* classification system that replaced the old alpha, beta, gamma system. NMS is a value expressed as a number of shares used to calculate the minimum quote size for each security.

Offer. The price at which the market maker will sell shares to investors.

Offer for Sale. A method of bringing a company to the market. The public can apply for shares directly at a fixed price. A prospectus containing details of the sale must be printed in a national newspaper.

Option. The right (but not the obligation) to buy or sell securities at a fixed price within a specified period.

Ordinary Shares. The most common form of share. Holders receive dividends which vary in amount in accordance with the profitability of the company and recommendation of the directors. The holders are the owners of the company.

Par. The nominal value of a security.

PEP. Personal Equity Plan. This allows investment in a number of shares, and carries various tax benefits including the receipt of dividends without paying income tax on the income, and sales free from Capital Gains Tax on the profit.

P/E Ratio. See *Price Earnings Ratio*.

Pink Form. See *Preferential Form*.

Preference Shares. These are normally fixed-income shares whose holders have the right to receive dividends before ordinary shareholders, but after debenture and loan stock holders have received their interest.

Preferential Form. The London Stock Exchange allows companies offering shares to the public to set aside up to 10 per cent of the issue for application from employees and, where a parent company is floating off a subsidiary, from shareholders of the parent company. Separate application forms, usually pink (hence the nickname), are used for this.

Premium. (1) If the market price of a new security is higher than the issue price, the difference is the premium. If it is lower, the difference is called the discount. (2) The cost of purchasing a traded option.

Price/Earnings Ratio. The current share price divided by the last published earnings per share, where earnings per share is net profit divided by the number of ordinary shares. The P/E ratio is a measure of the level of confidence investors have (rightly or wrongly). Generally the higher the figure, the higher the confidence.

Privatisation. Conversion of a state-run company to public limited company status, often accompanied by a sale of its shares to the public.

Private Company. A company which is not a public company and which is debarred from offering its shares to the general public.

ProShare. An independent organisation which promotes share ownership among individual investors, including employees.

Prospectus. Document giving the details that a company is required to make public to support a new issue of shares. See *Listing Particulars*.

Proxy. A person empowered by a shareholder to vote on his behalf at company meetings.

Public Limited Company (plc). A public company limited by shares and having a share capital, and which may offer shares for purchase by the general public. Only plcs may qualify for listing or trading on the London Stock Exchange.

Put Option. The right to sell stock at an agreed price at or within a stated future time.

Quoted. Securities admitted to the *Daily Official List* of the Exchange.

Redemption Date. The date on which a security (usually a fixed-interest stock) is due to be repaid by the issuer at its full face value. The year is included in the title of the security; the actual redemption date being that on which the last interest is due to be paid.

Renounceable Documents. Temporary evidence of ownership, of which there are three main types. When a company offers shares to the public, it sends an allotment letter to the successful applicants; if it makes a rights issue, it sends a provisional allotment letter to its shareholders, or in the case of a capitalisation issue, a renounceable certificate. All of these are in effect bearer securities, and are valuable. Each includes full instructions on what should happen if the holder wishes to have the newly issued shares registered in their own name, or if they wish to renounce them in favour of somebody else.

Rights Issue. An invitation to existing shareholders to purchase additional shares in the company.

Scrip Issue. See *Capitalisation Issue*.

SEAQ. The Stock Exchange Automated Quotations system for UK securities. A continuously updated computer database containing price quotations and trade reports in UK securities. *SEAQ* carries the market makers' bids and offers for UK securities.

SEAQ International. The Exchange's electronic price quotation system for non-UK equities, similar to *SEAQ*.

SEATS. A service which supports the trading of listed UK equities in which turnover is insufficient for the market making system. Distributed via TOPIC, the service shows current orders, company information, historical trading activity for each stock and the sole market maker, where only one is registered.

Securities. General name for all stocks and shares of all types. In common usage, stocks are fixed-interest securities and shares are the rest, though strictly speaking, the distinction is that stocks are denominated in money terms.

SEPON (The Stock Exchange Pool Nominee). An account into which stock is registered during the course of settlement.

Settlement Day. The day on which bought stock is due for delivery to the buyer and the appropriate consideration to the seller.

SFA. The Securities and Futures Authority. The Self Regulating Organisation responsible for regulating the conduct of brokers and dealers in securities, options and futures, including most member firms of the Exchange.

Shares. See *Securities*.

Shorts. See *Gilts or Gilt-Edged Securities*.

SIB. Securities and Investments Board. The agency appointed by the government under the Financial Services Act to oversee the regulation of the investment industry.

SRO. Self-Regulating Organisation. An organisation recognised by the SIB and responsible for monitoring the conduct of business by, and capital adequacy of, investment firms.

Stag. One who applies for a new issue in the hope of being able to sell the shares allotted to him/her at a profit as soon as dealing starts.

Stamp Duty. A UK tax currently levied on the purchase of shares.

Stocks. See *Securities*.

Talisman. The Exchange's computerised settlement system that acts as a central clearing house for transactions in equities.

Tender Offer. In an offer by tender, buyers of shares specify the price at which they are willing to purchase.

TOPIC. The London Stock Exchange's own videotext information system used for disseminating, among much other information, *SEAQ* and *SEAQ International*.

Touch. The best buying and selling prices available from a market maker on *SEAQ* and *SEAQ International* in a given security at any one time.

Traded Options. Transferable options with the right to buy and sell a standardised amount of a security at a fixed price within a specified period.

Transfer. The form signed by the seller of a security authorising the company to remove his/her name from the register and substitute that of the buyer.

Underwriting. An arrangement by which a company is guaranteed that an issue of shares will raise a given amount of cash, because the underwriters, for a commission, undertake to subscribe for any of the issue not taken up by the public.

Unit Trust. A portfolio of holdings in various companies, divided into units and managed by professionals.

White Knight. A company which rescues another which is in financial difficulty, especially one which saves a company from an unwelcome takeover bid.

Yield. The return earned on an investment taking into account the annual income and its present capital value. There are a number of different types of yield, and in some cases different methods of calculating each type.

Index

annual step 134
auditor's statement 111, 126

bargain 8, 56, 57, 74
bearer shares 39
bed and breakfast 161, 162, 163, 164, 169, 223
benchmarks 242
bid 72, 73
bonus issue 38
broker nominee designated account 28
broker nominee pool account 28
broker services 12
buying in 8, 39, 40

call option 53, 57, 60, 61, 62
capitalisation value 10
capital reconstruction 13
capital shares 113
CGT 11, 44, 48, 49, 50, 51, 138, 142, 144, 154, 155, 156, 159, 160, 161, 162, 163, 164, 165, 193, 201, 212, 214, 223, 230, 235
chairman's report 110, 126, 256
charts 93, 104, 237, 238, 239, 240, 241, 252
client agreement 14
contingent liabilities 110, 126

contract 6, 56
contract note 10, 11, 12, 24
convertible preference share 47, 201
coupon 41, 42, 43, 48, 66
CREST 20–32
cumulative preference share 46, 47

dealing 7, 21
debenture 47, 49, 132, 201
denomination 37
depot 40, 263
derivatives 52
discount 131
dividends 37, 39, 46, 48, 61, 77, 132, 159
dividend cover 78, 79, 86
double bottoms 254, 255

earnings 80, 81, 101, 102, 103, 116, 182, 185, 223, 265
electronic registration 29, 30
EPS 114, 115, 121, 126, 127, 185, 205, 265
ex dividend 61, 77
exercise price 58, 61, 64
extended settlement 10

Financial Services Act 3
frozen pool 156, 158

FT-Share Index 92, 99, 113, 203, 204, 219, 250
futures 65, 67

gearing 132
gear up 40
gilts 7, 41, 42, 43, 44, 45, 49, 52, 113, 211, 214
giver 54, 55

head and shoulders 253
highs 74, 75, 80, 95, 136, 209, 213, 214
hurdle rate 133, 134

IC/Coppock Indicator 92, 97, 98, 99, 100, 104
income shares 134
indemnity 11
indexation 154, 156, 157, 158, 169
indices 246, 248, 250
information technology 234–257
interest rate 6, 41, 42, 43, 50, 108, 112, 113, 126, 184
intrinsic value 59
investment trusts 130, 131, 132, 133, 134, 135, 136, 142, 164, 202

LIFFE 57, 65
loan stock 37, 46, 48, 49, 50, 51, 66, 132, 201, 224
London Stock Exchange 3
lows 81, 95, 136, 209, 214, 220, 222

managed funds 130, 142
market maker 4, 5, 6, 74
moving average 96, 246

NAV 125, 131, 132, 138, 139, 144, 218
nominal value 13, 37, 38, 42, 49
nominee company 9, 192

offer 72, 73
options 37, 41, 48, 52, 53, 55, 57, 58, 62, 64
ordinary shares 37, 39, 41, 46, 47, 48, 51, 53, 54, 56, 65, 66, 115, 125

participating preference 47
payment, rolling settlement 9
PEPS 144, 145, 146, 147, 148, 149, 150, 201, 212
PER 70, 80, 81, 86, 92, 95, 101, 103, 104, 182, 209, 251
pool 155, 156, 157, 158
PIBS 48, 49, 214, 224
portfolio 5, 37, 42, 155, 156, 194, 199–215, 215–220, 220–223, 223–225, 225–226, 226–229, 235, 265
pound cost average 137
preference shares 46, 52, 224
premium 42, 43, 58, 59, 60, 61, 131
put option 53, 54, 55, 57, 60, 64
redemption 41, 42, 43, 133, 134, 139
registrar 10, 11, 15, 38, 47
regulatory authority 3, 260

rights issues 159
ROCE 121, 123, 124, 125, 126, 265
rolling settlement 1, 9, 15, 192
RPI 115, 158, 200

scrip 38
sectors 250
settlement 2, 5, 7, 10, 13, 21, 25, 26, 45
settlement day 9
SFA 3, 4, 7, 112
share ownership 27
share price data 236
share registration 27
share registry 10
signals 244
split capital 132, 202
sponsored member 29
stepped preference 133
stock 39, 42, 215
stop loss 219, 220
striking price 58

taker 54, 55

TESSA 224, 225
time value 59, 60
traded option 53, 55, 56, 57, 62, 65, 66, 95, 192, 226
trader 95, 191, 225
trading range 95, 96, 210, 213, 220, 244, 245
traditional option 53, 55, 56, 57, 66
transfer document 6, 14
trends 242

unit trusts 130, 138, 139, 142, 144, 150, 164

volatility 49, 60, 61, 65, 71, 136, 193

warrants 36, 66, 67, 136

yield 43, 198, 203, 211, 225

zero dividend preference 132, 133